W
WILL
TELL
OUR
OWN
STORY!

WE WILL TELL OUR OWN STORY

The Lions of Africa Speak!

EDITORS

Adebayo C. Akomolafe
Molefi Kete Asante
Augustine Nwoye

Universal Write Publications LLC

We Will Tell Our Own Story: The Lions of Africa Speak!
Revised Edition

For information:
Submissions@UWPBooks.com
Website at www.UniversalWrite.com
IMPRINT: The Academy

Mailing/Submissions
Universal Write Publications LLC
421 8th Avenue, Suite 86
New York, NY 10001-9998

ISBN-10: 0-9825327-6-8
ISBN-13: 978-0-9825327-6-8

Contents

PREFACE

African scholars from throughout the world will see this book as a statement of what Simphiwe Sesanti refers to as "placing African culture at the core" of our thinking. I think that the authors in this book provide some of the most compelling answers to the issues that we have faced in the Academy. To begin with the writers are confident that they are going to tell their own story! In the past African writers and scholars have been so fascinated with the stories of others that they have abandoned their own ancestral wisdom in such as way as to leave the world, the African world especially, in the hands and minds of those who have been against the best interests of our people.

These authors are committed to righting the wrongs of intellectual inquiry by setting upright the standards, criteria, and assumptions that have often been avoided by Eurocentrists of any complexion. These authors are not all Afrocentrists but they are all deeply dedicated to the telling of an African story. Without us speaking and writing about our narratives we are leaving the field in literature, philosophy, social science, history, and psychology to those who have the slightest idea about adding to the African knowledge base. They seek always to increase the information wealth of Europe and America often by creating the impression that Africans have nothing to say. Thus, we will speak in our own voices loudly and we will write deftly and definitively in our own style with a view toward erecting a new phalanx of liberated minds.

Generally aware of the historical role Africa played in civilizing the world the authors in this book have started from a position of Africa as the central continent in the construction of the modern world. It is not a false claim, nor something that is wildly thought, but in the most rational of ways the authors have proceeded with the aim of stating cultural, social, economic, political, and literary facts regarding African people. Fully engaged with the issues of the times these authors seek to explore what it is that Africans have said and will say.

The authors of this book correctly perceive the world as important and powerful when people tell their own stories. Nothing in our narrative, neither the good nor the bad, can remain unsaid if we continue to bring into existence the most Afrocentric orientation possible in a complex world of competing ideas. It is not enough for Africans to be in a conversation with other cultures and not have anything to say. No longer will our truly energized scholars permit others to talk for us; our narratives will explain our lives and demonstrate how we have interpreted reality.

Extraordinary ideas are often found in casual conversations with other scholars. Herein is the beginning of this work. Augustine Nwoye and Molefi Kete Asante attended a conference held in Panang, Malaysia, on decolonizing universities on June 27-29, 2013. At that time we met a young man, Bayo Akomolafe, who was at Universiti Sains Malaysia. He was completing his doctorate degree and had many things to say to the four or five

African scholars assembled with a mostly Asian group of scholars. He shared his dream and impressed Professors Nwoye and myself. Bayo was intense and he thought that we should publish a book of original essays on African initiatives. We reluctantly agreed and asked him to gather as many people as possible for this adventure. He worked to get the authors. It was not difficult but then we saw that publishing such a radical project would not be easy either. Unable to find a publisher in Africa I understood the task of securing a publisher in the United States. Of course, it was only after getting Universal Write to publish the work that I was able to relax. It would be a product available to all Africans and it would be a work without compromise. I am pleased that Universal Write accepted the proposal that the book be published with the idea that it is a service to African intellectuals and scholars. The enriching and enlightening conversations held in beautiful Panang have now given expression to this volume with the iconic image of Seshat's headdress on the front cover, and Tehuti with his pen and pallet on the back cover. These are the first deities of writing in the world and it is appropriate that they come from ancient Africa.

Molefi Kete Asante

Chapter One

Beyond Truth: The Subversion of Story

Adebayo C. Akomolafe

There is no story that is not true, said Uchendu. The world has no end, and what is good among one people is an abomination with others.

—Chinua Achebe (Things Fall Apart)

Introduction: Truth as Global Industrial Complex

We today, as a human community, collectively face a constellation of planetary crises so riveting, so unparalleled, that our most granted realities, and our most unstated givens are being disturbed and, in most cases, discarded.

In response to the mass disenchantment created by these multi-systemic upheavals, something subversively *human*, something deeply exciting and, yet, unsettling is afoot today – and yet

1

we do not quite have the words to describe these changes or what they portend for our collective futures. We catch glimpses of these seismic shifts in our collective consciousness when the pixels of our computer screens are animated by the images of the Egyptian cum Arabic uprisings of 2010, by scenes from the Occupy movements across the globe, or stories about the *Den Plirono* ('I will not pay') Greek insurrection against that country's austerity measures. What seems to aptly describe these uprisings across the globe is a 'great unravelling' of some sort – wherein socio-political and ethical templates by which subjectivities have historically been shaped and conditioned are resisted and revolted against. Almost suddenly, new conversations are brewing in radically irreverent arenas, sustained by persons and groups walking out of the once ineluctable orthodoxies of our time; there has been as a result a tremendous increase in the number of non-profit organizations, neighbourhood associations and social justice movements, co-created by everyday folks without degrees or *expertise* – revealing a grassroots phenomenon without precedence.

What is this civilizational upheaval taking place around the globe? Why are people around the world coming together to resist – for instance – the very institution of schooling, to disrupt the economics of national currencies, to voice out their disen-chantments with the nation-state as *the* purportedly inevitable form of social cohesion? We are still coming to terms with what is now unfolding, but these tremors of discontent are compelling a radical repurposing – a bringing to light – of the institutions and metanarratives that have shaped human experience. Yet somehow, in spite of the revolutionary implications of these trans-local experiments, these changes and the growing disenchantments they allude to still linger on the threadbare edges of mainstream attention as glitches in a larger global system that assumedly does not require changing. The deep problems associated with the global debt-based monetary system, compulsory public schooling and the academy, the way food arrives at our tables and the ecological disasters left in its wake, and the very idea of a nation-state, escapes our common experience of our world. Why do we have to work so hard today? Why does schooling feel more tethered to the ideas of assessment and certification than to the free-flowing exploration of wisdoms and life-affirming conversations? Why do we have to be conditioned by a unitary monetary system that is defined by artificially induced scarcity and interest? Aren't there other ways of conceiving wealth other than in terms of accumulation of 'capital'? Is it possible to escape the poverty/wealth antinomy? Is the metanarrative of progress and infinite growth, and its concretization in terms of neo-liberal economic development, the only way to frame collective aspirations for a better world?

These questions and more have helped energized new conversations calling for a reframing of our shared possibilities – yet these calls, albeit plural and decidedly hesitant, have largely echoed out into deaf city hallways and back into the fringes and arenas of irreverence from whence they came. For instance, new experiments in creating complementary currencies in local communities that valorise wealth as 'flow' or gift (a practice that is very popular in some parts of Mali, and is being adopted in small contexts across the globe), not as 'capital', have barely made a bleep on the radar of mainstream consciousness – in spite of their resilience and ability to withstand the pitfalls of boom and bust paradigms. Concomitantly, the ancient gift cultures of indigenous communities in Africa (in which the notions of ownership and property were traditionally conceived in terms of the collective, and not in terms of the isolated individual conditioned by today's capitalist work ethic) do not inform critical policy development in the governments of African nation-states, which seem unavoidably trussed to the received discourse of sustainable economic growth.

What seems clear to contributors to this growing trans-local demand for alternative futures is that traditional top-down solutions have failed critically in answering our deep-seated questions about the things that really matter to our wellbeing, and may even be casting our world into greater peril: we are learning that our universities are not neutral arenas of life-affirming conversations we probably assumed them to be, but sites of power inequalities that have served as social sorting mechanisms perpetuating the hegemony of the elite and offering 'learning' that is fundamentally tethered to the service of a problematic global system; the development goals of international bodies and trickle-down policies derived from their predilection to neo-liberal market theories were once conceived as the most articulate way of spreading capital in a meritocracy of expertise – what is *really* the case, at least from the perspectives of these contributors, is that these policies and practices have served more to legitimize the growing divides between the 'poor' and the 'rich' by actually creating poverty through the on-going commodification of the commons and transformation of once sacred relationships into paid services.

Today's so-called solutions represent a failure of imagination, a reluctance to revisit the complex assumptions that actuate our collective livelihoods. Perhaps, the virulence of the multidimensional crises resisting today's conventional answers is a beckoning invitation to problematize the 'real', to reimagine the possible, and to defamiliarize the 'apparent' – the stickiness of the idea that the world *is*, that there is nothing conspiratorial about the way the world is framed, and that events more or less will continue in their prosaic, predictable, 'normal' way. On the streets of metropolitan Lagos in Nigeria, they have a saying that applies to this abiding, resolute faith in the regime of the non-extraordinary – a way of re-affirming trust in the way things are: 'Nothing *dey* happen!'

As I write this chapter, I am made increasingly aware – thanks to technology around me – of just how much the survival of our civilization seems imperilled: the Eurozone and her debt crisis spirals into deeper levels of recession – threatening the very existence of the global financial machine; the American dollar faces an unprecedented test of its legitimacy as the world's preferred currency; climate collapse discourse reveals alarmingly high levels of damage on the earth's ecosystems in part perpetuated by the monoculture of industrialism and rampant consumerism; the intractability of poverty continues to mock the most pristine demonstrations of individual or national philanthropy; public schooling and higher education fails to address the lived experiences of the world's incredible diversity of peoples; the energy crisis is borne out in the revelation that the world has reached 'peak oil' and, as a result of this depletion, can no longer easily power the global engine that provides food and livelihood to potential billions of earth's citizens; indigenous livelihoods and cultures are surreptitiously phased out by the encroaching paraphernalia of modernity and the political correctness of 'progress'; *and the world spins madly on.*

In Africa, a place I call home, the story of broken neon-lighted landscapes and panting asphalted roads riddled by potholes rages on. Gripped by the tyranny of the apparent and no less affected by these radical disturbances, the trajectory of political discourse and governmental praxis in Africa (as mentioned earlier) is oriented towards the realization of 'sustainable development', economic independence and technological supremacy – a choice of paths that is often a very cerebral way of saying 'we should strive hard to look like the West'. So, labouring under debt peonage, African governments convince themselves that they must undertake gargantuan infrastructure projects, celebrate the privatization of our commons, erect skyscrapers, and fund the construction of more universities – anything to catch up with the unquestionably 'more advanced', but deeply troubled, West. This capitulation to existing structures, to the silencing of hidden alternatives buried in our own rich histories, is our failure of imagination.

A causal argument that can be made, which is very critical from the point of view of my partial elucidation of the today's challenging situations, is that from mapping our civilizational crises an *ideological complex* emerges that may be employed as an analytical tool for integrating the seemingly disconnected issues that are of critical concern today (such as the ecological crisis of climate change and the financial crisis caused by spiralling levels of debt), and, principally, the subversion of which may be employed for weaving a new politics of departure and of hope for a new world – one 'our hearts tell us is possible', as Charles Eisenstein so memorably said. This complex is the notion of Truth (with a capital 'T'), and the discussions that ensue will serve to distinguish this 'Truth' as deeply held assumptions about and consciousness of the nature of reality, human experience, and the notion of the self. It is probably helpful to think of this complex as a civilizational curriculum; a colonising plot that is gradually encroaching on other spaces of performance and weaving characters that benefit its actualization; a *story* that has influenced our rhythms, values, purposes and practices. While playfully risking the accusation that such subsuming constructs only tend to over-simplify or particularise the general and generalise the particular, it is my contention, as we will see, that the aptness of this causal argument is to be found more in its rhetoric force than in its empirical adequacy. By suggesting that we playfully perceive our multifaceted problems as *symptomatic* of an even more fundamental *cause* – namely our collective consciousness of Truth, I intend to weave not another monologue of *facts*, but a reflexive concourse that implicates the reader as a co-creator of those *facts*, and invites new ways of seeing that reify new *facts*. Posing the claim that the *perceptual apparatus* we have employed to experience our world is problematic serves to highlight, dramatize, and focus attention on our experiences – and not so much on *solutions,* which often tend to reinforce the same assumptions that have yielded the *problems* in the first place.

Truth itself is evasive as singular concept – and there are many senses in which it is employed, an extensive analysis of which is not proffered. I do not speak of the situated ethical spaces that orient an individual's relationship with the mysterious; I do not speak of 'truthfulness' or 'honesty' or anything remotely related. The 'Truth' I refer to, is the one with a capital, the performance of which animated the incursion of the first colonial lords into Africa, the establishment of the social sciences, and the troubling myths that founded our global order. Let it suffice the reader that

I distinguish between the many uses of truth (which may be spiritual, philosophical, or poetic) by using a capital 'T' here – to highlight it as a political articulation. However, this does not suggest that its use radically contradicts spiritual, philosophical and poetic employments of the concept. My use of truth here is more readily concerned with the ways knowledge is produced and valorised, with power dynamics that insist on certain aspects of reality as valuable and others as superstitious and trivial, and more potently with global institutions, purportedly inevitable social structures and disciplinary arenas that constrain and demonize indigenously African assumptions about the world.

A most effective way to understand Truth as employed here is as the promulgations of and assumptions that support the global industrial complex. This 'Truth', conditioned by a convoluted history arguably located in the West, can be seen as a 'consciousness grid', a creed of inescapability – the Thatcher-ian declaration that 'there is no alternative' to the way the world is framed. This Truth, borne out prominently in the elitist perpetuation of the capitalistic ethos and the development-progress paradigm (the McDonaldization of society), the proliferation of consumerist economies and genocide of local ecologies of wellbeing, the homogenization of identity and culture, is placed in contrast to *story*, which exemplifies more fragile, more holistic, less intrusive, more local, and more sacred articulations of what it means to be human and in the world.

These indigenous cosmogonies adduced respect for the land, an interconnectedness with all things, a sensitivity to other worlds and the fragility of the veil that divides normal consciousness from shamanic consciousness, as well as community-based understandings of 'self'. In colonial moments past, Truth, riding on the deep psychic banners of Judeo-Christian conquest narratives and the dualism engendered by Cartesian coordinates of reality, entered into African homelands and subverted these stories – leaving in its wake a collective self-hatred and a caricatured attempt to approximate foreign identities and 'standards' sanctioned by the global market. The most lasting grip of colonization is felt today when African nation-states continue to solidify their boundaries, invite foreign direct investment, and think of prosperous futures only in terms of gross domestic products (GDPs) and conventional indices of market-induced growth. Meanwhile the shamanic fringe lies neglected, and the communal ways of living and being – the magical consciousness that defined our co-habitation with, and respect for, 'nature' – rots away in the hidden corners of our collective awareness. Hence, by problematizing our present dominator consciousness and the processes by which our subjectivities have been shaped, I hope to highlight a politics of neglect, the marginalization of *story* in favour of Truth.

The idea that our collective failures are deeply connected contrasts sharply with the ways we might have been attuned to understanding the world. Many would thus observe the turmoil in the markets, the economic crisis of recent times, the inequity in global resource allocation, the failure of schooling to translate into meaningful social change, the utter disconnect of the nation-state from the citizens it was supposedly created to 'protect' and 'serve', and many other worrisome features of our troubled times as unrelated events – mere glitches in an otherwise well-tuned system or splotches on a painting that continually needs a few fingered adjustments here and there. The world cannot be conceived in any other way, it seems.

They fail to connect the dots to reveal another gripping picture.

When we see that the many crises we recognise today are but symptoms of an even deeper anomaly, it becomes easier to focus our gaze on the issues that matter, which I represent as a 'crisis of consciousness'. Many activists and commentators are thus learning to see the world differently – not as a static reality, concrete and removed from us, but as a shared projection of our collective consciousness, a co-creation made alive by the breath of our participation. In other words, the world is not 'real' as such, but a narrative encounter, a relationship. The world is as we dream it.

I hope I do not get ahead of myself when I say this, but it is just as appropriate to mention that this evolving vision of an interconnected pluriverse, this radical reinterpretation of the world as a *performance*, is making room for an equally subversive insinuation: that behind the veneer of banality and mundaneness, behind the innocence and taken-for-grantedness of our most abiding concepts and institutions (such as development, schools, progress, growth, money and jobs) are deep political processes that have historically served a minority and that have created the multidimensional crises we now witness today. It is the recognition that we often speak of 'development', money and 'going to school' as if they were somehow built into the very structure of the world, as if there were no other ways to frame our lives. By reinforcing these metanarratives about what it means to be human, about what it means to live in the world, we in Africa have inadvertently perpetuated a monoculture that has torn us apart from our sacred communities, our worldviews and ourselves. However, if our givens are no more 'real' than the social constructions that valorise them, then we can co-create new realities and values, tell new stories, and perform new relationships that exemplify our vulnerable grasp on 'social justice' and 'meaningful living'.

So, in Africa, we may ask the questions: *do we really need our kids to go to school? How has 'development' made our lives any more meaningful? Why do we educate our children in factory-like settings with topics and issues that have nothing to do with their questions, hopes and aspirations? Are our national currencies really value-neutral or have they conditioned us to think we do not need each other?* The echoes of these irreverent queries are now bouncing off universities hallways – grappling with the 'official' answers that have been prepared by the social sciences; and, in this chapter, I will not only highlight the contours of this civilizational story which I have called 'Truth', but I shall attempt to demonstrate how the social sciences, legitimized by a gargantuan academic apparatus spanning the globe, and taught in African universities are complicit in perpetuating a dangerous monopoly on alternatives for the continent, and are leading to the loss of our own local cosmologies and ways of being. I limit my analysis to their influence on the African subject, knowing – however – that most of what is argued here applies to other indigenous cultures struggling to reclaim their voices – which of course is not limited to contexts in the Global South.

The 'reality' is that the world as we know it is crumbling, fading away into the dreamlands that once bore it. The old global arrangements of conquest, debt-based money, inequitable power structures and planned obsolescence are gradually giving way to thrilling experiments with local exchange technologies and networks that replace centrally planned systems. In the context of a discussion about the historicity and evolution of Truth as a way of seeing and being with the world, I discuss what these changes mean for the beautiful peoples of Africa and the continent's quest for better conditions. It is my intention to defamiliarize the status quo, and present our common ways of seeing as a discourse, a *received* imperative that has instigated new problems, and then inspire a politics of failure – one that allows for new ways of understanding the world, one that re-enchants indigenous 'low theories' and one that strongly suggests that the way *out* of our predicaments is the way *in* to our own stories.

In a truly exciting sense that is crucial to this quest for a revitalised Africa, the evolutionary pressure being exerted by this global crisis may be read as a usurpation of truth and the revitalization of *story*. Making sense of the fundamental shifts in perception that are now exploding in irreverent ways across the planet will not be 'complete' (not as if anything ever is complete!) without approaching the tense arena – primarily in the so-called social sciences – where truth and its hegemonic grip on how we live is now being contested, where the syllables of the idea of a platonically distant referent outside our subjective experience were first uttered, where *story* was first wounded.

THE SOCIAL SCIENCES AS TRUTH

Here might be an excellent place to write about the parable of the fish: it is said that though a fish is born in water, grows in water, derives its nourishment from water, mates in water, and eventually dies in water, it does all of this without knowledge of water – that is, in a most ironic way, a fish doesn't know it's wet. There are a thousand other possible parallels one might playfully draw on to further illustrate the deep lessons we could learn from this fishy parable – my most favourite of which is derived from the historical invasion of the 'White' man into Africa; that is, the 'Black' man only recognised himself as black when the white-skinned Europeans landed on their seashores. There was nothing else to compare him to.

Far from merely revealing that identity is often shaped in the circumstance of its own contradiction, the fish's parable teaches us the power of blind spots: that seeing is not a given; it is not a fixed, uncontested event. We were instructed in school to observe the intricacies of vision, to marvel at the miracle of sight and the many processes that make it possible. Now many understand that seeing is not merely a brain-based coordination of electrochemical energies coasting through our optical nerves and the visual cortex. Seeing is an instance of colluding ecological circumstances, a political event, called to being, *stained* and shaped by the context within which it is. The paradox of sight is that it often reveals as much as it conceals. In an absorbing sense, seeing is a story, and we are taught to see, conditioned to see, and rewarded (or punished) for seeing the world in a particular way. This monoculture of sight, this unstated assumption about what is 'real' and what is 'not' influences how we go about our lives and what we think is possible.

Consequently, the world is populated with competing visions of the 'real', contradictory stories about what is valuable and beautiful and worth coming to terms with. In the process of trying to dominate other contestations, certain ways of seeing the world are established as natural, as obvious and essential, 'even though they are often entirely counterintuitive and socially engineered'. Thus, for instance, in the 'rush to bureaucratize and rationalize an economic order that privileges profit over all kinds of other motivations for being and doing', many local knowledges and comparable systems of sharing that emphasize gifts and connection are immediately *disqualified*. Further still, and more dangerously, Africans have learned to internalize these dominant ways of seeing – which means that 'we begin to deploy and think with the logic' of global status quo.

It is here that the problematic influences of the social sciences – particularly (in my experience) psychology and philosophy – on the subjectivities of Africans are revealed. It is also from here that an interesting conversation about what is possible today can originate.

Often taken to be the expert's (and therefore the only legitimate) take on the systematic workings of the human person, her society, and the world she abides in, the social sciences taught fervently in African universities today silently promulgate the regime of a single story disguised as a universally consistent appellate. What is hidden, what is usually not seen, what is lost in high-strung academic attempts to wield more bombastic accounts of orthodoxy, is the 'fact' that orthodoxy itself is a ruse, a game with very human players and very intense political interests.

A discussion surrounding how the social sciences and their Eurocentric leanings have pressed upon us a culture-specific, history-specific way of being – and *this* under the guise of being universally applicable – is crucially important to the attempt to address the 'African situation'. This is because how we *come to be* in the world today (largely the product of the monoculture of being I am talking about) feels so intuitive, so commonplace, so incontrovertible that to question this shared experience is to be branded 'abnormal'. In Africa (as in most parts of the world), our notions of the concrete and isolated self, inhabiting a concrete body, experiencing a concrete world, for instance, fosters itself so tightly to our imaginations that it is a wonder our forebears once said, 'Because you are, I am'. What now stands in the place of that ancient 'African' valorisation of community is Descartes' insistence that 'I think, therefore I exist' – a decree about human *be-ing* we have been trained to accept as the only legitimate way to frame our unwieldy human experiences. Consequently, this concrete ego that exists must accrue to itself scarce resources, and must compete for relevance in a world that has already condemned it to be alone in its prison of experience.

It is difficult to miss the prognostication we derive from this account of the universe: there is Self and there is the Other; there's the Rich and then the Poor, the Right and the Wrong, Inside and Outside, Truth and Heresy, and on and on into a spiral of more troubling dichotomies we have grown to accept as 'normal'. However, the social sciences have bequeathed Africans with much more than far-reaching dualisms; today, we more or less attune our lives, most times without knowing this, to the streams and currents of thought emanating from the conversations in the disciplines. When we speak about 'getting to the top', 'living the good life', 'making it big', 'settling down', 'being successful', 'being a *man*', or just 'hustling', we are weaving our experiences, developing our language, and co-constructing meaning from the narratives and compulsions of these disciplines. The motivation towards social ascension or upward mobility, and the common-sense notion that we are separate, distinct, rational consumers cast in a world of scarce resources, whose most important tasks are to outwit the 'other' and keep growing in order to thrive, are probably taken for

granted and believed to be part of our normative understandings
as humans. It would probably shock not quite a few to realize that
these 'understandings' are artifices of an antiquated story – con-
cocted, invented and not in the very least inevitable.

This is the glory of most of the social sciences today; and while
it might be naïve to suggest that the academic industry in Africa
has had such an impact on lived experiences and social life outside
its ivory fences, we must take into account the many years of
plunder and cultural colonisation performed by a multi-systemic
complex (including the media), of which the Western-type university serves as its intellectual base. In less ungainly words, the
social sciences (comprising of, but of course not limited to, psychology, mass communication, economics, history and philosophy) as taught in the universities across Africa have more or less
defined our experience of ourselves today. Whether intentionally
or inadvertently, the social sciences, emerging from their historical
heartlands in Enlightenment-era Europe, have helped propagate
a belief that an objective reality exists 'outside', and independent
of, our subjective experiences – a universe of atoms, bricks, stones
and persons caught in a web of potentially understandable laws
and principles, access to which is denied to the uninitiated (those
unschooled in the intricacies of the scientific method). They have
fostered themselves so strongly to our imaginations that it is near
impossible to think of living without money, to think of education without schooling and the provinciality of disciplines, to
think of social organization without the instrumentality of the
nation-state and its various apparatuses of control, to think of
wellbeing without pharmaceutical corporations, psychotherapy
and prisons, to think of wealth without its synthetic opposite

– poverty, to think of work without jobs, to think of togetherness without the illusions of *sustainable development* and *progress,* to think of ourselves without creating the 'other'.

To this claim of complicity in creating a flawed mercantile civilization – one which we can no longer tolerate, a counterclaim may be offered – that the social sciences have just as well provided alternative visions that do not support the idea of an objective reality, and that, even more crucially, it is quite immature to represent the disciplines concerned as a monolithic template of uniform doctrines – instead of a multi-faceted arena of contested concepts and unresolved controversies. For instance, positivistic approaches to reality and knowledge often stand in sharp contrast to social constructivist accounts of the universe; and there are critical traditions within these disciplines housed in our universities that challenge most of the assumptions of mainstream studies. In this wise, how can the claim that the social sciences have acted as vessels of this pervasive ideology be adequately sustained?

Halberstam notes, in a Foucaultian reading of the techniques of modern power, that the problem is disciplinarity itself.

> This is not a bad time to experiment with disciplinary transformation on behalf of generating new forms of knowing, since the fields that were assembled over one hundred years ago to respond to new market economies and the demand for narrow expertise, as Foucault described them, are now losing relevance and failing to respond either to real-world knowledge projects or student interests.

The social sciences and other forms of disciplinarity within established academic contexts are not merely implicated in the encouragement of a global monoculture by virtue of content alone – but more due to structure. Disciplinarity, as defined by Foucault, 'is a technique of modern power; it depends upon and deploys normalization, routines, convention, tradition, and regularity, and it produces experts and administrative forms of governance' that are conducive to the modern project of progressive disenchantment. The critical traditions in academic culture are 'not the answer to encroaching professionalization but an extension of it, using the very same tools and legitimising strategies to become "an ally of professional education"'. In other words, the very occurrence of academic disciplinarity – regardless of content, critique, and intention – is at once an instance of modern power, of the global industrial complex, of *Truth*.

This is easier to see when we recognize that these disciplines are substantiated within teaching and research contexts by protocols, techniques, designs, and traditions that often militate against African traditional systems and values. For instance, I recognized early in my psychological research career that the way knowledge was framed and accessed abused and belittled deeply African sentiments about the sacred holding frameworks and initiation rituals believed necessary for valuable knowledge. The research encounter converted my participants into mere recipients to be discarded later, objects to be sucked from for the glorious objective of 'adding to knowledge' – as I was told. The sacred traditions that shaped the encounter were placed in the back-seat, relegated to trivial and vestigial concerns that merely irritated the 'pristine' task of doing research. Ultimately, as in my experience, most research outcomes end up feeding the university system's scarification, desacralization, rationalization, and corporatization of 'knowledge'. By concretizing knowledge as scarce resource which is only legitimately accessible at the end of a linear path of schooling and professional certification, universities, via the instrument of disciplinarity, lend a strong hand in creating a monoculture of learning, a global context of cultural genocide, hegemonic systems of relevance, and binary structures that serve elitist 'high agendas'.

Thus, the social sciences, which are the form of disciplinarity this chapter is concerned with, help entrench knowledge production agendas that are disruptive to local and autonomous ways of knowing and being. The performance of disciplinarity – a modern attempt to atomize experience and categorize learning in ways that ease the social sorting preoccupations of an increasingly stratified social order – might then be read as a resistance of diversity, as discomfort with the chaos that comes with allowing plural articulations of the world, and as a politics of correctness – which conveniently serve the vested interests of the global order socially engineered to legitimize the *one* and the disqualify the *other*.

In many implied senses, the social sciences and their critical strands can be appropriately read as a cultural quest for *one world,* a global Apollonian order of manufactured knowledge and estranged practices. This tendency towards imperialist ethos is not ameliorated by the growing accommodation of indigenous studies in university curriculums, since this 'accommodation' is more readily a patronizing 'occupation' of such wisdoms for dispatch in a world socially engineered by scarcity and corporate profit motivations. This further instils the notion that these disciplines are the only legitimate, objective and relevant ways of knowing:

> Belief in an external world, an objective reality that exists 'out there', disguises the cultural construction of ontologies

as external, unbiased and naturalised... The assumption that universal truths can be discovered, and that Eurocentric knowledges have revealed at least some of them, means the idea of knowledge itself is often not problematised in academic discourse. This renders invisible processes that construct knowledge, and many of their consequences. Eurocentric knowledges, boundaries and relationships are conventionally treated in the academy as the only possible knowledges and as universally relevant.

Concomitantly, this hegemonic construction of knowledge as objective referent has by implication delegitimised other forms of knowledges possible in the world today – and all this in the name of 'Truth'. By silencing indigenous knowledges and damning them to the fringes of collective consciousness, the social sciences as truth have invaded our cultural spaces, giving the impression that western culture is objectively superior to other cultures.

The social sciences are of course a Trojan horse. They are not at all neutral, depoliticised attempts to gain entrance into a platonic heaven of explanations; the only 'truth' they carry are the limited Eurocentric perspectives that have floated around Eurocentric concerns. How questions are framed, how research is carried out, how data is conceptualized and gathered, how reports are storied, how conclusions are reached, and how knowledge is produced and archived are echoes of Euro-American interests and assumptions about the world. The social sciences are vessels carrying the historical anxieties of Euro-American moments, their cultural assumptions, and their hopes. This they have, in imperialist might, branded as universal truth, law or principle; so that when a mainstream clinical psychologist diagnoses his client as schizophrenic, he believes his judgment (which leads to further action in attempting to treat the client) actually corresponds with the 'true' state of things about that client's mental health, a platonic ideal he has accessed thanks to his battery of tests and procedures, thanks to the rationalistic scientific method.

It is even more damning for the cause of disciplinarity in Africa when the historically bigoted, anti-racial agendas of the social sciences come to light. The original impetus and evolutionary (almost religious) fervour of the social sciences were partly derived from derogatory, research-validated ideas about Africans and races different from the Caucasian. Indeed, the histories of the disciplines, such as sociobiology, psychology and history, now celebrated in African universities today are replete with instances of purportedly verified commentary about African agency and identity. I will not repeat some of these ideologically repugnant comments here – in the hope that in merely alluding to them I can demonstrate how these disciplines were informed by ideological and cultural values, in this case the colonizing agendas of 'developed' nations.

Today's unravelling of our common consciousness, of what is deemed 'real', of what we see and do not see, begins with an examination of the 'performance' we have conveniently called Truth. Contesting the social sciences as an avatar for the myth of Truth could have radical socio-political implications for African communities and their knowledge systems.

A BRIEF HISTORY OF TRUTH

We live in times of excitingly disturbing but promising irreverence defined by a morbid suspicion for normative metanarratives.

Paradoxically, this irreverent re-inspection of cherished concepts, spurred in part by an Age of Interpretation – instead of absolutely stripping knowledge of the power it once held – is gradually leading to the re-sacralisation and re-enchantment of our common experiences. Case in point, history may no longer be viewed as the painstaking recapturing of events as they occurred regardless of any observer, but simply as a perspective, a narrative that potentially tells us more about the *narrator* than the *narrated*. History is thus a political event, always porous (and not for a lack of details) and compellingly allegorical – a storytelling enterprise, not a fact-finding expedition.

While this might immediately suggest that lethargy and sloppiness are definitive markers of our transient times, it need not be so: telling stories is not any less engaging or gripping than our previous fixation with 'facts'. Indeed, there are more to 'facts' than immediately meet the eye: facts and theories do not just gloss over aspects of human experience that are princely captured by stories, they hide the 'vulnerabilities' and 'paradoxes' that come with seeing and claiming to know. Like 'truth', they rob the world of its diversity and sacredness by insisting on the valorisation of one means of knowing. It is this sensitivity to the utter fluidity of knowledge and the contradictions inherent the claim to know that shapes today's discourse of what is possible, and brightens our chances of reinventing ourselves as Africans. However, it is important to note that the construction of 'facts' have also been beneficial in helping us sustain a creative tension with the world around us, with helping us achieve technological sophistication and social coherence. Facts' are not 'bad' things; they are simply not as 'stubborn' as previously supposed. Examining truth's history as a colonising concept is thus for me an allegorical attempt at producing a powerful narrative that does not fall for the anxieties hidden in seeking actuality, finality or 'what exactly happened', but transcends these fixations with an intent to provoke conversations and movement (this is why I think the so-called 'African situation' and its many crises is a call for poets and heretics, not more experts and 'leaders'). I can choose to devote my energies into weaving narratives, possibilities, and hope into a rich quilt, an ásó-òkè of power that energises 'Africans' to reclaim their agency and worlds.

So how did Truth become such a powerful concept? What have the social sciences as practised within the university got to do with it? And what could transcending Truth mean for Africa?

Even asking those questions is a powerful thing because it problematizes knowledge and suggests that the world is not just 'there', waiting to be discovered – alive outside our conscious observation of it. Asking these questions suggests that truth is co-produced, like a battery-operated torchlight is manufactured – it is not sunlight, assumedly natural and 'there', but a way of seeing in a complex, ever-dynamic and always participatory vortex pregnant with other (possibly contradictory) ways of seeing, and none more valid than the other.

It is worth repeating that Truth is considered here as the knowledge system and global order of connected assumptions and myths about the world, a dominant culture that is reified in terms of escalating economies of scale, the conversion of otherwise healthy ecological systems and relationships into commodities and paid services and, generally, the social structures that are complicit in sustaining this state of affairs – including, but not restricted to, schooling, medicine, religion, the scientific method, disciplinarity and the monologue of development and progress. In other words, 'Truth' put out as reality. This 'Truth' influences how we see ourselves and the ways we behave to each other. It is what instructs us to build more and more schools to 'help' *poor African communities;* it is what compels us to print more money without questioning how this monoculture of learning and currency impacts on our societies, our diverse ways of knowing, and the health of the planet. 'Truth' is the story of our disenchantment and disconnection from each other and from a holistic interdependence on and co-existence with our lands; it is the replacement of our carnal, fleshy, sacred, in-tune, and local narratives with the harsh contours of a machine, a mercantile totalitarian system that is blind to our stories.

Greenwood traces this mechanization and disenchantment of society to the deep social changes that occurred largely due to the conversion of Constantine to Judeo-Christian faith:

> Disconnection is largely due to the fact that in Western history there has been a progressive withdrawal of divinity from the natural world accompanied by a devaluation of human experience. This started in the period of Late Antiquity between the accession of Marcus Aurelius and the conversion of Constantine to Christianity. Aided by Copernicus's transferral, in 1543, of many astronomical functions previously attributed to the earth to the sun, a fundamental change was made regarding human relationships to the universe and to God, creating the transition from a medieval to a modern Western view. The Copernican revolution facilitated the seventeenth–century mechanistic conception of nature developed by philosopher René

Descartes (1596–1650) who separated the thinking mind from the material world and thus laid the ground for an objective science; this contributed to the view that human relationships to the world were in opposition to nature.

The emergence of Judeo-Christian religion led to the entrenching of potent categories of thought, which served to distinguish between the created order and the Creator – a duality that influenced and shaped Descartes' separation of consciousness and matter. By stripping nature of its sacredness, by casting man as lord and master over the created order, Descartes provided the grounds for its exploitation for the glory of man's designs, which in turn were exalting to the transcendent Creator, *outside* and *above* nature.

The allusion to the ensuing 'Cartesian coordinates of reality' corroborates the potency of this Eurocentric version of reality that has shaped modern civilization – but more readily valorises the politics of control that has since characterised human engagement with the mechanized *other*. Greenwood writes that

> ...the notion of nature as a mechanical inanimate system may be comforting for some, giving the idea that human beings are in control of nature and confirming the belief that science has risen above primitive animistic beliefs. However, this view comes at a cost. A superior sphere of reason was constructed over a sphere of inferiority; the former was a privileged domain of the master, while the latter, which formed a category of nature, comprised a field of multiple exclusions created by racism, colonialism and sexism. Racial, ethnic and sexual difference were cast as

closer to the animal and the body, a lesser form of humanity lacking full rationality or culture

The machinations of Truth are therefore forcefully borne out in the downgrading of other endemic ways of being in the world, and lend themselves to the establishment and preservation of an elite group over and above a perpetually exploited other.

THE SOCIETY OF THE ASSEMBLY LINE AND THE MARGINALIZATION OF OTHER WAYS OF KNOWING

The fixed agenda of Truth, this capitulation to a universal narrative, this static reasoning that legitimized colonization, has led to the marginalization of other ways of being and done violence to indigenous cosmologies. Owing to the on-going mechanization and commodification of relationships, our social orders may be characterized as a 'society of the assembly line', wherein a single collective treatise is reified as real, and a homogenizing linearity is imposed to organize the problematic existence of alternatives and competing narratives about life. All of human experience is subsumed under the rationalistic enterprise of producing – under very repressive, machinated circumstances – a certain kind of outcome, which itself vindicates the raison-etre for the 'machine'.

The programmed bureaucratization and reduction of life into convenient rational symbols strips communities of their rich local powers, their local freedoms, and their situated sacredness – replacing these 'messy', diverse contexts with easily recognizable logos and language that situates these otherwise thriving settings on a universalist ladder of global progress. Hence, the continent of Africa immediately found the need to 'develop' when the measuring tape of progress was stretched out against it. Our cultures of learning, sharing, and relating with the divine and the other-worldly were immediately thrown into the newly minted fringes to make way for the central positioning of a hostile doctrine. Today, we have forgotten our ecologically sensitive and techno-logically advanced mud-houses in the doomed quest to build taller skyscrapers than our Western counterparts; we have become entrapped in the false dualisms of creating wealth versus eliminating poverty – unable to see that the very system of wealth-creation and capital reification exists because money (fiat currencies based on scarcity economics) and the global finance mechanism acts as a siphon, drawing life currencies away from the many in order to feed the few. In the place of situated indigenous learning and playing, we have planted schools that churn out certified drones regurgitating lessons that are valueless to their communities – the very lifeblood of a globalist machine that seeks to create 'powerless places and placeless powers'. When, once in a while, a spirited reformer speaks about revamping the education system, he is unfortunately calling for more schools – or worse, schools with Trojan curriculums and cute green gardens beyond wooden windows.

Accordingly, normal waking consciousness is now become the commerce between schooled childhood and occupied adult-hood – a linearity of hustling, a compulsion towards upward mobility, the mindless conversion of everything sacred into profit or avenues for profit-making, an atomistic preoccupation with 'making a living', and the tragic forgetting of the flowers by the side of wearied asphalted road. To reward our disillusionment and perpetuated participation in sustaining the system, we are rewarded with luxury (the common name for things we only enjoy because others do not have them), the promise of greater power and control – all the while blind to our enslavement and isolation from the things we really crave: each other. We are assured that the global arrangement is necessary for the disinterested pursuit of knowledge, of freedom, of democracy, of human rights, of happiness and increasing technological sophistication. However, what is hidden behind these rarefied memes of collective conquest is a repressive regime of marginalization as Steven Best (2011) eloquently articulates:

> The dark, ugly, bellicose, repressive, violent, and predatory underbelly of the "disinterested" pursuit of knowledge, of "reason," and of "democracy," "freedom," and "rights" as well, has been described through a litany of ungainly sociological terms, including, but not limited to: secularization, rationalization, commodification, reification ("thingification"), industrialization, standardization, homogenization, bureaucratization, and globalization. Each term describes a different aspect of modernity—reduction of the universe to mathematical symbols and equations, the mass production of identical objects, the standardization of individuals into the molds of conformity, the evolution of capitalist power from its competitive to monopolist to transnational stages, or the political and legal state apparatus of "representative" or "parliamentary" democracies. Each dynamic is part of a comprehensive, aggressive, protean, and multidimensional system of power and domination, co-constituted by the three main engines incessantly propelling modern change: science, capitalism, and technology. In industrial capitalist societies, elites deploy mathematics, science, technology,

bureaucracies, states, militaries, and instrumental reason to render the world as something abstract, functional, calculable, and controllable, while transforming any and all things and beings into commodities manufactured and sold for profit.

George Ritzer, in a resounding critique of modern life, called this process 'the McDonaldization of society' – a global process in which 'society and culture come under the logic of mass production, standardization, mass consumption, and capital markets. As McDonaldization spreads insidiously, it dulls consciousness, destroys diversity and difference, and integrates people into the global factory system in spheres of production and consumption, work and everyday life, while spreading markets and commodification imperatives in all directions, always with the intent to amass capital and power for the minority elite.'

Because of popular trends, it is probably worth mentioning that major colonial religious systems on the continent of Africa and specifically in some parts of West Africa (where variants of Christian Pentecostalism are rampant) – especially revivalist, charismatic strands of evangelistic Christianity – are complicit in the sustenance of this mercantile agenda of homogenization. Of course, Christianity is itself a child of the state, born in the historical moorlands of political motivations to centralize systems of belief and create a monotony of sacred relationships. We can easily draw parallels between the logic of dualism that animated the project of Enlightenment and Cartesian expansion and the present widespread capitulation to the 'prosperity message' – the idea that God desires Christians to prosper materially and spiritually, though with practiced and desired emphasis on the former.

The 'prosperity message' colludes with the compulsion towards upward mobility – creating masses of people who continue to internalize the master's rule, subjectivizing populations and motivating people to strive for the 'top'. While creating the mirage of an *escape route* from the disenchantments of modern life, these institutionalized belief and praxis systems – founded on the substructure of Truth – are actually a *detour*, offering the hope that with devotion to some enunciated sacred practices, anyone can enjoy the best of modern life (and its preoccupations with bigness, ownership and profit) with the added benefit of a heavenly life beyond the pale of human existence. The prophets of this system display stunning degrees of wealth, and stand as avatars of hope in the system. Messages to congregations comprise of stylized promulgations about the sanctity of 'work' (a rehash of the Protestant ethics that linked salvation to work), legitimizations of ownership and property, the demonization of competing cosmologies and ways of life, the celebration of 'testimonies' that vindicate upward mobility, and support for conventional institutions of global cohesion.

This narrative of economic evangelism is suspiciously similar in motivation to the capitalist ethos – the impulse to create a monoculture of belief, a consuming population beholden to the global market, the discountenancing of competing stories, the casting of the 'other' as one needing saving, and the commodification of life itself. In a sense, the former sacralises the latter, acting as a magnet to the disillusioned – those that fall off the superhighway of contrived modern life. Further still, these institutional avatars of Truth help dissolve communal ties, isolating the pilgrim in a 'personal' quest for 'salvation' (which of course, as has been alluded to in mentioning the 'prosperity message' above, has been expanded over the years to include incremental material abundance, the absence of disease, and a prepared place in heaven). While new communities of belief inevitably cohere around these promises of economic/spiritual expansion, the heteronormative status quo remains unchallenged and these communities actually turn out to be 'persons in close proximity' – each individual/family unit merely employing new spiritual tools to gain a place in an economic meta-structure that is itself insane.

What the politics of salvation does to indigenous gift culture stories about our connections to the earth and our interdependence with everything else, the politics of correctness in the academy replicates in the arena of conversations about education, knowledge and meaningful learning. It then becomes not too difficult to see how the social sciences, religion, healthcare, the nation-state, the scientific method, and the global finance system together conspire to create a collective regime of Truth – or the 'growing influence and dominance of corporations, bureaucracies, and technological control models' at the expense of ecological health, vital learning and empowering wisdom, local power to determine one's life, real abundance, a wholesome appreciation of the 'present', and a nourishing magical consciousness about the possibility of other worlds.

SUBVERTING TRUTH: A 'SHAMANIC' URGENCY

Steven Best has written,

> As the corporate machines continue to slash and burn the planet, inequalities widen and power grows, logics of profit and control spread through social institutions, human

numbers and the insatiable appetites of the global consumer society swell as the biodiversity of flora and fauna
steeply declines, it is easy to become not only cautious or
pessimistic about the prospects for planetary peace and
freedom, but fatalistic and nihilistic. In the schools and
social movement discourse, we are beginning to hear from
some who appear resigned to the catastrophe playing out
on this planet. Others, however, remain oblivious to this
incredible moment in time and the epic tragedy of resigning
humanity's fate to be a failed primate species because of its
inability to harness the evolutionary advantages of a large
forebrain or overcome its predilection to tribalism, xeno-
phobia, hubris, hierarchy, violence, alienation from nature
and other life forms, and uncontrolled growth...

There are no easy solutions to the complex crises of today,
and this chapter offers none. Moreover, this is not the time for
solutions as such, but a reconceptualization of the problems that
beset us. We are dealing with paradigms and conditioning metanarratives here, and the effort to come to terms with the governing systems of our time is important. However, a certain urgency
is needed today, for as the global monoculture of Truth gains
momentum – squelching relationships under its metallic boot of
profit, commoditizing value, distorting indigenous stories, producing hypnotized populations of isolated consumers, loosening
our connections to the lands that bore us, and creating ever escalating technologies and pyramidal hierarchies of elite control – it
is becoming gradually difficult to stop in our tracks, to turn the
wheel towards more holistic directions. Even well-meaning resistance efforts designed to inspire people to localize, and embrace

'ancient futures' have hardly been able to slow down the destruction of the planet, the destruction of our collective futures, and the destruction of our stories.

There is therefore something of a shamanic urgency to recognize Truth as a colonizing creed and reclaim the fluidity and Dionysian beauty of our own stories. I use the word 'shamanic' in reference to indigenous healers whose roles in their communities across Africa and the world historically served to bring new ways of seeing from other dimensions and wisdom for living in tune with the present. Though thoroughly relegated to the backwaters of irrelevance and often seen as relics of a dark, unenlightened past, the shaman is a traveller of invisible distances and an agent of transformation, of a shift in consciousness or an expanded sensitivity to the worlds and possibilities usually hidden behind our blind spots. The shaman, through their connections to plants and other-than-human entities, represents fragility, possibility and playfulness. This concluding section is however not a treatise on the shaman as it is a siren call for the revitalization of shamanic consciousness – what Greenwood calls 'magical consciousness', the basis of which is 'participation, as an orientation to the world that is holistic and 'mystical'':

> Magical consciousness, as an aspect of human cognition, may be equated with what Lévy-Bruhl has termed 'the law of participation'. Lévy-Bruhl saw participation as a psychic unity, a fundamental state of mind, that included individuals, society, and the living as well as the dead; he described it is a type of thinking that created relationships between things through unseen forces and influences. Magical consciousness is based on analogical rather

than logical thought, and involves the association of ideas, symbols, and meaningful coincidences. Described variously as 'altered states of consciousness' (ASCs), shamanic states of consciousness (SSC), or non-ordinary reality, magical consciousness is usually brought about through the application of one or more techniques, such as dancing or drumming (or a combination of these); it may occur in or out of a ritual setting. Primarily concerning a shift in consciousness to an expanded awareness, it may involve the invocation of spirit beings.

Magical consciousness thus represents a disruption of conditioned ways of thinking and programmed attitudes occasioned by the modern civilizational complex. It represents a revitalized way of seeing and being in the world that valorises connection instead of distance, community in paradoxical juxtaposition with the individual; it restores local power and indigenous stories and storytelling dynamics – not in a static sense of recapturing Kodak representations of culture and mindlessly seeking to practice them, but more in a way of providing a familiar field for conversations about the ways we live. Magical consciousness restores agency to the African, disabuses her mind as to the preached inevitability of the global industrial complex, and invites experimentation with new ways of being together – woven from the material threads of our once-buried cosmologies. For an extended treatment of magical consciousness, the reader is happily referred to Greenwood's *The Nature of Magic*, in which she astutely expands upon the soft, feminine, indigenous consciousness about life and our relations as a 'pan-human' awareness, a story that could redeem us from the inevitability of the status quo. Let it suffice the reader to know, in the context of this chapter, that magical consciousness is another paradigmatic way of being in and with the world – one which emphasizes participation and performance. The Copernican revolution and its ideological descendants facilitated the mechanization of life, leading to the creation of vast mindscapes characterized by creed, conquest, conversion, commodification, control and crisis. If, in simpler terms, the gradual colonization of human futures under this rigid atmosphere of global compliance represents a particular way of thinking, then magical consciousness, no less the subversion of Truth and the reanimation of *story,* is its disruption. Above all, 'magical consciousness concerns the awareness of the interrelatedness of all things in the world', Greenwood writes.

More than ever, we in Africa need to tell our own stories. The stories lost in the asphalted regimes of modernity need to find new tellers, new maroon communities of practice, new performances. The crisis we face is no less a crisis of consciousness; the root of the problems we face is not our incompetence, corruption or our inadequacy, but our surrender to the contested practices of development, urbanization and consumerism.

Though we do not recognize it, our disenchantments are our greatest treasures, our most faithful allies – not our orange-tinged skies or wild festivals of divine performances, and definitely not the fact that we are currently striving hard to climb the ladder of global reckoning. By our disenchantments, I refer to our collective pain that is often borne by apparently negative, all-too-familiar feelings of despair, of disgust, anger, failure, irritation, rank cynicism, and depression. Most of the time, we are taught through our cultural conditioning and some of the social sciences that we must treat these feelings as militant viruses that must be spotted quickly and disarmed. We are told that there is something wrong with us if we become 'too negative', if we forget our place, if we cannot see that people are working hard to give us the 'good life', and we are offered easy ways we can deal with these feelings through pills, through the adoption of labels, through feeding off the glamour of celebrity culture, and, most of all, through the dumbing down of hope.

But other traditions suggest to us that the universe is fragile, indeterminate, playful, arbitrary and connected; our pains are creative aspects of being, invitations to transform our experiences and emerge from the reality grids we are currently trapped in.

Across the world, there is a general yearning today for these indigenous wisdoms – as if the promises of modern civilization – in contrast to the smallness and sacredness of these cultures – have been tested and found wanting. Thanks to shamanic arts and local voices from the fringes, trans-local communities are seeing a revitalization of the feminine, a reclamation of ancestral reciprocity, a valorisation of a new sense of holistic sacredness and a depathologization of profane, carnal, gooey traditions; they are seeing a recovery of our beautiful insignificance, a rejuvenation of our multidimensionality and astounding sacredness, a trouncing of boredom and a penetration of the politics of the normal.

Thanks to these cosmologies, new social technologies are emerging – ones that change the parameters we have grown used to, replacing them with new ways of being. A shamanic urgency would call for a return to gift cultures, a return to built environments that respect the earth as a living 'thing', a return to a conception of learning that is not dependent on the reification of grades and certificates, and a turn to wisdom from instrumental information. In these shifts lie our collective hope for new landscapes – away from the messages of disciplinarity and the social sciences, into the unfettered, ever-dancing arenas of magical consciousness.

Sometime early this year I sat with strange looking men, who live and practice their art on the edges of social acceptability, in the borderlands of despair. I had beaten a dangerous path out of the arenas of conventional, 'safe' research by seeking them out. As a clinical psychologist, I had quickly grown disenchanted with my practice, which seemed to me a commoditized, tongue-in-cheek, legitimization of modern civilization and its discontents – a way of entrenching the status quo by patronisingly pathologizing the exception...a way of taming possibility. Bursting with a restless quest for alternatives, I sought out these Yoruba traditional healers – to learn their stories, to understand what we have collectively forgotten, and perhaps to recognize faint tunes about my own journeys which I had not yet danced to.

In their unbecoming shacks, I saw bottles, countless bottles with sticks and strange smells, dusty amulets hanging on cobwebbed threads, the horns of cows, and calabashes half-filled with viscous red palm oil and floating cowrie shells. They had all been trained informally, under the strict and sacred supervision of their fathers. They were shamans – conjurers of other worlds, scribes of songs only plants could sing. Thanks to the rich conversations with them, I began to notice remarkable differences in the ways I had been taught to operationalize mental illness and in the ways these men saw the phenomenon. In one of my sessions interviewing one of these men, after exploring the diagnostic dimensions of his sacred practice with mentally challenged persons, I asked the question that I had been struggling to articulate for some time:

"What do you know", I muttered through my interpreter, ashamed I could not speak my own language "that we in the West-inspired world seem to have forgotten? How can we live healthier lives?" Here, in essence, is what he said to me:

"You have forgotten that everything is alive and connected, and you have rested in your faith that your pills will solve all your problems. Your modern projects have chased away the spirits – so we have to go deep into the forests to find them again. But you will find them again, you will find new ways of living when you find the courage to embrace the dark and lose your way."

CHAPTER TWO

Telling an African Social Sciences Narrative: An Approach

MOLEFI KETE ASANTE

Africa is full of surprises and nothing stuns a conscious, assertive, self-assured African any more than to see mature, adult African people rushing to become new victims of Western stories whether they are Harry Potter or Jesus Christ or Michel Foucault. It is as if we have forgotten our own stories and the names of Imhotep, Chaminuka, Oduduwa, and Okomfo Anokye. There were, of course, philosophers in Africa before the Greeks (Asante, 2000). Almost all humans in every part of the world, and particularly in Africa, have converged at the most aware and conscious moment since the beginning of European hegemony with the will to tell their own stories. I am optimistic that Africa, with its intellectual and moral engines for power, will help establish a world civilization that takes into consideration the plural contributions of humankind. This is just one of the stories that is possible.

My personal story is one of liberation and victory over oppressive academic brainwashing and brutish social situations. I was born in the racist Deep South of the United States during the 1940s near the nadir of African American history when the lynching of black males was an epidemic and the brutalization of African women was quite common. Our education was an indoctrination of the worst form because we were basically taught that African people were inferior to whites by content and symbol. White racial domination was the theology of all Europeans and there were no white voices, that I could hear, railing against the false ideology. The content of our education glorified white achievements and we learned that the slave-holders George Washington and Thomas Jefferson were great men, almost without peer. Our language was called backward, ignorant, and unsophisticated – although we were able to use it for the most intricate of conversations and the most intimate of emotions. The white supremacist view was delivered to us by black teachers in segregated schools with second-handed books, too old and used to be in the hands of white children, but just good enough for African students. My friends later had these same messages delivered to them by white teachers in predominantly white student schools. The impact was similar; we were taught that white was better and that black was inferior. We were made to question our African experiences, histories, and behaviors and to deny what was truly African. We grew to dislike being identified with a continent that we had been told did nothing, achieved nothing, and was going nowhere. This situation did not change when the educational transformation occurred during the era of school integration where blacks and whites had to sit in the same classrooms. The information given to the students remained white supremacist in content.

For me, a radical, rambunctious, angry young man, nothing that was given to me was accepted at face value because I believed that the doctrine of white supremacy was false and spurious. I knew that I was innately as intelligent as any white person I had ever met and consequently the fact that I had not been exposed to some information only made me want to read more. Therefore, I questioned and challenged the style of presentation and the content of my classes. Western social sciences emerged from the same racist grounds as Western arts and humanities. I knew intuitively that the Greeks were not the first philosophers; how could they be when Greece did not exist before Egypt, Nubia, India, or China? I despised the white racists who constructed the system of separation in the first place because they were afraid of African people (Ani, 1994). They did not want to compete with us because they knew that our students were equal to any of them. However, they also knew that they had the economic, military, and political power to thwart the will of any African people in the American South. This was the continuation of the system of unbridled disrespect of a people who had been drastically removed from their continent of origin. Consequently social sciences, as conceived by such a society, had to be racist inasmuch as educational systems are proscribed by the political ideology of a society.

Consequently what was taught on the African continent or in the Caribbean or South America, wherever black people lived, was the same aggressive white ideology. When a student left the classes at the largest African universities in Kenya, Uganda,

Senegal, Nigeria, South Africa, Zambia, Congo, Ghana, and other nations he or she left with 'European' on their minds. They had been brainwashed, completely deprived of the thousands of years of information and knowledge collected by African people, and therefore they had often become self-hating and self-deprecating Africans.

THREE IMPORTANT POINTS

There are three propositions that might elucidate the issues confronting us in dealing with the hegemonic Eurocentric worldview in social sciences. It is essential that we confront a system that has trapped our own narratives and often wrestled them to a standstill. First, I think that *we have to undo much of the structure* that has been erected by European scholars who have advanced a whites-only agenda of world knowledge. Secondly it is necessary to *unhinge the social sciences from the capitalist project* of service to the property classes that was greatly augmented during the era of enslavement and colonization, and continues to be a problem. Thirdly, we have to *propose a more human and open system of learning informed by the sage narratives of the indigenous peoples* of the earth. As Africans it will be necessary for us to begin with our own life stories, revealing the strong underpinnings of our knowledge about the world. We did not have to wait for the Greeks to build the pyramids, the *dzimbabwes,* the Eredo fortification, or to master herbs and numbers.

What we know is that these three critical issues will not run alone; they must be encouraged, managed, and motivated by thinkers who are devoted to human interests, freed from attachments to personal gain and professional careerism. In addition,

there must be bold social scientists who must be willing to con-
ceptualize in new ways, to find innovative paths to knowledge, to
discover in the sage methods of African people our own truths,
and if necessary, to rename themselves. There is nothing sacred
about the use of the term "social scientists" and any genuinely creative African cadre of scholars can approach the manipulation of
experiments, the gathering of data, and the interpretation of data
from an African perspective.

Undoing the Structure

I have concluded after much reflection based on my reading and
inquiries that we must advance on two fronts to unseat the driver
in the traditional Western social sciences vehicle that has brought
us to the brink of social, economic, and political disaster. We must
understand that the marginalization of African lives and experiences in the social sciences is due to the prosecution of a fierce
Eurocentric agenda that promotes Europeans as the standards
of the world. Consequently we must abandon all talk of "tribes,"
"pygmies," "natives," and other pejorative terminologies that still
appear too regularly in our discourses. The key to undoing the
Western racist constructions is to confront every instance where
Africans have been moved off of philosophical and cultural terms.

The second point that we must understand is that the values
of Europe have been foisted upon the academic community as
the "best" values in the world, and hence the normative ideal of
Europe becomes one of the most aggressive ideas assaulting the
minds of African scholars. We must proceed from the staging of
intensive critiques of European social sciences to the posting of
assertive alternative intellectual projects that not only chastise

imperialism, racism, and capitalism but provide a different scale and space of work.

In thinking about what new forms of social sciences will emerge from an Afrocentric perspective I am reminded that the brilliant Senegalese genius Cheikh Anta Diop once said that had Africans studied the idea of families and launched this study internationally the notion of social sciences would have been called Family Sciences. I know that our constructive possibilities are numerous and that we have an opportunity to advance a more practicable agenda if we are committed to confronting our conceptual imprisonment based on our acceptance of the European model. Already we have seen at the political level various indigenous populations rising up to demand their own liberation. Thus, there are resistances everywhere to colonialism, imperialism, capitalism, and corporate definitions of success. Who are we as human beings if we are un-free to explore our own cultures, arts, sciences, and behaviours because we have been smothered by an aggressive and violent culture of clashes? One must understand that we have often allowed the massaging of our minds away from our traditions, experiences, histories, and ancestors in such a way that we become heretics against our own interests. This is why the indigenous cry to be left alone, actually to be able to stay free of the clutches of the West or any other region, is important for psychological and ethical health. How can we create global alternatives to the reigning hegemony of Europe must be our main task? Fortunately as we are confronted by this challenge the entire world appears ready to renounce the continuing hegemony of whites. I think it is possible to announce the end of the ideological doctrine of neo-liberalism that has been promoted as a progressive Western stance against the old European Order. The reason I think we can make this announcement is because of the rise of consciousness everywhere in the African world.

Young African Colombians, African Peruvians, African Brazilians, African Ecuadorians, African Bolivians, African Mexicans, and African Venezuelans have joined with people of African descent in the United States, Jamaica, Haiti, Cuban, Costa Rica, Panama, and other Diasporan communities to move from critique of the West to posing their own alternative ways of seeing reality. This is not the abandonment of knowledge or science but rather the re-orienting of science, arts, humanities, and social sciences away from the imposition of Europe as universal. They are in search of a transcendent Africa as source and inspiration for innovation, myth, motif, and ethos. Without this response to the African condition we will never be able to transform the minds of African youth. A culture that cannot teach its children its traditions is a dead culture; a civilization that has forgotten its own names and narratives is an enslaved civilization; and people who no longer sing in the languages of their people are condemned to confusion in the modern age.

Clearly, contemporary events have helped to radicalize the thinking of African people throughout the world. For example, the North African Uprising of 2011, largely among the Arab populations of the region, has brought in its wake a shocking awareness of the racism that was being held back by the Gaddafi Regime. Under the Rebels, supported by NATO, there has been an unleashing of Arab mobs against the numerically smaller groups of indigenous and immigrant blacks in Libya. Whipped up by rhetoric that accused Libyan blacks of being mercenaries the

Rebels of the East massacred many blacks, some of them defence-less Toubou people. Thus, it must be said that the traditional reaction against white racism must now be applied to Arab racism (Deng, 2016). Resistance! This has to be the African's response to every form of racism whether overt or covert. One must find in the historical record of ancestral achievements the strength and inspiration to stand down the threat of hierarchical oppression from any quarters. But this can only be done when we have a revolutionary cadre of intellectuals willing to confront the marginalization of Africans in the social sciences. Of course, there is some hyperbole in the preceding statement because we are developing that cadre all over Africa and the African world. From Brazil to Benin and from Colombia to Cameroun, and from United States to Uganda, African social scientists are rewriting the texts on many issues. We have learned to do as Ama Mazama contends to question everything that Europe proposes if it is not based on an African paradigm (Mazama, 2003). Question often and questions deeply must be one of our mottoes.

The tasks at hand are numerous and cover many intellectual fields. For example, if we take the fields that are usually considered the central social sciences in the West we see that they all must be re-oriented by an innovative group of African scholars. If one looked at geography from the standpoint of an Afrocentric position it would necessary be necessary to modify the construction of the world where Europe is at the centre of everything. Of course, the reality is that on the ground Europe has managed to control the air, space, oceans, radio waves, Internet, and natural resources of the world yet we are on the verge of new national and international challenges to this hegemony. China, among Asian nations, and South Africa and Nigeria, among African nations, are headed in the direction of spreading influence from the European center. In 40 years Nigeria will become the third most populous nation in the world. This movement will be accelerated in the future. In Anthropology, sociology, psychology, history, and political science we need a reframing of the discourse away from the narrow, provincial idea of Europeans as the universal people by which all knowledge is measured.

If we look at history as taught in the West we see that almost all *periodization* relates to something in the West. One can readily see this problem with BC and AD references as the split in time between the ancient world and the current era. Why not use the founding of the nation of Egypt in 3400 BCE as a defining period in humanity's march through time? The West is self-centred in its understanding of human history but the problem is in our hands; Africa must operate in its own interests to understand the world from its perspective, not to burden others with our perspective but to suggest our own sense of agency as it relates to our experiences. There are many key points in African history that might be used for markers of periods. For example, the end of the Pyramid Age, Ramses' conquest of Kadesh, King Tutankhamen's return to Waset and the temple of Amen after his father Akhenaten had violated the traditions of the people, Piankhy reuniting of Kemet and Nubia, the end of Great Zimbabwe, the Fall of Timbuktu, and numerous other markers could be used to frame time periods. Yet almost no African writer or scholar has seen fit to employ a period strategy that utilizes African markers. This is the objective of Afrocentric philosophers who want to redress the slavish allegiance that African scholars hold to European notions of time.

African historians who have been trained in the Eurocentric manner for the past fifty years have rarely ventured to re-organize their conception of periods; this is one of the monumental failures of African historiography.

The classical narrative is fundamental to a resurgence of African ideals. Africa cannot articulate its own narrative without having some idea of the beginning of the major ideas of the continent. When did people organize themselves into societies and nations? Who defined the nature of architecture? How did the ancient Africans arrive at the use of sailboats on the Nile? What method did Africans use to disseminate behaviours, values, and spiritual concepts? During what time period did Africans create geometry and mathematics? How did medicine and philosophy come into being in the Nile Valley?

Obviously the plethora of questions that can be asked and should be answered about African narratives is endless. How we tell these stories in a way that advances human knowledge, not for any imperialistic reason, will add to the collective memory of Africans. Without an appreciation of early civilizations in Nubia and Kemet no African child can have any way to make sense of his or her own specific national or ethnic histories. We are connected to a large global collectivity of humans who originated in East Africa and spread to the rest of the continent before moving out of Africa into Europe and Arabia.

UNHINGE SOCIAL STUDIES FROM THE CAPITALIST PROJECT

The capitalist project is a five hundred year old activity that is now crippled by its own reach for greed. Based on the idea that greed is the fundamental motive for good and that profit at all costs should be the basic economic model of the world this bankrupt system of exploitation has now reached its most major crisis point. There have been crises before but the fear now is that the system organized to dominate the world by crushing competition has come home to roost in the West itself. In one sense the European world has played the game as if they were the only ones to matter and so long as the West controlled all of the commodities of the world, the banking institutions, the airwaves, space, the oceans, gold, diamonds and other minerals, it could rest assured that one day the West would capture petroleum as well. The model had been practiced in Africa from the earliest moment the Europeans entered the continent. This was the economic model of enslavement. It was practiced during the 300 years of slave trade as well as during the white occupation of Africa. The Congo Free State under the Belgium king Leopold and his tyrant, Henry Stanley, sought to prove that the West could drive its engine on the backs of hardworking Africans.

Capitalism needs chattel; this is its inherent nature. Whether that chattel was a human being or a factory did not matter to the makers of this system; the idea was to work the property to its fullest extent so that it would bring the highest yield. In our narrative research must not be for its own sake and it cannot be for the sake of profit; it must be for the sake of transforming human beings so that they can live safer, cleaner, and more rational lives. This means that social sciences become connected to something more than careerism. I do not want the themes of our social sciences to be dictated by the needs of the Western professors entering African and African Diasporan communities as explorers with trinkets to give to the poor African person willing to sell his knowledge or skills to assist the white person in his or her research agenda. 'What is Africa's agenda' must be the question that must be asked each time someone comes with a request. If the Westerners are able to accommodate an African agenda then perhaps assistance could be arranged; but it is time for Africans to stop being dictated to about what is important to research in Africa. If the people will not stop them, then the Westerners will continue their inquiries and requests because they assume that their agendas are more important than those of Africans. They have received their grants and research commissions for subjects with are often outside of Africa's needs and interests; however, these research projects for which they invariably need African assistance have often set the agenda for research by Africans. I mean, why is it that we know more about Africa and France or Africa and England than we know about Africa and India or Africa and China?

Given the fact that humans have been building, learning, conceptualizing and debating on the African continent longer than on any other continent our primary burden as intellectuals is to explore indigenous knowledge. There is a story told of a young man who left a small village in the rain forest and travelled thirty days toward the Sahel where he had been told that there was a wise woman who knew how to decipher an inscription he had received from his grandfather. Although he had tried several times to find someone who could tell him the meaning of the inscription along the way, he had failed to get an answer and at last he found himself in the Sahelian village in the north of Niger. When he was introduced to the woman she gave one look

at the inscription and told him that it was impossible to understand the meaning of the writing. He was sad, disappointed, but
took leave of the place and went back to his own village, another
thirty day journey. When he returned home and told the elders
what he had done they were amazed. One of them said that he
should have asked at home. He had never thought that anyone
at home knew the meaning. However, when the elders looked at
the inscription several of them knew the meaning and even knew
the original creator of the inscription. The lesson here is that one
can sometimes find the answer in one's own village. What existed
before Capitalism and Marxism? What were the inadequacies
of those pre-European systems? Why have we been so eager to
assume that they are better than what Africans decided or could
possibly have decided? These questions must be asked in any
re-evaluation of social sciences if we are to disconnect from the
European wagon that has dragged us a long ways from our own
traditions and cultures. Indeed, Europe has essentially degraded
and despised African cultures and customs by proposing a social
sciences system that failed to consider African human beings as
a part of the process of creation of knowledge. Europe's problem
is that Africa seeks revolution in the study of African history,
culture, spirituality, societies, languages, and economics. All
revolutions are essentially social because they involve a conscious
people dedicated to transforming their situation. Do European
or America social sciences want to see this type of revolution in
African thinking? This question is significant because almost
every social science in the West, from anthropology to sociology,
from political science to psychology, has been constructed with
Europe in mind.

UNIFYING SAGE AND INDIGENOUS THINKING

What we need to do as scholars and intellectuals is to begin a drastic rewriting of the current narratives about social sciences. In fact learning from the historic Haitian Revolution we could seek a total break with the enslaving system of the West. This means that we must make dramatic breaks with the uni-global system articulated by an aggressive Eurocentric core. Indeed, if we learn from the Haitian departure we can apply it to politics and social sciences. I am not calling for isolation but rather for a collective African sense of worth that allows us to rely upon our own communities and ideas.

Europe has presented itself on the stage of human history long enough for us to understand something about its manner. It has disclosed itself for the past five hundred years and we know lots about its values and prospects. If you take styles of relationship it appears that the West presents itself with these values: confrontation, experts, polarization, blame and shame strategies, divisiveness, rights and victims, focus on the other, and the leader as a hero. In general, African people tend to see relationships as cooperative, facilitator-led, participant-centred, unifying, positive, with shared responsibilities, introspective, and with the leader as an advisor, a colleague, brother or sister. This is not some statement about blood or biology but rather about the ways we have been acculturated in the places where we have spent the most time. Africans, spending time in African communities, have developed certain patterns and responses that are recognizable from one place to the next. If we cannot utilize our own information, knowledge, and experience then our own contributions to human understanding lie dormant while we explore those of others. This is a complete sell-out of our ancestors in the sense that we have refused to modify their ideas, transform their suspicions, and investigate their hypotheses.

In every aspect of human life, from the discovery of new techniques for ordinary daily activities to the most complex ritual creations dealing with initiations, metal-making, and reproduction of dramatic history, Africans people have made some important declarations of the activities. We may not know them but we must investigate, discover, and where we cannot discover we must reason backwards knowing that if a certain thing exists today that it must have had precedents an those actions coming before the present helped to create what we hear, see, and do now. Our genius must be to ferret out the truth, to remove the curtain across the stage of our history and allow new attitudes and facts to emerge. I hope, in fact, I know that this will happen because already the Afrocentrists are demonstrating their agency in the act of discovery. They are finding new avenues for discovery and asking more powerful questions about the building of civilization. If each scholar searches in his or her own culture for new leads, new personalities, long forgotten facts, and inquiries from the living elders what they know about processes, relationships, families, kinship, and social creations we would reveal to ourselves and the world new ways of telling our own narratives.

We must determine the purpose of knowledge. If our aim is to liberate our people and provide them with information that can assist them in making a proper decision about their lives then we need to make social sciences or the study of human social and family issues central to our task of empowering the people. One does not necessarily do this by supporting the building of Western social sciences or by referring to those who have written and studied Western social sciences. This is a process that does nothing but build on the Western mound of information by making it the keystone of human understanding. I do not believe that a true social scientist in the African tradition has any business studying or teaching alienating narratives to African people, nor should we be supporting a racist construction that has been used to stranglehold our visions of the future. What has to happen now is that we see the value of proverb wisdom, *sebayets*, and sage knowledge as ways to combat political and social ignorance and conceptual illiteracy. There is no question in my mind as it has been in the minds of Paulo Freire, Ama Mazama, Claude Alvares, and Abdias do Nascimento that you cannot win mental freedom by depending upon a type of social sciences that has imprisoned the thinking of African people. Why would European or American social sciences be used to liberate African people?

The research narrative that seeks to escape human reality by masking itself in abstractions is far from what we need as African intellectuals. Those of us who practice "social sciences" cannot be neutral and hope to bring about change. Transformation of the masses into a phalanx of participating democrats about their own conditions and futures must be the objective of our social sciences. In effect, for me, the journey has to be one where I seek no refuge in obfuscating abstractions but where I engage reality with the authentic responses of proverbial wisdom from my ancestors. Perhaps this is a journey that we can all share. May these words be justified.

REFERENCES

Alvares, Claude (1992) *Science, Development and Violence: The Revolt Against Modernity.* London: Oxford University Press.

Ani, Marimba (1994) *Yurugu: An African Centered Critique of European Thought and Behavior.* Trenton: Africa World Press.

Asante, Molefi Kete (2000) *The Egyptian Philosophers.* Chicago: African American Images.

Deng, Bol Gai (2016) *Arab Racism in Kush.* New York: Universal Write.

Freire, Paulo (1996) *The Pedagogy of the Oppressed.* New York: Penguin

Mazama, Ama (2003) *The Afrocentric Paradigm.* Trenton: Africa World Press.

Nascimento, Abdias do (1979) *Brazil, Mixture or Massacre: Essays in the Genocide of a Black People.* Buffalo: Afrodiaspora

Chapter Three

Afrocentricity and the Critical Question of African Agency

Ama Mazama

A frican people have often been made invisible by 500 years of Eurocentric oppression and suppression. Eurocentrism, for the sake of our discussion here, is defined as the interpretation of all reality from the Western perspective, especially as it emerged during the so-called European Enlightenment period. This perspective developed both internally, with the development of a meta-paradigm specific and relevant to Europe; and externally, in opposition to "others," especially African people. Thus, there are at least four assumptions of that European meta-paradigm which have played a major and negative role as far as African people are concerned: 1) all human beings evolve along the same line; 2) the European experience is universal; 3) Europeans are superior; and 4) "others" are defined by their experiences with Europeans.

In other words, the European meta-paradigm rests, among other things, on the belief in the superiority and universality of the European experience.

European social sciences, informed as they are by Eurocentric assumptions, have played a major role in making Africans secondary, even to ourselves. It is my purpose in this chapter to review social sciences' approach to African phenomena, and argue for an Afrocentric corrective, namely, the exercise by African people of our agency in all arenas, especially the intellectual/mental one.

SOCIAL SCIENCES' PROBLEMATIC TREATMENT OF AFRICA

In his brilliant essay on "social science as imperialism," Claude Ake (1979) had already observed that much of what passes for scientific, objective studies of Africa, is nothing more and nothing less than an attempt at maintaining Africa under European yoke. Indeed, by imposing an analytical framework that creates mental and conceptual dependency upon Europe, and by presenting the latter as both the norm and ideal model, thus fostering feelings of African inadequacy and inferiority toward Europe, European social scientists enable the exploitation of Africa by Europe. But this is not all, since in a very concrete way, social scientists also engage in pro-capitalist propaganda, hence facilitating the integration of African societies into global capitalism. Ake focused his analysis on political science, sociology and economics, revealing how, in fact, the concept of development reigns supreme in the Eurocentric paradigm shared by these disciplines.

First, explains Ake (1979: 109), there is the tendency to classify nations as advanced (developed) and backward, and to present the former as "good" and the latter as "bad, or, at any rate, undesirable.

Second, there is the tendency to hold up the Western industrialized countries as the model for the economic development of the underdeveloped countries. Third, there is the tendency to regard the present condition of the underdeveloped countries as a moment in their evolution towards the present condition of the developed countries. Fourth, there is a preoccupation with the possibility of making the Third World countries more like the Western industrialized countries.

The conclusions drawn by Ake after his review of sociology, political science and economics apply to most if not all other social sciences. Linguistics, for example, is no exception. As I demonstrated elsewhere (Mazama, 2003), although linguistics officially claims that all languages are equal, Language Planning Studies, a field within sociolinguistics whose aims are to address the "language problems" of "developing countries," postulates nonetheless a linguistic hierarchy reminiscent of the hierarchies established in other social sciences. At the very bottom of the continuum, one finds "preliterate languages," followed by "unstandardized languages," "young standard languages," "archaic standard languages," "fully developed small group standard languages," and finally, at the top, "mature standard languages" (Kloss, 1968: 82). Needless to say, most Western European languages, the so-called world languages, belong to the last category.

Thus, in the context of Language Planning Studies, for a language to become part of the mature standard languages club, it must undergo "development," the first step of which being the elaboration of an appropriate script, preferably one using the Roman alphabetic conventions. This emphasis on the elaboration of a script for a language to be considered on the path

to "maturity," is part and parcel of the Western "literacy myth,"
(Graff 1979), the locus of incredible and extravagant speculation in the West about the liberating effects of literacy. Indeed,
according to many, literacy plays a key role in cognitive, group,
and social mobility. The most dramatic effect of the introduction
of writing into a particular community, according to the literacy
myth, is that only through writing can a community become part
of history: in other words, history starts with writing (Goody &
Watt, 1977; Stubbs, 1980). Any event taking place prior to the
use of writing by a particular group is dismissed as "prehistorical"
(Prieswork & Perrot, 1978: xxi). The criterion of transmission of
knowledge through the written medium has certainly been used
to disqualify Africa as a place where any meaningful history could
have occurred, as pointed out by Keita (1977: 141):

> Until quite recently it was generally believed that the
> concept of history was alien to African societies. Barring
> unsubstantiated stereotypical views about African society
> in general, evidence of the argument that African peoples
> were traditionally ahistorical was produced by pointing
> to the fact that there was no tradition of written history
> in Africa.

WHITE RACIAL INTELLECTUAL SUPREMACY AT WORK

This imposition of Europe, under the guise of objectivity and
universalism, one must realize, is part and parcel of a narrative
of white superiority, a "racial mythology," based on the "rather
strange belief on the parts of whites that they are superior to Africans, that they have a right to establish and maintain a hierarchy
over blacks by force of arms or customs or laws or habits" (Asante

2007: 136). It is rather easy to see, however, how this strange belief is inseparable from the self-serving notion that only Europeans are capable of agency, or at least to a much higher degree than other people in the world.

In his insightful book *The Colonizer's model of the world*, Blaut (1993) explains how, starting in the 16th-17th centuries and culminating in the 19th century, Europeans embraced diffusionism to account for their self-proclaimed superiority. According to this metatheory, the world is made up of two parts, one characterized by cultural and intellectual inventiveness, the other by uninventiveness. Quite predictably, the uniquely creative human communities "remain the permanent centres of culture change, of progress" (1993: 14). Consequently, "at the global scale, this gives us a model of a world with a single centre – roughly, Greater Europe – and a single periphery; an Inside and an Outside" (1993: 14). The rest of the world is therefore condemned to consume European intellectual and material products, due to its own creative impotence. Worse yet, the rest of the world is to depend on Europe to be rescued from its cultural and historical lethargy.

So dormant have the Africans been that some Europeans went so far as to suggest that not only had we failed to progress (that is, to become like Europeans), but we might even have been regressing when Europeans stepped in and saved us from sinking back into sheer bestiality. Likewise, Hegel's theory about Africa's ahistoricalness was also generated by the diffusionist metatheory paradigm. Since one of the central pillars of this metatheory is that Africans are deprived of agency, it was a foregone conclusion that African history could not exist. It is worth pausing to examine Hegel's paradigm, given Hegel's outstanding influence on Western thought, and indirectly then, African thought. As convincingly argued by Tibebu, although repudiated in its most outrageous forms, "the *subtext* of the discourse on Africa continues to remain essentially Hegelian because Africa is still perceived through the prism of essential otherness" (2011, p. 174).

Hegel explains that what he calls "Black Africa" "has no historical interest of its own," since "man as we find him in Africa has not progressed beyond his immediate existence." For Hegel, in fact, the African is best understood as being outside not only the historical realm, but outside the human realm altogether, the African is 'animal man', a 'cannibal' by definition (Tibebu 2011, p. 180). Unsurprisingly, Hegel finds great fault with every aspect of African life, for the latter is nothing but a mere reflection of the African state of deleterious consciousness deprivation. Thus, African religion is reduced to sorcery and magic; the African marriage and family are not worthy of the name, but provide simply the context for the sensuous debauchery to which Hegel intimately associates the Africans as 'animal men'. It could not be otherwise since, according to Hegel, Africans are incapable of experiencing love, and cannot appreciate life; etc. In fact, in Hegel's view, the Africans could not have minded being enslaved in the Americas, given their profound disregard for life, including their own! Hegel goes so far as to argue that their enslavement on American soil constituted 'a leap forward in Africans' education for the attainment of absolute freedom' (Tibebu 2011, p. 202).

Thus, within the diffusionist perspective, it is only when Africans encounter Europeans that they truly start to exist as human beings, admittedly retarded ones. This explains labels like "under-developed," "developing." Truly, Africans (and other "others") are defined by their experiences with Europeans. Whether acquiescing or resisting to them, Africans somehow only exist as a result of Europeans' interventions in our lives, as those brutal and aggressive acts of imposition are always and implicitly assumed to be *the* defining moments in the African experience. The common division of African history in two periods, 'pre-colonial' and 'colonial', attests to this Eurocentric historiography. European disruption of African societies is assigned a central place in "African" history. The white American historian, Trevor-Ropper (1973: 9) expressed as well as any this idea: "Undergraduates, seduced, as always, by the changing breath of journalistic fashion, demand that they should be taught the history of black Africa. Perhaps, in the future, there will be some African history to teach. But at present there is none, or very little: there is only the history of the Europeans in Africa. The rest is largely darkness, like the history of pre-European, pre-Columbian America. And darkness is not a subject for history." Further echoing commonly accepted Eurocentric ideas of social Darwinism and linear universalism, the same author (1973: 9) also stressed how, "Then indeed we may neglect our own history and amuse ourselves with the unre-warding gyrations of barbarous tribes in picturesque but irrele-vant corners of the globe: tribes whose chief function in history, in my opinion, is to show to the present an image of the past from which, by history, it has escaped."

Thus, through a racist and arrogant discourse that claimed European monopoly over cultural and historical agency, European social scientists (as well as others operating within the same paradigmatic confines) contributed to the establishment of a discursive space that effectively places Europe at the centre of the

world, while relegating Africans to a marginal position. The violence that this process of imposition entails can hardly be under-
estimated, and nor can its psychological and mental ravages be
ignored. What happens here is that Europe attempts to occupy all
human space. The European experience becomes the yardstick by
which other people's humanity (or lack of) will be evaluated. Yet,
the European experience is nothing more and nothing less than
one experience among many. Parading and hiding as "universal"
and "objective," the European cultural and historical experience
becomes invisible and infiltrates African people's consciousness.
Its European specificity has become, to a large degree, unrecogniz-
able. Yet, as Molefi Asante remarks, what passes for universalism
amounts to nothing more than "Eurocentric ideology" (1998:1),
while so-called objectivity is better understood as "a kind of collective subjectivity of European culture" (1998:1). Asante further
notes how "the aggressive seizure of intellectual space, like the
seizure of land, amounts to occupying some else's territory and
claiming it as one's own. When this happens, cultural analysis
takes a back seat to galloping ethnocentric interpretations of phenomena" (Asante 1998: 10).

What educational institutions, schools or universities, functioning within the Eurocentric premises deliver is not true
education, Asante contends, but Eurocentric triumphalist propaganda, "a racist education, that is, a white supremacist education"
(Asante 2007: 82). In such a context, the development of history,
philosophy, mathematics, writing, arts, religion are automatically,
and without any questions, attributed to Europe, as a result of the
so-called Greek miracle. Yet, closer scrutiny of the facts would
compel advocates of the Greek miracle theory to far more humble

and reasonable claims.

THE PRICE OF AFRICAN NEGATION

One of the consequences of the denial of African agency has been the conspicuous absence of African people, whose presence became invisible even to us, and whose existence was denied: "Africans have been negated in the system of white racial domination. This is not mere marginalization, but the obliteration of the presence, meaning, activities, or images of the African. This is negated reality, a destruction of the spiritual and material personality of the African person" (Asante 1998: 41). Consistent with this denial of Africa was its inferiorization: "With regards to African literature, history, behaviour, and economics, the Eurocentric writers have always positioned Africa in the inferior place with regards to every subject field. This has been a deliberate falsification of the record. It is one of the greatest conspiracies in the history of the world because what was agreed upon, tacitly, writer after writer was that Africa should be marginalized in the literature and downgraded when it seemed that the literature spoke with high regard to Africa" (Asante 1998: 45). As a result of this overall obliteration and inferiorization, Africans have often "lost sense of their cultural ground" (2007: 35) and often live in a state of mental and cultural exile. Africans are described as a people who have been "relegated to the fringes of the society" (Asante 1998: 39), "de-centred" (Asante 2003: 5) and "dislocated" as a result of European cultural (and intellectual) imperialism. Indeed, what else could happen to those Africans who internalize the debased Eurocentric image of Africa, who believe in African cannibalism as a natural African condition, who buy into the myth of Christianity's universalism and worship a white god, or who accept European epistemological categories, such as "underdeveloped," "non-whites," or "Third World"?

THE AFROCENTRIC METHODOLOGY FOR LIBERATION: THE EXERCISE OF AFRICAN AGENCY

It is out of great concern for African disenfranchisement and marginalization in the intellectual arena, as well as other spheres of life, that Molefi Asante (1980) developed the theory of action and liberation known as Afrocentricity, which he explained most recently as seeking to "obliterate the mental, physical, cultural and economic dislocation of African people *by thrusting Africans as centred*, healthy human beings in the context of African thought" (2007: 120; italics added). The purpose is to "escape from the anomie of fringeness" (1998: 41). Asante believes that it is only in the process of reassuming in a most conscious manner our sense of historical and cultural agency that we, Africans, can hope to put an end to our invisibility, debilitation and powerlessness. Asante's rhetoric of liberation, through which he attempts to create and reclaim space for African people, therefore stresses the African as actor and victor. In fact, "the Afrocentric idea is unthinkable without African agency," explains Asante (1998:19) who defines agency as "an attitude toward action originating in African experiences" (2003:3). More specifically, "an agent, in our terms, must mean a human being who is capable of acting independently in his or her own best interest. Agency itself is the ability to provide the psychological and cultural resources necessary for the advancement of human freedom" (1998: 40). The Afrocentric African is acting, not acted upon, for she is no longer satisfied to be "the dark toy/in someone else's carnival/or in someone else field/the obsolete scarecrow" (Césaire, 1957; my translation). Instead, she stands strong and tall in her own centre.

Agency is the activating principle that allows our centre to be a true home, that is, a source of nurturing existential paradigms. Africanity is not to be confused with Afrocentricity. Being born in Africa, living in Africa, does not make one Afrocentric, as explained by Asante himself: "Only those who are consciously African, given to appreciating the need to resist annihilation culturally, politically, and economically, can claim to be adequately in the arena of Afrocentricity" (2007:47). Again, one may be culturally exiled although living in Africa. This happens, for example, when one practices alien traditions, such as worshipping foreign gods, or defending and promoting alien concepts.

The source of agency, as defined Afrocentrically, is consciousness. Agency must be understood as an expression and a manifestation of consciousness. As such, it has particular attributes. For example, it is quantifiable: "What we can argue about in any intellectual discourse is the degree to which Africans are weak or strong agents, but there should be no question that agency exists" (1998: 32). The relative strength or weakness of one's agency is directly correlated to the development of one's consciousness. According to Asante, indeed, consciousness develops through time, as one's awareness increases. Five phases are identified by Molefi Asante (2003: 62): skin recognition, environmental recognition, personality awareness, interest-concern, and Afrocentric awareness. While skin recognition represents the lowest form of consciousness, each subsequent phase is marked by enhanced consciousness and therefore increased agency.

In addition to being quantifiable, consciousness can also be typified. According to Molefi Asante, there are two types of consciousness, consciousness of victory and consciousness of oppression. Both types correspond to the levels of development identified above. Consciousness of victory represents the highest level and consciousness of oppression a much lower one. In fact, only the first one qualifies as Afrocentric consciousness, for only a consciousness of victory is capable of being "stimulating in a progressive sense" (2003: 65). Asante thus continues (2003: 65) "No Afrocentric person can ever have merely a consciousness of oppression, pain, and suffering. The present and the future must be lived victoriously. To be conscious of how difficult the European has made one's life is to be conscious at a very elemental level."

Another significant attribute of agency is that, while agency is a given, basic human feature, it can be exercised or given up. Asante (1998: 35) talks about those Africans who "had denied, lost, or given away agency in order to become different from our historical selves." The price for not exercising one's agency is mental and psychological bondage, even accompanied at times with physical bondage: "When the Afrocentrist says that it is necessary to discover one's location, it is always in reference to whether or not the person is in a centred or marginal place with regards to his or her culture. An oppressed person is dis-located when she operates from a standpoint, that is, location that is centred in the experiences of the oppressor" (Asante 2007: 42).

Consciousness being the source of agency, what determines consciousness (that is, Afrocentric consciousness) itself is our relationship with Africa. This relationship develops along a vertical and horizontal axis. In its vertical dimension, consciousness emanates from the quality of one's relationship with one's ancestors. Afrocentricity requires a "commitment" to an African "cultural base" (Asante 2003: 62), and ancestral veneration is undeniably a most important pillar of the African cultural base.

The person who fails to develop and maintain a relationship with their ancestors is most dislocated and bound to engage in destructive behaviours as they "will attack mothers and fathers, disparage the very traditions that gave them hope in times of hopelessness, and trivialize their own nobility. The person's images, symbols, lifestyles, and manners are contradictory and thereby destructive to personal and collective growth and development. Unable to call upon the power of the ancestors, because one does not know them; without an ideology of heritage, because one does not respect one's own prophets; the person is like an ant trying to move a large piece of garbage only to find that it will not move" (Asante 2003: 3).

This focus on the ancestors as the originators of consciousness is demanded by African culture itself. It is the ancestors who are primarily responsible for the welfare and the thriving of the community, by bestowing protection and guidance to the living. They ensure the flourishing of the community by blessing it with fertility. They are also the zealous moral guardians of the social order upon which the society rests. It is not exaggerated to state that the purpose of African life is to become an ancestor, since such a high status is reserved to those who have lived an ethical life – that is, those who have abided by the community's norms and traditions, thus effectively contributing to its continued and enhanced existence. In the African cultural context, one's ability, personally and collectively exercised, to maintain harmony, peace and balance in life is largely predicated upon one's relationship with the ancestors. This is why consciousness of self as an African necessarily entails, according to Afrocentricity, an active and respectful relationship with the ancestors. This is then also why ancestral veneration is posited as the ultimate source of Afrocentric consciousness, which translates into agency. Thus, Afrocentric consciousness is, in the end, a function of our relationship with our ancestors.

In its horizontal dimension, one's relationship with Africa includes the embrace of the Pan-African community as one's community since, in the African context, existence is conceived as first and foremost a social experience. The exercise of agency, as an assertion of African existence, is therefore also primarily a social phenomenon with intended benefits not just for the person exercising agency but for the whole community. In a political sense, collective consciousness and agency are linked to a commitment to Pan-Africanism. The latter, Asante (2003: 80) observes, "is a political perspective and a political ideology as well as a social theory. The one does not negate the other. Actually when we speak of the political dimensions of the concept we are also talking about *how Africans see themselves as social units*" (emphasis added). As we engage in the transformation of our consciousness, as a collective rather than an individual affair, "we seek to break out of our isolation and distance and come closer to our African brothers and sisters" (Asante 2003: 91).

AFROCENTRICITY AND AFRICOLOGY

Applying Afrocentricity to the academic arena, Asante suggests that the proper study of African phenomena –assuming that the goal of such study is to help liberate African people's "suppressed and oppressed truths," could only be Afrocentric, that is, ground-ed in the observation of the African experience from the stand-point of African people as agents rather than objects, and as victo-rious rather than victims: "Africology is defined, therefore, as the Afrocentric study of phenomena, events, ideas, and personalities related to Africa. The mere study of phenomena is not Africology but some other intellectual enterprise. The scholar who generates questions based on the centrality of Africa is engaged in a very dif-ferent research inquiry than the one who imposes Western criteria on the phenomena" (Asante 1990; 140).

Two important questions are raised here. One is the impera-tive for the African scholar to realize that scholarship *is* praxis. As such, one's scholarship cannot claim to be "neutral," or "objective": much to the contrary, it must be consciously oriented in such a manner that it will be of service to the African community, out of obligation to one's community. Given that Afrocentricity was identified as the indispensable remedy to end our disenfranchise-ment and inferiorization, African scholars must exercise their own agency, that is, embrace the Afrocentric paradigm.

The second question that is being raised concerns a most criti-cal epistemological issue: the paradigm that one uses is bound to determine the configuration and the outcome of the intellec-tual inquiry under way. Kuhn, a Western philosopher of science interested in identifying the process through which a particular mode of scientific thought and practice becomes established as an accepted or dominant mode, helped make explicit the existence of premises upon which all intellectual inquiries are necessarily based, thus rendering the idea of scientific neutrality untenable. Any paradigm represents by definition a conscious or unconscious commitment to a set of metaphysical assumptions, beliefs, a particular methodology, certain methods and techniques, etc. This is why, as discussed in the beginning of this essay, the Eurocentric metaparadigm can only produce imperialistic studies, be they economic, sociological, political or linguistic. It is therefore imperative for African scholars to engage in studies that truly illuminate and enhance African lives.

REFERENCES

Ake, C. (1979) *Social Science as Imperialism. A Theory of Political Development*, Ibadan, Ibadan University Press.

Asante, M. (1990) *Kemet, Afrocentricity and Knowledge*, Trenton, Africa World Press.

Asante, M. (1998) *The Afrocentric Idea*, Philadelphia, Pa.: Temple University Press.

Asante, M. (2003) *Afrocentricity: The Theory of Social Change*. Chicago, African American Images.

Asante, M. (2003) `African American Studies: The Future of the Discipline`, in Mazama, A. (ed.) *The Afrocentric Paradigm*, Trenton, Africa World Press.

Asante, M. (2007) *An Afrocentric Manifesto: Toward an African Renaissance*, Malden, Polity Press.

Asante, M and Mazama, A. (eds) (2009), *The Encyclopaedia of African Religion*, Thousand Oaks, Sage Publications.

Blaut, J. (1993) *The Colonizer's Model of the World – Geographical Diffusionism and Eurocentric History,* New York & London, The Guilford Press.

Césaire, A. (1960) *Ferrements*, Paris, Editions du Seuil.

Goody, J. and Watt, I. (1977) `The consequences of Literacy', in Goody J. (ed.), *Literacy in Traditional Societies,* Cambridge, Cambridge University Press.

Graff, H. (1987) *The labyrhinths of Literacy. Reflections on Literacy past and present,* London, Falmer.

Keita, L. (1977) `Two philosophies of African history : Hegel and Diop', *Présence Africaine,* 91: 41-49.

Kloss, H. (1968) `Notes concerning a language-nation typology' in J. Fishman, C. Ferguson, & J. Das Gupta (eds), *Language Problems of Developing Nations*, New York, Wiley.

Mazama, Ama. (2003) `An Afrocentric approach to Language Planning', in Mazama A. (ed.), *The Afrocentric Paradigm*, Trenton, Africa World Press.

Priestwerk, R. & Perrot, D. (1978) *Ethnocentrism and History: Africa, Asia and Indian America in Western Texbooks,* New York, NOK.

Stubbs, M. (1980) *Language and Literacy: the Sociolinguistics of Reading and Writing,* London, Routledge & Kegan Paul.

Tibebu, T. (2011) *Hegel and the Third World, the Making of Eurocentrism in World History*, New York, Syracuse University Press.

Trevor-Ropper, H. (1968) *The Rise of Christian Europe,* London, Harcourt, Brace & World.

CHAPTER FOUR

Social Sciences and Academic
Imperialism in the Global South:
Some Reflections on Africa

GORDON ONYANGO OMENYA

In *The Idea of Africa*, Mudimbe (1994) asks the following question: 'Which idea of Africa does today's social science offer?'
Sall (2010) grapples with the answer to this question and argues
that the social sciences as we know them today came to Africa
through encounters with the West, particularly during the colonial era. Autonomy and hegemony became an issue for the social
sciences for at least two reasons. One is that in the immediate
aftermath of the wave of decolonization that swept through the
African continent in the late 1950s and early 1960s, the formation of epistemic communities was regarded as a condition for
and a logical sequence of the struggle for political independence.
Autonomy was perhaps as important for social sciences in Africa as

political independence was for the continent generally. The dominant epistemological order in Africa which informed academic imperialism, as in the rest of the world, was that of the West, and the first and second generations of African scholars were trained in the West (Mkandawire, 1995, 1999). Many of the new universities established in Africa read Global South, in the late 1950s and early 1960s were for a time affiliated with French and British universities. The heavy dependence on resources from the West, particularly in the 1980s and 1990s, made the autonomy of social sciences in Africa a major issue of concern. Beyond the question of resources, the question posed was who sets the research agenda? Social sciences were thus born in the West and reflected the experiences and hegemonic interests of an expanding socio-economic, political and cultural Western world (Mlambo (2006). The counter hegemonic currents by social scientists within the African continent were thus a resistance to forms of knowledge authored and authorized by the West.

In the five decades or so that have elapsed since the wave of decolonization against academic imperialism swept through the continent, and almost sixteen years after the official abolition of apartheid, the institutional and demographic bases for social science research, teaching and related activities have undergone deep transformation. From a very small number at the end of the colonial era, African universities are now close to a thousand, and still growing at breakneck speed. Both governments and private providers are setting up new higher education institutions. Research centers, institutes, networks and NGOs are also mushrooming (Sall, 2010).

However, the Euro-America epistemological orders still remain central in the African Academy. Since the colonial encounter, the construction of scholarly knowledge about Africa has been internationalised both in the sense of being an activity involving scholars in various parts of the world and the inordinate influence of externally generated models of African scholarship (Zeleza, 2007). The challenge of autonomy, hegemony, and of developing interpretative frameworks that are scientific, universal, and relevant – that is 'suitable' for the study of Africa and of the world from the standpoint of Africans themselves – is still very real.

From the late 1950s to the early 1990s, the African social science community grew in size, but still remained relatively small. In most countries, the institutions of higher education and research were few in number, and often new and weak. The research environment was less than ideal, given the poor socio-economic and political conditions that prevailed. This led to poor funding for higher education and research, and to violations of academic freedom. The key concepts and theoretical frameworks with which most African scholars worked were 'made in the West'. Western interpreters, as well as African analysts, have been using categories and conceptual systems that depend on a Western epistemological order. Even the most explicitly 'Afrocentric' descriptions and models of analysis, explicitly or implicitly, knowingly or unknowingly, refer to the same order (Mudimbe, 1994). My reflexive question in this chapter, therefore, is this: what academic image do we as African scholars want in the social sciences and how can critical re-interpretations of hegemonic knowledge create decolonising, emancipatory postcolonial knowledge and practice in the Global South? In this chapter, Africa is taken as a case study in understanding and interrogating academic imperialism with the view of trying to restore the hitherto subdued African identity within the social sciences.

The explicit purpose of this chapter is to encourage academics within the Global South to move out of a Eurocentric worldview in the sphere of knowledge production, especially in the social sciences, and to help regenerate or create fresh models of intellectual enquiry and research more in touch with their own realities and intellectual traditions. It is an undisputed reality of our times that most academic knowledge has been hegemonised by the Western world. The hegemony has extended to even the perception of what constitutes knowledge. This situation of tyranny has prevailed now for over 200 years. Efforts are even now underway to expand further the reach and influence of existing social science models from European and American universities and to intensify dependence of the academic community located within the Global South on these. The issue is that, we must develop our own intellectual, autonomous tradition for the simple reason that academic colonialism and dependence fashion us in the image of what is thought to be best.

Mlambo (2006) observes that accompanying Northern colonialism in the Global South and Africa in specific was an epistemology that validated Northern presence in Africa and presented colonialists as 'saviors [sic], initiators, mentors, arbiters' in what was, in the words of Ake, 'imperialism in the guise of scientific knowledge' (Nyamnjoh, 2002). This tendency continues to manifest itself in these days of globalisation where Africa continues to be marginalised and to be subjected to Western paradigms, research methods, knowledge production and dissemination, and the measure of what should be regarded as 'authoritative scholarship'.

In any case, Africa's dependency on knowledges imported from the North has serious implications for African people's self-image and pride in African institutions and practices. As Mugambi (2000) correctly observes, where knowledge is generated and packaged is very important because of the cultural, ideological, political contexts which it embodies and conveys. Africa, as a net importer of published knowledge generated abroad, runs the danger of losing its identity and of underdeveloping and undervaluing its own unique forms of knowledge. This is because, when textbooks used in schools and universities in Africa are generated from abroad, they are not likely to speak to the lived experience of the African students or to help them come to terms with their own identity as Africans. In the words of Mugambi, Northern-based publishing houses with outlets in Africa have been:

> ...exporting into this continent, books that are culturally intended for schools, colleges and universities in Europe and North America. Education is a cultural enterprise. Ideally, the publishing industry ought to support that enterprise. Thus, the ... publishing industry has contributed immensely towards the alienation of the African élite from its own culture, by providing texts that are culturally uncontextualised...

How can Africa's élite chart the future of this continent when its education is based on policies and ideas intended for other cultures? How can Africa's youth develop new insights to solve problems in the context of its own culture, while it is exposed only to literature coming from other cultures? The time has come for Africa's élite to contribute towards shaping the future of this continent through publication of the knowledge and experience accumulated at home and abroad.

The emphasis on imported knowledges is at the expense of a rich fund of indigenous knowledge, which has yet to be tapped, transcribed, recorded and published. Indigenous knowledge is 'the common sense knowledge and ideas of local peoples about everyday realities of living which form part of their cultural heritage. It includes the cultural traditions, values, belief systems and worldviews of local peoples as distinguished from Northern scientific knowledge' (Dei. 1993). Indigenous knowledge in Africa has generally been side-lined and denigrated as Northern knowledge has been privileged, especially in the development discourse. Yet, such knowledge is perhaps more appropriate for the needs of African societies and is, certainly, more acceptable to them than imported knowledge, since it emerges out of their lived experiences, traditions and collective wisdom (Mlambo, 2006).

The inferiority complex induced by colonialism in Africa has persisted well into the post-colonial era when the structures and systems of formal colonialism are no longer in existence, particularly among Africa's social scientists and academics. Thus the production of knowledge by postcolonial elites continues to be based on western epistemological schemes and theories deeply rooted in and informed by colonial thought! Therefore, a form of intellectual and academic imperialism continues to this day, an imperialism to which the victims willingly succumb to by perpetuating an intellectual dependency on former colonizers. This intellectual dependence also generates a negative self-image among African scholars (Mlambo, 2006). How do we get ourselves out of this situation? The answer to this question requires a brief historical background on the academic imperialism and the colonization of the social sciences, read education, as well as the genesis of the struggle to assert African identity in the process of knowledge production within the realms of social sciences.

HISTORICAL BACKGROUND OF ACADEMIC IMPERIALISM AND EARLY FORMS OF AFRICANITY AND AFROCENTRICITY IN THE SOCIAL SCIENCES

With regard to the African continent, the colonial episode profoundly affected every aspect of African life as colonialism brought with it certain ways of reconstructing (or distorting) African social reality. Education, for example, was a powerful weapon used in transforming African society during the colonial encounter. Consequently, institutionalised or formalised Western education in Africa is a product of the colonial legacy. The thrust of colonial education was to deny the colonized useful knowledge about themselves and their world and, in turn, transmit a culture that embodied, and was designed to consolidate dependency and generally enslave and undermine the colonized capacity for creativity in all spheres of life. In destroying these institutions, the whole colonial machinery's thrust was the depersonalisation of Africans or de-Africanisation. This process took cruder and deepened forms in the case of those African countries with extensive white minority colonial settlerism. In lieu of Afrocentricity, the colonialists tried to establish European conceptions of social reality, social knowledge and social truth which have continued to enslave and undermine African intellectual independence. The universalising pretensions of such conceptions during the colonial inroads have been a major source of tensions and conflicts in their encounter with indigenous African philosophical traditions and practices. This was inevitable since European moral, intellectual and cultural traditions had very little theoretical resources to cope with diversity. Western postmodernism, which tinkers with such a problem, is illustrative of the problematic and historical nature of Eurocentrism (Teboa and Mmabotho 2001:23).

According to Noor (1999:56), a pivotal issue confronting African social sciences is the nature of the relationship between it and the Western academy, and particularly what should be done to overcome the assumed secondary status of African social science. The legacy of colonialism has always posed problems for the autonomy of the colonized regions in all spheres of life, including the academy. The anti-colonial struggles and the post-colonial struggles against economic domination strongly influenced the evolution and character of social science, infusing it with strong tendencies to be independent and oppositional. Now, it appears that forces of global domination once again threaten to subvert the development of endogenous African social science (Appandurai, 1998:2).

The relationship between the postcolonial state and African academia has been a complex one and has gone through a number of stages. Immediately after independence, the new universities that mushroomed throughout the continent signalled a new phase in the educational development of the continent. The political leadership viewed with pride these new institutions that would provide the necessary 'manpower' for indigenisation and development. In these initial phases, teaching was the main task of the university and whatever research was being done, was largely an exclusively expatriate activity precariously attached to the universities. The student community was generally passive, with relatively good material conditions, high social standing and bright career prospects (Omenya, 2010).

Since then, a critical issue has been the definition of what is a suitable role for the intelligentsia in society. The broad consensus in the immediate post-independence moments was that African intellectuals would contribute to the 'development' of their respective countries, but defined by the state. However, as the national consensus of what were the common interests crumbled and 'development' became more elusive and as the distributional outcomes of the unfolding, socio-economic processes were contested, the role assigned to the intelligentsia became problematic. Research and teaching, which had been hitherto an isolated academic activity, entered the public domain, leading in some cases to conflict and violence between scholars and the state (Omenya, 2010).

In contrast, in the West, the creation of a material base for an autonomous intelligentsia went hand in hand with the development of a national bourgeoisie and the creation of civil society. That national bourgeoisie is, however, absent, or at best, only nascent in most African countries. The corollary of this absence is that, outside of the State, the only other significant source of financial resources for academic work is external; the donor community in Africa is exclusively foreign. This position opens a chance for the West to continue with their academic imperialism and academic dependence by African academia. The presence of foreign donor agencies in Africa provides opportunities and raises a number of questions. On the one hand, the presence of external funders has enormously expanded the space for social science research in Africa. It is clear that in a number of fields only their presence has made research possible. By being free from a number of domestic political constraints, foreign donors have been able to set research agendas in Africa and to fund research themes that no local authority would dare or wish to encourage. Additionally, the high moral standing of some of the donors has shielded grantees from the repressive measures by local authorities. On the other hand, foreign funding brings with it its own constraints. First, the substantial contributions they are making to social science research has given the donor community power, a situatio which has brought with it a number of intended or unintended constraints on social science research. These can and do take a variety of forms. This observation goes well with Alatas' (2003) argument that the condition of academic dependency is related to the global division of labour in the social sciences which plays a significant role in maintaining the structures of academic dependency. In this kind of arrangement the Global North looks for fund to support their research agenda while social scientists in the Global South effect or carry out the actual research.

By giving priority to projects over programme funding, donors can shape the research agenda and can thus eliminate work in certain areas by merely indicating areas of their interest that they consider fundable (Sall, 2010). They can, by their explicit or implicit ideological preferences, nurture forms of self-censorship among (African) researchers who are in dire need of funding. Research may be constrained by bureaucratisation of evaluation procedures where 'doability' narrows the areas that can be safely funded to meet certain bureaucratic schedules and goals. The shifts in donor interests could have much effect on the sustainability, continuity and accumulative prospects of African research than donors and even recipients may be fully aware of (Omenya, 2010).

Considering the above, Kenyan and African scholars have readily created space for theories manufactured in research and higher learning institutions in the North without subjecting them to critiques. Consequently, we have toned down our radicalism and left others to determine our destiny. This intellectual amnesia goes hand in glove with our craze to attain intellectual acceptability in the faddish western scholarship that has become widespread (Ochwada 1997).

But looking at colonialism and its imperialist agenda in Africa, Kisianga'ni (2000) argues that it was during the era of colonialism that Africans came to learn that what was often seen as universal and humanity had been exclusively and purposefully derived from the culture and perceptions of Western European person. As a result, the imperial project in Africa trained colonial subjects to perceive things only from a European standpoint. Effectively the colonial enterprise undertook to criminalise and atomise the culture and values of the African, with the result that Western ideals came to inform all the intellectual discourses about the African people both during the formal and hegemonic phases of colonialism. This intellectual propensity, according to Kisiang'ani, has tended to influence the way in which the African people confront the many problems facing the continent. It is the perception of their (African) conditions of domination that is vital to their being able to develop strategies for resistance. This also formed the basis of decolonization processes in Africa.

It is this perception of viewing things from the Western world view that needs to be changed by embracing and inculcating a scholarly relationship which is mutually beneficial among social scientists both in the so-called Global South and the Global North. Scholarly or academic relations are something very different from academic colonialism or academic imperialism. Scholarly relations means that you write to each other to say that you want to do this or that, that you request help, that you acknowledge help received from other scholars, that you treat people with respect when you ask them questions, that you give each other the results of investigation and all those sorts of things. We in the Global South must certainly, therefore, strengthen our own ideas and we must put these forward as alternatives. This will help us overcome academic colonialism and will thus help us to regain our self-image in scholarly world in the Global South (Gutkind 1977).

The worst result of this colonialism was the intellectual reliance of the developing nations. Altbach (1995) noted that the paradigms that we use in our learning techniques in almost all colleges and universities were from the West. Other features that continue to influence our education from the West, he noted, were the themes chosen to be studied, medium of education or the language policy. This academic dependency as a matter of fact needs to be dismantled. This is because literature by the colonizing culture distorted the experience and realities of the colonized people thereby condemning colonial subjects to an inferior status. It is therefore important for the social sciences in Africa to demonstrate the ability of the Africans to articulate their identity.

Colonial education was premised on Western intellectual, cultural and philosophical prejudice. Manifestations of this prejudice were seen in the way the colonialists dealt viciously with any form of indigenous social knowledge and practices. Those social sciences dealing directly with social and human conditions and public policy issues were highly susceptible to abuse as colonizing social instruments. Their core postulates, key concepts, basic methodologies, undergirding theories and guiding models were drawn from and essentially represented extrapolates of discrete Euro-American socio-historical experiences and cultural specificity. As such, the social sciences are not only a reflection, but more importantly, an intellectual production of this particular experience in the ethnocentric sense. Therefore this kind of imperialism needs to be toned down. The social struggles against colonial and neo-colonial rule and Western hegemony remained *pari passu* struggles against the intellectual dependency ushered by the colonial experience. The colonial and neo-colonial crises in social reality corresponded to and precipitated the crises in, organized intellectual ones. The message was quite clear: not only were Euro-American traditions parochial, they were also fundamentally anti-universal and their practices of intellectual *patriae paren* were to be dispensed with. Given the African conditions, the social environment of vexing social problems should inevitably constitute raw materials for African intellectual discourse and representations. This does not mean that African social scientists should shed their international dimensions and be characterized by particularist perspectives and imperatives only. What it means is that there is a great need to decolonize the social sciences (Teboa and Mmabotho 2001).

Looking at the development of social sciences from a different perspective, Mamdani (1998) argues that the characteristic features of African social science as represented through the activities of CODESRIA have been its autonomy from governments and the social sciences imposed by the metropole. Furthermore, he argues that African research has been defined not by local or field studies but more by comparative studies. Mamdani did, however, also point to some of the problems which have plagued social science production in Africa namely a 'weakly institutionalised intelligentsia and a tradition of 'African Studies' given to theorising Africa through analogies. These criticisms go to the heart of the challenges faced by African social science in an increasingly globalized world.

Contributing to the rise of Africanity, Mafeje (2000:70) argues that this has spelt doom for African studies for the simple reason that African studies is an American institution run by Americans for their purposes, good or bad. African studies are an anomaly in Africa found only in South Africa, the vortex of white racism then. He further argues that to study themselves, Africans do not need African studies as a separate intellectual or political endeavor. In instituting African studies, both the Americans and the White South Africans were politically and ideologically motivated. African scholars have been in the forefront in rebelling against such kinds of white domination in African studies. The Africanist antithesis, as can be seen in *'Out of One, Many Africas'* vindicated the position of those American scholars who had been arguing for developing a new concept of African studies by putting an end to white American hegemony in African studies. Although there are some Africanists such as Jane Guyer, who sincerely believe that African studies 'made in the USA' can still be redeemed, it is apparent that the rise of Africanity and Afrocentrism is its ultimate negation. This in itself does not mark an end to the study of Africa by white American scholars. It marks the end of their taken-for-granted intellectual hegemony and institutionalized domination in African studies. It's conceivable, Mafeje argues, that the institutional void created by the disappearance of African studies 'made in the USA' will be filled by such African organizations as CODESRIA, OSSREA, AAPS etc. These are potentially democratic institutions because they are run by Africans themselves and not beholden to any government.

The growth of African universities since 1948 has made possible the production of members of the African elite who are not as enamored by things European as their predecessors, who obtained their university education in Europe during the peak of European colonialism in Africa. The foundation in 1948 of university colleges in Freetown, Accra (Achimoto of Legon) Ibadan and Kampala laid the foundation for the development of universities in English speaking Africa. Furthermore, it meant that more university graduates were available to enter into the colonial service. It also meant that many African graduates were no longer under official pressure to take on a job in the colonial bureaucracy soon after graduation. The result was that many Africans entered postgraduate studies for their M.A and PhD degrees in a multiplicity of subjects and disciplines. This development is important in any assessment of the role of Africans and their contributions to the development of African studies since the mid-1950s (Obichere, 1976).

With the policy-oriented studies of European and Americans dominating their own thought and their own brand of African studies, there emerged in Africa itself a new breed of Africans who began to write books on Africa history, politics, literature, and so

on. The works of those Africans went along way to correct the mis-
understanding of Africa by the European and American scholars
who suddenly turned to the African continent from what president Julius Nyerere of Tanzania called the new intellectual parti-
tion of Africa. Significant books which appeared in this period
include: A. Adu Boahen, *Topics in West African History* (1966),
J.F.A Ajayi, *Christian Missions in Nigeria, 1841-91* (1965), C.G
Baeta *Prophetism in Ghana* (1962) and B.A Ogot, *A history of the
Southern Luo, 1500-1900* (Obichere, 1976).

The reaction of early African intellectuals to the denigration of
and western onslaught on Africa was not always a resort to mime-
tism but to a robust defence of the African past. Early black writers
like James Africanus Horton fought hard to combat the false theories of modern anthropologist, while others, the most prominent
of whom was Cheikh Anta Diop, advanced an Afrocentric interpretation of African history. A committed defender of the dignity
of the African past which Western social science was dismissing,
he was convinced that 'only by re-examining and restoring Africa's
distorted, maligned and obscured place in world history could the
physical and psychological shackles of colonialism be lifted from
our motherland and African people dispersed globally'. Among
his publications *African Origin of Civilisation: Myth and Reality*
(1974) and *Civilising or Barbarism: An Authentic Anthropology*
(1981) are good examples of scholarly effort to restore to the
African past what Western social sciences had taken from it.
What they all had in common was their determination to correct
western misunderstandings and distortions about the nature of
the society, history and being of the African (Mlambo, 2006)

Other Africans who echoed their sentiments against academic

imperialism under the disguise of African studies included Dr. Kwame Nkuruma in his work *Towards Colonial Freedom*, Jomo Kenyatta- Facing Mount Kenya, Dr. Nnamdi Azikiwe-*Liberia in World Politics,* Mbunu Ojike- *My Africa,* Nwafor Orizu A.– *Without Bitterness: Western Nations in Post War Africa,* and Mwalimu Julius Nyerere among others. This crop of people influenced the development and direction of African studies from the mid-1950s through their contribution of ideas to the pool of African thought about African studies. The significance of these publications was that African authors were no longer a rarity. Moreover, nationalist and progressives could be heard by a wider audience. A cursory glance at the newspapers of this period would reveal that African writers dwelt on subjects like education, colonial oppression, poetry, religion culture and racial discrimination (Obichere, 1976)

The above discourse provokes Diop's (1996) resistance to the colonial displacement of history in Africa. In particular he advocates for an intellectual development in Africa with an understanding of the African context. His overall findings and argument are that Western scholarship in the social sciences has suppressed the history of civilization in Black Africa and that there is dire need to rediscover Africa by African scholars guided by African ideology and culture. Social science, as introduced in Africa was thus imbued with essentialism and racism (Matshedisho 2005:6).

The loss of the African's sense of identity and self-esteem can be said, therefore, to have resulted from several factors: Colonial rule not only disrupted the natural evolution of Africa's cultural values and traditions, but also debased and denigrated those cultural values that constitute an essential basis of the identity of a people, the loss of our independence to foreign rulers and concomitant dehumanisation of our people unleashed by colonialism and imperialism; our reluctance; on one hand to attempt to create our own institution, have confidence in them, and nurture them, and our readiness, on the other hand, to borrow such institutions from alien sources; the besetting political and economic failures and frustrations of the postcolonial era that seem to raise questions about our own abilities to confidently and satisfactorily solve our problems, making us most times to depend on others; the fact that we do not seem to have made much progress in our political and economic life since regaining our political independence: all this has generated a crisis of identity and self-esteem (Mbembe 1998, Ndulu 1998).

This crisis has also spilled over to the social sciences where colonial methods have been used both in the writing and teaching of the social science disciplines. But how can we restore our sense of self-esteem and dignity? The restoration of Africa's sense of self-esteem within the postcolonial thinking will require: building African societies from their cultural roots to give African people a sense of authenticity and rootedness; putting in place educational structures aimed at developing the intellectual capacities of our people and developing in the educated African attitudes and perceptions that are positive and respectful not disdainful of African values; building educational structures that will emphasize creativity and innovativeness, not imitation, and will close the gap between the elite and the mass of the people; evolving adequate language policies to ensure greater use of African languages in education and public life, for the long term development of a people, their culture, and a sense of identity can hardly be achieved through the medium of foreign languages pursuing such policies and measures as will reduce the intellectual, cultural, and economic dependence of Africa on other peoples and cultures of the world, and, thus to remove the paradox of Africa's independence deepening its dependence on others (Ibid)

Post-coloniality therefore engages the constitutive illustrations and legacies of slavery, colonization, imperialism and apartheid. This way, it constitutes the unifying discursive intellectual practice embodying the self-reflexive desire of the denied and objectified African to know itself and its community, re-write its own history, re-capture its destiny and sovereignty, and belong to itself in the modern world–in the context of independence and actual autonomy (Mbembe, 2002).

But studying the effects of neo-colonial domination in the contemporary world also means studying the ways neo-colonial hegemony is constantly reproduced, legitimized or contested through the actions, knowledges, and political subjectivities of those living in postcolonial contexts. there is a possibility to bridge postmodern or poststructuralist thinking with postcolonial thinking in the way how 'an other science' is to be practiced, if at all (Soko, 2010). De-linking thinking from the epistemology of modernity and all the universal categories that follow implies according to Mignolo a re-inscription of subalternised knowledges from a differential locus of enunciation that undoes the Eurocentric practice of science. A possibility of de-colonizing social sciences and the Global South from academic imperialism can be achieved by positioning ourselves and our research projects in a differential locus of enunciation that engenders the epistemological break with the epistemology of modernity but at the same time renouncing the attempt of 'representing' subjugated knowledges from the position of a totalising theorist as Foucault would warn us. Henceforth, the recognition of the epistemic colonial difference which is lacking in postmodern thought can be complemented with the practice of the intervention/reinscription of suppressed knowledges that resist institutionalisation, or unitary theorisation (Soko, 2011).

Mkandawire (1997) also observes that the critical point of departure in getting out of academic and intellectual subservience lies in the establishment of a distinctly African intellectual tradition. By this, we mean that it is important for Africa social scientists to reject the scholarship that proceeds from the premise that Africa has no civilization, methodologies, theories, history or traditions. Africanisation as a specific civilization or cultural expression of indigenisation is a clear statement that theories, concepts and methodologies in the social sciences (as elsewhere) can be derived from and nourished by African historical conditions and socio- cultural practices. Addressed in this way, Africanisation can also be a corrective that could help in eradicating African scholars' imitative tendencies and dependency attitude. Such dependency has actually alienated African social scientists from their roots and incapacitated them from coming up with creative and original thoughts and solution to problems. This has created a condition where we find ourselves grappling with the legacies of colonialism that is neo-colonialism within the social sciences. From the point of view of the sociology of knowledge and sociology of education, the specific and unique continental objectives demand that the social sciences be sensitive to the legitimate needs of the great masses of the African people. To this effect, the social sciences normally modeled on the disciplines of the universities of the former colonial powers-need to shed their cultural alienation and social responsibility. Nevertheless, they will still have to be nourished by progressive and revolutionary elements derived from other socio- cultural environments. The call for Africanisation of the social science is a clear reflection of a long held dissatisfaction at the disdain which anything African is perceived. It is also a clear sign of the continued endeavor on the part of African scholars to privilege African scholarship and to disengage from academic imperialism of the West. Teboha and Mmabotho (2001) states that the social sciences in African universities have never been grounded on African experiences and aspirations and do not reflect African hopes, wishes and aspirations, dilemmas and predicaments.

It is important, therefore, that ^knowledge of Africa must make its own unique contribution to world knowledge and forge the theoretical and philosophical lenses through which Africa can be truthfully understood. Africa needs to develop its own knowledge production centers and knowledge producers, recognized not only locally but internationally as well. Africans also need to be encouraged to publish in the local journals. Theoretical frameworks that they should develop independently of the north must address African realities and challenges and help develop appropriate policies that resolve African issues in ways that reflect the lived experiences of Africa's societies (Mlambo 2006)

LIBERATING SOCIAL SCIENCES FROM ACADEMIC IMPERIALISM AND EUROCENTRISM

The fight against academic imperialism and oppression of the

Global South will only be won by changing our mindset. But the question is whose mindset do we want to change and how? This is where the question of agency comes in. Who is it that needs the change and who is going to be the agent of change. If you want to change the mindset you have to change the mindset of the culture determining group, the mindset of the so called elites and the intelligentsia. This is the diseased mind we are dealing with as Paranjape (2008:7) puts it. The problem with the African elites is that they are unable to recognize the work of any of their colleagues. They are very busy observing and reading the latest developments in the West. It is therefore important that we accord this recognition to our fellow African scholars, to read, cite one another as a process of disengaging from the yoke of academic imperialism an creating our own image in the social sciences.

It is however, my worry that such process disengagement from academic imperialism may not happen or likely to begin from Cheikh Anta Diop University, University of Nairobi and/or University of Ibadan because these by and large are actually centers of neo-Colonialism. There is need therefore to create new universities which do not suffer from colonial hang ups and baggage and which can afford to take these risks. But we should also note that the processes of both decolonization and (re)colonization are complex and polyphonic processes. Therefore decolonization of social science from Western academic imperialism cannot be effectively achieved through a single way or approach.

Just like we have to change the ideology and mindset of our elites and scholars, we also need to have a look at our institutional structures. This is because for us to decolonize we need to appropriate institutions. We are in desperate need for institutional reforms. Our schools, colleges and universities for instance need to be revamped because they are so stultified. Our libraries (colonial libraries) need to be restocked with books authored by African scholars. This therefore is a wakeup call for Africanists to lead the way in local knowledge production if we actually want to dismantle forms of knowledge authored and authorized by the West. This should be accompanied with a radical change in the content and courses being taught in our various institutions in keeping with our goals, needs and objectives.

Kisiang'ani (2004:8) asserts that today, in Africa the sophistication of the African intellectuals is measured in terms of the way in which he/she commands such European languages as English, Spanish, German and French. This he argues has to change. The fight against Eurocentrism should also be linguistically based. Ngugi Wa Thiong'o, Kenya's foremost intellectual powerhouse has not only called for a linguistic overhaul of Africa's education system but he has also cried out for the decolonization of the African intellectual mind. Social sciences in Africa have so far been written and conducted through these alien languages, yet, the majority of people in Africa have only elementary grasp of European languages. These two scholars therefore front for the use of African languages if we really have a dream of decolonizing social sciences and ensuring Afrocentrism. Ngugi bids farewell to English as a vehicle 'for any of my writings. From now on it is Gikuyu and Kiswahili (Ngugi, 1986). I agree with these views. However, to the contrary my argument is that African scholars need to know that decolonization cannot only be achieved through the creation of opposite binarism of We/ Other, Us/ Them English/ African as Said (1978) postulated within the postcolonial set up.

Decolonization and Afrocentrism for that matter, as opposed to Eurocentrism, does not necessarily mean one has to be rigid, be confined, make do with little, fail to explore, or fail to venture, and so on. African scholars have to do better than this. That is why the challenge is greater and that is why we need to have original and multiple notions of what we mean by decolonization freedom from academic imperialism and Afrocentrism. Going back to our discussion on English as a medium which needs to be dismantled as a way of fighting academic imperialism especially within the social sciences, I partly agree with both Ngugi (1986) and Kisianga'ni (2004). However, we should look at alternative ways of suppressing not only English as a form of (neo) colonial hegemony in the teaching of social sciences but also western theoretical formulations. This is because for us to decolonise, and taking English as a medium of expressing our decolonization agenda to the West, then, it would be prudent for us not to have an English dominated multilingualism or in the case of East Africa, a Kiswahili dominated multilingualism but rather a pluralistic multilingualism in which no single (English) language dominates over all of African languages. For instance, both English and Kiswahili should be given an equal weight in the African context. But for this approach to work, Africa must first and foremost speak an African voice before Europe listens and deals with Africa as an equal partner. Through this approach, we can definitely move as far as resisting academic imperialism in the social sciences in Africa is concerned.

As indicated elsewhere in this paper, most of our texts, theories and even funding mostly come from the West. All of these are part of the educational neocolonialism, meaning, there is still the continuing impact of former western imperial and colonial regimes and some advances on poor or developing nations in the Global South in the areas of educational system and knowledge production. As a way forward, there should be a continued effort of reforming and modifying the social sciences until it reaches its goal of freeing itself from the (neo) colonial powers. This should start at the early years of education as this is the stage where we incorporate our African knowledge to the young. This is the stage also where people are prone to various forms of knowledge. This should go along way with orienting African scholars in a proper way to teach the social sciences, and other areas of knowledge in such a way that we promote our own social science, culture, history among other social science subjects rather than the West. This will lay a stronger foundation for our students in the universities as far as asserting our subdued African identity in the social sciences is concerned. Africans should assert themselves the right to develop freely without the aid or influence of the West this is because African scholars have the intellectual capacities to do what were hitherto deemed to be the domains of the West, a position which has been strongly supported by Garces (2007:3).

A number of scholars in the Global South have echoed similar sentiments. The efforts of regional social science council such as CODESRIA and OSSREA, and professional associations of sociologists, anthropologists, political scientist and the like, to address the problems of autonomy have therefore been geared towards building a networked, self –aware community of scholars. Some explicitly sought to participate in the building of what has been called an 'African library' to replace what Mudimbe called the 'colonial library'. The modern African library would of necessity be made up not only of written texts, but also of oral and visual 'texts' (Sall, 2010 and Olukoshi 2010). Groups of scholars and activists from various disciplines in the developing world have been influential in raising the issue of the state of the social sciences in their countries. However varied they are- we cannot as yet speak of a unified intellectual movement (probably this book could be the beginning of that movement)–their calls for endogenous intellectual creativity, an autonomous social science tradition (Alatas, 2003), decolonization, globalization sacralisation, nationalization, or for the indigenization of social sciences share similar concerns. But it also involves the construction of 'alternative traditions. In today's social sciences, Eurocentrism no longer involve blatantly racist or prejudicial statements, based on simplistic dichotomies between South and North, Orient and Occident, progressive and backward, or civilized and barbaric. Instead they take the form of a marginalization of non-Western thinkers and concepts, and the desire for analytical constructions resulting from the imposition of European concepts and theories (Alatas, 2010, Alatas 2006). The call for alternative discourses thus suggests that the social sciences take place in a social and historical context and must be relevant in this context. One way to achieve relevance is to develop original concepts and theories on the bases of the philosophical traditions and popular discourses of these societies. Any claim to universality must respect the extent of the differences between the Global South and admit that in some instances distinct theoretical backgrounds are required (Alatas, 2010)

Alternative discourses according to Alatas (2010) set themselves in contrast to, or even oppose what they consider to be mainstream, Euro-American 'universal' discourses. The aims and objectives of alternative discourses are not merely negative. They do not simply break with metropolitan, neocolonialist influences and hegemony. The defenders of alternative discourses do not reject Western knowledge in *toto*. More positively, they are genuine non-Western systems of thoughts, theories and ideas, based on non-Western cultures and practices. They can be defined as discourses which are informed by indigenous historical experiences, philosophies and cultural practices which can be used as sources for alternative theories and concepts in social sciences. Alternative discourses are relevant to their surroundings, creative, non-imitative and original, non-essentialist, counter-Eurocentric, and autonomous from the state and other national or transnational groupings. Alternative discourses are attempts at correcting what is perceived as the irrelevance of mainstream, Euro-American theories and models for the analysis of non-Western societies. Irrelevance can be of different types, including unoriginality, redundancy, disaccord, inapplicability, mystification, mediocrity and alienation. These types of irrelevance impinge on all facets of social science knowledge, including its meta-analyses, methodologies, theories and empirical and applied studies. Alternative discourses can be developed for each of them for instance, development of local theories adapted to the study of one region, mixing of local and Western theories adapted to the study of one region and the development of a universal theory on the basis of the study of one region.

Without empowerment, Africans will remain victims of other people's machinations, for as UNESCO (1981) correctly observes, 'those who lack knowledge see their fate shaped by others in the light of their own interests'. Similarly, societies that lack knowledge are doomed to perpetual manipulation by others. This demands, in part, that relevant knowledge generated from African realities and which speaks to the African people's lived experience be made available. It is the duty of African social scientists to make this knowledge available to their societies rather than continue to echo imported wisdoms from Western social sciences. It is therefore, important for African scholars to develop an independent and truly African social science tradition to enable them to reflect on African problems, address the challenges confronting African societies and economies and help undo some of the distortions that resulted from centuries of Western academic imperialism and domination (Mlambo, 2006).

The call for alternative discourse in social sciences in the Global South does not imply any cultural homogenity or that there is anything like say an African or Global South branch of social sciences. It does suggest however, that the social sciences, like any form of knowledge, take place in a social and historical context and must be relevant in this context. In Africa for instance, social sciences must be relevant for the study of African societies. The same applies to other societies in the Global South. One way to achieve relevance is to develop original concepts and theories on the bases of the philosophical traditions and popular discourses of these societies. To achieve such relevance is but one aspect of broader efforts to free social sciences from cultural dependency and ethnocentrism, and to achieve genuine universalism. The goal is not to substitute Eurocentrism with another ethnocentrism per se. But any claim to universality must respect the extent of the differences between Global South and Western societies, and admit that in some instances distinct theoretical backgrounds are required (Alatas, 2010). It is through such bold moves that the Global South will be able to free themselves from academic imperialism and dismantle forms of knowledge authored and authorised by the West among our scholars, students, academic disciplines, and in our universities.

CONCLUSION

It was the objective of this chapter to interrogate academic imperialism and the oppression of the Global South and to critically re-interprete how hegemonic knowledge in the social sciences can be decolonised. This chapter has also explored ways of regaining the African image and identity from academic imperialism of the Global North. It has been demonstrated that social sciences in our continent suffers from neocolonialism, a condition which was necessitated by the installation and presence of western institutions and forms of Knowledge in Africa. The paper has argued that for African scholars and stakeholders to effectively liberate themselves from this form of imperialism within the social sciences, there is an urgent need to re-define the term decolonization and get into its deeper meaning. This is because, I believe, that decolonization does not necessarily mean resistance, being rigid and closing our mind. By this I mean we can also use some European values as agents of decolonization. The paper recommends that we need to change the ideology and mindset of African scholars since they are the culture determining group. This should go along with institutional reforms and creation of new institutions of higher education which do not suffer from colonial hang over. Finally we need to delink the politics of knowledge production and publishing from foreign publishers in case they attach unrealistic conditions to publishing. This can only be achieved by establishing publishing houses committed to African knowledge production without necessarily pegging such endeavours on profit making. But also social science should be geared towards addressing African realities and conditions not just for the sake of knowledge production. Through such critical re-interpretation and re-thinking of Western forms of knowledge, social science as an academic discipline together with our universities and scholars in the Global South will be able to liberate themselves from academic slavery of the West.

REFERENCES

Alatas, S.F. (2003) 'Academic dependency and the global division of labour in the social Sciences', *Current Sociology 51(6) 599-613*

_____(2006) *Alternative Discourses in Asian Social Science: Response to Eurocentrism*, New Delhi, Sage

_____ (2010) *The Call for Alternative Discourses in Asian Social Sciences*, Paris, UNESCO

Altbach, P. (1995) 'Education and Neo-colonialism' in Ashcroft, B. (ed) *The Postcolonial studies Reader*, London, Routledge

Appandurai, A. (1998) 'Globalisation and the Research Imagination' Paper presented at the International Symposium on Globalisation and Social sciences in Africa, University of Witwatersrand, Johannesburg, 14-18 September

Dei, J.S.G. (1993) 'Sustainable Development in The African Context: Raising Some Theoretical and Methodological Issues, *African Development* 18 (2) 97-110

Diop, C.A. (1996) *Towards the African renaissance: Essays in African Culture and Development:1946-1960*, London, Karnak House

Garces,S. (2007) *Decolonizing Knowledge, Decolonizing the Social Sciences: Issues Concerns and Recommendation*, (http://www.ss180-jf. blogspot.com accessed 10/10.2011

Gutkind, P.C.W. (1977) 'The Western Academic Abroad : An African Response' *Quarterly Journal of Africanist Opinion* 8 (2) 8-13

Kisiangani, E. (2000) 'Decolonizing Gender Studies in Africa' in Kisiang'ani, E. and Signe A. (ed) *African Gender Scholarship, Concepts, Methodologies and Paradigms,* Dakar: CODESRIA

Kisiang'ani, E. (2004) *The Youth and African Heritage: Some Reflections*, CODESRIA bulletin no 3 and 4

Mafeje, A. (2000), Africanity: *A Combative Ontology*, CODESRIA bulletin No 1

Mamdani, M. (1998) 'Preliminary notes on Political Science in Equatoriql Africa' Paper presented at the International Symposium on Globalisation and Social Sciences in Africa, University of Witwatersrand, Johannesburg 14-18 September

Mamdani, M. (1998) 'Is African Studies to be Turned into a New Home for Bantu Education at UCT? Paper presented during the Seminar debates on The African Core of the Foundation Course for the Faculty of Social Sciences and Humanitie, University of Capetown 22 April

Matshedisho, K. (2005) *Reinterpreting and Reconstructing Africa: The Challenge for Social Science Scholarship,* Dakar: CODESRIA

Mbembe, A. (1998) 'The Idea of Social Sciences' Paper presented at the International Symposium on Globalisation and Social Sciences in Africa, University of Witwatersrand, Johannesburg 14-18 September

Mbembe, A. (2002) *African Modes of Self –Writing,* CODESRIA Bulletin No1

Mkandawire, T. (1995) *Three Generations of African Scholars,* CODESRIA Bulletin No 2

_____ (1997), 'The Social Science in Africa: Breaking Local Barriers and Negotiating International Presence', *Africa Studies Review* 40 (2) 12-36

_____(1999) Social Science and democracy: Debates in Africa', *African Sociological Review*, 3(1)

Mlambo, A.S. (2006) 'Western Social Sciences and Africa: The Domination and Marginalisation of a Continent', *African Sociological Review* 10 (1) 161-179

Mudimbe, V.Y. (1994) *The Idea of Africa,* London, Indiana University Press and James Curry

Mugambi, J.N.K. (2000) 'Challenges to Publishers and Writers of Scholarly Books Intended for African Readership', A Paper Delivered at the Workshop on Academic Publishing and Book Distribution in Africa Durban, 5 August

Ndulu, B., and Mbembe, A. (1998) *Toward Defining a New Vision of Africa for The 21st Century* CODESRIA, Bulletin no 1

Ngugi Wa, T. (1986) *Decolonising The Mind,* London, James Curry

Noor, N. (1999) *Globalisation and Social Sciences in Africa,* CODESRIA Bulletin 1 and 2

Nyamnjoh, F.B. (2002) 'African Universities in Crisis and The Promotion of a Democratic Culture: The Political Economy of Violence in African Educational Systems', *Africa Studies Review* 45(2) 16-17

Obichere, B.I. (1976) 'The Contribution of African Scholars and Teachers to African Studies 1955-1975', *Quarterly Journal of Africanist Opinion* 4 (2) 27-32

Ochwada, H. (1997) *Intellectuals in Kenya and The Crises in African Studies*, CODESRIA Bulletin no 4.

Olukoshi, A. (2010) *The Contribution of Social Science Networks to Capacity Development in Africa*, Paris, UNESCO and International Social Science Council

Omenya, G.O. (2010) 'Social Science and African Resistance o Academic slavery' Paper presented at the World Festival of Black Arts and Culture, Dakar, 10-30 December

Paranjape, M. (2008) Decolonizing English Stuudies: Attaining Swaraj, http://www. Infinity foundation.com/mandala/s_es_paran_swaraj_frameset.htm , accessed 18 October 2011

Said, E. (1978) *Orientalism*, London, Routledge and Kegan

Sall, E. (2010) Council for the Development of Social Science Research in Africa (CODESRIA), Paris, UNESCO and International Social Science Council

Sokol, L. (2011) 'Decolonising the Social Sciences and the Humanities', Paper presented at the International Graduate Conference on Colonial Legacies, Postcolonial Contestations held at Goethe University Frankfurt , 16th-18th June

Teboha, J and Mmabatho, M. (2001) *Africanisation of the Social Sciences Within the Context of Globalization,* CODESRIA Bulletin no 1 and 2

UNESCO, (1981) *Domination or Sharing: Endogenous Development and the Transfer of Knowledge*, Paris, UNESCO

Zeleza, P.T (2007) *The Study of Africa, Vol 2: Global and Transnational Engagements*, Dakar, CODESRIA

CHAPTER FIVE

In Search of Becoming Whole: Moving the Center in Social Science Research

AUGUSTINE NWOYE

CONTEXTUALISATION

The initial inspiration for this chapter came from an invitation I received from the officials of Covenant University in Nigeria, to take part, as one of key speakers, in a special Workshop organized by the Department of Psychology of that University – and conceived and designed specifically by a young member of that Department, Mr Adebayo Akomolafe (the initiating editor of this book), whose radical explorations of alternative ways of framing research and knowledge production inspired bold new conversations about the subtext of the academy. The Workshop took place in February 2011. It was designed to help impel the motion that it is time to challenge the current dominance of quantitative research methodologies in African universities. And the overall goal was to work towards making that research paradigm to loosen its exclusive hold on the imagination of our students and scholars so that some deserved attention can be directed to other methodologies best suited for the study of lives and other related themes in the modern African context.

In highlighting the need for the shift in emphasis from the quantitative to the qualitative methodologies in African universities, I take as my specific point of reference the enduring dominance of quantitative methodologies in the practice of psychological research in Nigerian universities and the corresponding unfair marginalization of alternative research approaches in this venture. The thesis to be developed is that the currently unfair marginalisation of the qualitative research methodologies in psychology and other related programmes is no longer acceptable and needs to be halted. We must see it as a negative outcome of our continued unfortunate dependence and uncreative imitation of the patterns of research prevailing in mainstream Euro-American psychology.

One way to illustrate the operative signs of this prevailing anomaly is to draw attention to the list of undergraduate psychology courses prescribed and made compulsory by the Nigerian National University Commission (NUC), which shows that an enormous emphasis is still being placed in favour of the quantitative and experimental research paradigms.

Thus, the NUC approved programme for undergraduate psychology training (NUC, 1989-2010), in line with the structure of psychology programmes in some American and British Universities requires that Quantitative Methods in Psychology be offered as a compulsory course in the very first semester of the students' first year of study; a measure followed up by the same students being required to register for another compulsory course, entitled Basic Concepts in Experimental Psychology in the second semester of the students' first year of study. Similarly, in the first semester of the second year of the programme, students are required to register for another compulsory course, Introduction to Statistical Methods in Psychology, and in the second semester of the same year there is another course called Experimental Design which they are expected to register for and pass, that still places emphasis on quantitative procedures.

This means that for the first two years of the students' four-year degree programme, the foundation years, the incoming psychology students in Nigerian Universities are inundated or saturated with the false impression that the central preference for research in psychology is the quantitative and experimental paradigm.

The main discomfort that one feels in examining this apparent obsession in our context for the quantitative and experimental research approaches is that although such a structure may have been relevant in serving the interest and needs of Western societies under which it arose and drew inspiration, we need not stick to that paradigm, almost exclusively, since our national circumstances and aspirations, which our study of psychology is meant to serve, are largely different from those of the West.

More importantly, it appears something of an irony to note that this our continued subservience to the quantitative and experimental research paradigms is taking place at a period in the history of psychology when the formerly spokesperson of the behavioural sciences, namely, Professor B.F. Skinner of blessed memory, had already lamented (in an article entitled, Whatever happened to psychology as the science of behavior? published in 1987), the regrettable decline of interest in the promises of experimentalism in the study of human subjects. He blamed this shortfall on the rising tide of discoveries in the fields of cognitive, social, and humanistic psychologies. Yet despite this change in trend and attitude in Western psychology, we still go on in our own context, to adore and put enormous stress on the experimental and quantitative paradigms that initially, but no longer now, fully inhabited the centre of admiration in psychological research in the West.

Humanistic psychology that has for the past several years operated as the greatest rival of the behaviouristic and experimental psychology, has been noted by Tom Greening (the former Editor of the Journal of Humanistic Psychology), as a branch of Western Psychology that is completely unique in American Psychology due to its Five Basic Postulates that are, in my view, in synchrony with the central teachings of African Psychology; a psychology from where we ought to have drawn the governing initiative for our social science research practices. Among those humanistic postulates as summarized by Greening (2006: 239) include the understanding that: human beings are more than merely the sum of their parts; exist in uniquely human context; are conscious beings, aware of being aware; ...'are intentional, aim at goals and seek meaning, value and creativity'.

Of course, an important governing idea that is missing in the above list which has gained acceptance in much of current mainstream psychology, particularly in the area of the study of personality psychology, is the increasing recognition of the importance of the social environment in the making of the human subject. Thus, as seen by Ross Stagner, an individual's personality is embedded in a cultural milieu and could only be understood through reference to the cultural context. Hence according to Stagner, as cited in Nicholson (2009: 196), 'personality is a social product, [for]... ideas, attitudes, traits, desires, motives and urges of the individual are intimately related to and perhaps completely determined by the social environment in which he develops.' An observation such as this, suggests that a true knowledge of the psychological characteristics of the modern African subject cannot be achieved merely by the use of the quantitative research methodology.

This conclusion implies that unless a remapping of the centre of our social science research paradigms is seriously pursued, our psychology will remain at best a pale copy of Western psychology; rightly to be designated a "Euro-American product", in which what we do will have little relevance to the social reality as it prevailed in Nigeria, and the wider African world.

THE MARGINALIZATION OF AFRICAN PSYCHOLOGY

The important point to make under this heading is the current regrettable omission of African Psychology as a subject with a teachable content in psychological training in most African universities. In that way, there was nothing to distinguish psychological training in African universities from similar psychological degree programmes in Euro-American Universities. This anomaly is both regrettable and indeed an irony because such an awful omission is taking place in our age of identity and multicultural expression when even the American Psychological Association, the prestigious APA, has recognized the need for such a specialization in psychology, and had gone further to permit the establishment and inauguration of Division 52 (Indigenous Psychology) as a separate psychological organization whose objective is to promote the formal study and practice of Indigenous Psychology throughout the world.

The regrettable consequence of putting African Psychology on the back seat in our programmes is that up to this moment, students of psychology in African Universities typically complete a degree programme and do research in psychology knowing little or nothing about the meaning, content, and promise of African Psychology. Yet African Psychology is a course which, on account of its rootedness in the values, aspirations and epistemologies of our culture and tradition, promises to offer a fruitful basis for the practice of relevant qualitative research in psychology.

In contrast, it is something of a big relief to note that such anomalous placing of priorities, no longer obtains in such sister degree disciplines in African social science fields like Philosophy where we now have African Philosophy as a vibrant and legitimate area of study; English Literature, where the study of African Literature in English is now very well established throughout the world; and Religious Studies, where we have African Religion as an important degree area of study. This same positive trend extends to instances of degree programmes in History (African history), Anthropology (African anthropology), Music (African music), Archaeology (African archaeology), and Political Science (African political thoughts and systems); in each of which, as we have seen from the courses enclosed in the brackets, that the African approach to the study of the discipline is firmly recognized and established.

Now, because this chapter is intended to promote the moving of the centre of attention in social science research methodology in African universities, and because I am quite aware that often the most fitting method for the study of issues and problems in African psychology is the qualitative methodology (Nwoye, 2000; 2002, 2005), it would seem essential that an attempt should be made in this chapter to say something, however briefly, on the meaning and scope of African Psychology as a background to the task of sharing with the reader my own understanding of the importance and content of qualitative methodology, at least, as applied to the field of research in psychology in Africa. And so, to the notion of African Psychology, we now turn.

THE NOTION OF AFRICAN PSYCHOLOGY

Here, the first point to note is that for the purposes of this chapter I will like to use the term, African Psychology, interchangeably with the term, African Indigenous Psychology. This is to draw attention to another way of naming that aspect of psychology in the literature, both in continental Africa and in the Diaspora. And in terms of giving it a definition, I can say that African Psychology can be taken to refer to the systematic study of the complexities of human thought, behaviour and experience in the pre- and post-colonial African world.

The above observation means that the term, African Psychology, has both a pre- and a post-colonial reference. In its pre-colonial emphasis it refers to the systematic study of the patterned ways and rituals, theories and techniques, philosophies and assumptions, invented in indigenous African communities for understanding and addressing the psychological needs and problems of living in the indigenous African world. In its post-colonial concerns, on the other hand, it is interested in generating knowledge that will offer illumination and meaning, and information and education, to modern African citizens, enabling them to understand and appreciate the challenges of living in, and the means of successfully finding their way through the complicated and difficult terrain of contemporary African environments.

Each of the above two definitions, I agree, is a descriptive definition of the term, African Psychology. But the aim is to show that at the core of its meaning is the study of the thought, behaviour, and experience of the great African peoples, past and present; with its results ultimately inclined to heal and restore and to open new vision for many of our people (both young and old) still drifting, in search of a framework to give anchor to their lives (Nwoye, 2010). Understood in this way, African Psychology can be viewed as a branch of the discipline of psychology with traditions of its own, and one with an audience or researchable constituency separate and apart from the Euro-American ones.

I make this observation to emphasise the view that African psychology has never, and cannot operate as an imitation or replica or approximations of its Euro-American counterpart, employing the same techniques, and in approximately the same emphases, and urging the same values and practices in terms of research approaches. Yet African psychology is not antagonistic to the psychologies of other lands (such as American humanistic psychology earlier cited) that are of relevance for enabling our people to understand and address the peculiar circumstances under which they live and work.

African Psychology is rather a psychology essentially concerned, first and foremost, with achieving an understanding of the

African cosmology and worldview as a background for gaining a deeper appreciation of the African's perception of his or her world and his or her place within it. This means that the world of African Psychology is to be understood as a world defined by a religious worldview which embraces in its conception of human life and society, the interpenetration of realms of beings that encompass the physical, the abstract/the symbolic and spiritual realities. Hence, the African human universe, the focus of the study of African Psychology, is more inclusive than the empirical and the attenuated universe of post-Renaissance Europe, which poses as the continuing context of mainstream psychology. For this reason, the realities admissible for study and understanding in African Psychology and indeed in the entire African social science are much more diverse and broad than the realities admissible for psychological scholarship in Euro-American psychology with the latter's emphasis on the observed and the observable, and on application of the methodologies employed in the natural sciences, anchored on the philosophical investigations of the British empiricists and logical positivists (Nicholson, 2009).

What the above indications are intended to demonstrate is that given the above scenario of differences between the African and the official Euro-American notions of the human world and society, it would be surprising if there are no significant differences between the concerns and methodologies of research in African psychology and those of Western psychology. The truth is that there is. For, the view propagated in mainstream psychology that all incidents and characters mentioned in psychology discussions must be explainable from principles applicable to the physical order of things appears antagonistic to the proper appreciation and study of some of the yearnings and anxieties of interest to the physical and spiritual well-being of many members of the modern African communities.

This, in essence, means that to remain relevant, students of psychology and other aspects of the fields of the social sciences in Africa must push back the limits of Western psychological and other social science frames to accommodate the need for relevant psychological and other social science research methodologies in universities in Africa. In doing this, we must, as psychologists and social scientists in Africa try to reconnect our psychology and social sciences with the complexities of life as lived in our various African societies. Hence, the language and research paradigms adopted by authorities in charge of psychology programmes in Africa must be flexed and bent to allow relevant psychological idioms and registers to be invented and made use of, in our efforts to account for the peculiar challenges of the African environment. For this reason, in the examples to be offered below, I plan to focus attention on alternative methodologies for psychological research in Africa; with the effort to try to highlight those oriented to helping us to achieve a better understanding of the lived experience of the African human being in the contemporary world.

Importance of Qualitative Research in Psychology

Seen against the above, it is obvious that there is a crucial place for alternative research paradigms in psychological training in African universities. This is because the qualitative, more than the quantitative approach to the study of things psychological, has concepts and methodologies more flexible and diverse to accommodate the challenges of understanding the nature and complexities of human thought, social change and experience in the postcolonial African world.

To signpost the enormous benefits of such a research paradigm, embracing the qualitative approaches, the rest of this chapter will now be devoted to an attempt to introduce, as briefly as possible, the different aspects and methodologies of qualitative research in psychology. To do this, we should, first of all, devote some time and space to attempt a definition of the term qualitative research.

WHAT IS QUALITATIVE RESEARCH?

Qualitative research is an approach to research in which the researcher studies people or things in their natural settings. It is, in particular, a type of research approach in which the views and perspectives of those studied or the meanings which such people bring to things that happen to them are given priority. It thus often implicates the study and reporting of first-person experience, or of life as lived, in which the researcher can serve as an investigator and data generator in his or her own problem.

Thus, unlike in quantitative survey researches, in which a structured questionnaire or a standardized rating scale with preset answers to questions under study are presented to (often distant) respondents to choose from, qualitative research involves an open-ended research methodology in which the aim of the researcher is to gain access to the unbiased views or beliefs, assumptions or practices, fears or plans of the research subject/s on the phenomenon under investigation. Supporting the above, Welman and Kruger (1999, p.189) point out that the phenomenologists who usually follow the qualitative research strategy, 'are concerned with understanding social and psychological issues from the perspectives of people involved.' This means that, essentially, in qualitative research, the emphasis of the researcher is on the experiential and the personal dimensions of human experience (Crossley, 2000). For, according to Groenewald (2004, p.7) the principal beliefs in qualitative research are that '(a) data are contained within the perspectives of people, and (b) because of this (the researcher should engage with the participants) in collecting the data.'

Consequently, one of the vital differences between quantitative researches in comparison with a qualitative research is that, in qualitative research, there is absence of manipulation of variables, and there is no testing of hypotheses. Qualitative research is concerned with the lived experiences of people; and therefore, basically exploratory or auto-ethnographical in nature. Often, of course, the task of a qualitative researcher is an attempt to develop a model for understanding a given phenomenon or situation or to generate a theory, rather than to test an already existing theory.

Most importantly, in a qualitative research, there is an emphasis on triangulation. And by the term triangulation, I mean an approach to research that uses a combination of more than one research strategy in a single study. Hence, in qualitative research there are different types of triangulation that can be used. These include: (1) Data Triangulation, (2) Method Triangulation, (3) Investigator Triangulation; (4) Theory Triangulation; and (5) Multiple Triangulation, which uses a combination of two or more triangulation techniques in one study (Denzin, and Lincoln, 1998; Marshall, and Rossman, 1999; Schwandt, 1997). A few words on some of these are presented below.

The exercise of data triangulation, involves the qualitative researcher collecting data from different categories of stakeholders of interest to the research. In some other instances it may mean the need to collect data from more than one site, or community, region or country; or from more than one time period (this aspect often given another name, environmental triangulation). It is argued that conducting in-depth interviews to gain insight on a given situation will be much more reliable if representatives of each relevant target group or community who volunteer information on that situation are found to share a common view on the situation in question.

In mixed methods triangulation the qualitative researcher most often uses quantitative methods combined with qualitative methods in the study design. In that case the interview procedure can be combined with the questionnaire design. On the other hand, using methodological triangulation requires that the qualitative researcher make use of multiple qualitative and /or quantitative methods to study the problem under attention. In that case the assumption is that where the conclusions from each of the methods corroborate one another, the findings are should be more reliable.

Again, in qualitative research, investigator triangulation is suggested in situations where two or more researchers (such as colleagues) from one field of study can work together to study a given problem. In that case, each member of the research team will have to study the phenomenon using the same instrument (interview or questionnaire or focus group discussion) and at the end, the findings from each investigator would be compared to those of the other colleagues, to arrive at joint conclusions for the study. The process is believed to make the entire study and its findings more robust and reliable. At other times of course investigator triangulation might involve researchers with divergent backgrounds and expertise working together on the same study as happens in participatory-action research. For example, in participatory-action research, research planning and data collection can be undertaken by two or more investigators; one, the primary, and the other, a member or some members of the people or community, an aspect of whose problems or lived experiences, are being investigated. In this regard, each member of the investigator team must have prominent roles in the study and their reportage of the events studied is expected to be complementary. This is because each of the investigators should discuss their individual findings and they should reach a conclusion in their presentation, which includes all findings. In each of the above two examples, the difficulty to be confronted is that of being able to assemble different investigators with a common interest and time to work together on the problem.

Theory triangulation is also often essential in qualitative research, particularly at the level of giving theoretical explanation to the diversity of meanings encountered in the data collected. This is, for example, what happened in my study of African Family Behaviour in Illness, in which the goal was to determine why some African family members tend to devote enduring attention to the care of their terminally sick, while in other instances, family members tend to be on the run, deserting the sick one (Nwoye, 2001). In this way, through theory triangulation, diverse explanation is found to account for the variety of trends in the data collected; a feat that would not be possible if attention is placed in reference to only one theory (Holloway, 1997). Thus, with theory triangulation, the idea is not to draw a theory from the data collected, but to make use of multiple professional perspectives (many a time outside of one's field of study) to interpret or clarify or explain the meaning of one's research data.

MAJOR QUALITATIVE RESEARCH APPROACHES

Having come to this stage, we are now in a position to highlight the major qualitative research approaches, at least, as deemed applicable for conducting psychological research in Africa. Among such approaches the following can be mentioned:

Narrative research: In narrative approach, the focus is on studying one or two individuals, gathering data by collecting their stories (Gergen, & Gergen, 1983), or experiences of, and responses to, a significant event in their lives, for example, a chronic illness, and exploring the meaning of those experiences for the individual/s concerned. Examples of such studies are those made famous by Michele L. Crossley, reported in her important book, entitled, Introducing Narrative Psychology: Self, Trauma and the Construction of Meaning published in the year 2000; in which emphasis was placed on constructing, through research, of a new framework for understanding how people challenged by a difficult illness struggle to survive and find meaning in their battered lives (Crossley, 1999a; Crossley, (1998a).

Phenomenological research: This aspect of qualitative research focuses on the meaning of an experience for an individual, or a number of individuals. In phenomenological research, in other words, the emphasis is on discovering what all participants may suffer in common but often approach in a different way, such as HIV infection or being a left-handed person in a dominantly right-handed society. After generating accounts of the participants' lived experiences in this way, the researcher can develop descriptions and understandings of the underlying meanings which each participant brings to the experience.

In some phenomenological studies the main goal may not be that of understanding different people's approach and response to an illness or to a given problem, but that of exploring the basis for the unique personal orientation of, for example, unmarried school drop-out teenagers who relish at being mothers of children very early, when their parents and neighbours would consider them as regrettably greedy and unready for that role.

A similar goal like the above, was explored in my study of the differential behaviour of two married African women whose husbands suffered from a similar ghastly automobile accident, but in which the wife of one, came up with empathy and devotion to the hospital care of her afflicted husband, while the wife of the other man refused to show up for the care and support that was needed. In such a research, exploring the basis for occurrence of compassion fatigue in family care of the chronic hospital patient, the emphasis is on understanding the psychology of variation reflected in the differential attitudes and actions of the two women in the picture, and to learn from it.

These observations mean that in phenomenological (qualitative) research the effort of the researcher is to attempt to 'understand the world from the subjects' point of view, to unfold meaning of people's experiences' (Kvale, 1996:1-2). Concurring, Bentz and Shapiro, 1998: 96) point out that at the root of phenomenological research, 'the intent is to understand the phenomenon in their own terms,–to provide a description of human experience as it is experienced by the person herself.'

Grounded theory research: This is an approach to qualitative research made famous by Glaser & Strauss (1967) and Strauss & Corbin (1990). Grounded theory research is a type of qualitative research in which the ultimate goal is to move beyond description to generate or discover some links within a set of the data collected that can lead to the development of a theory. Thus in grounded theory research, like in all kinds of qualitative research, the goal is not that of theory testing but that of theory generation and development.

Ethnographic research: In psychology, like in anthropology (Bernard, 2006), ethnographic research approach can be used to study, describe and interpret the shared and learned values, behaviors, beliefs, and practices of a given institution, or community, such as among the leading prayer-church groups in most parts of Africa today. In conducting such a study emphasis is placed on trying to discover a pattern in the data collected; including identification of commonalities and differences in the rituals of healing provided to participants.

Case-study research: The case study approach is a popular qualitative research approach in the social science fields. In the field of psychology, a case study can be done on an individual, or an institution, or a group or a community. A typical example of such a qualitative research approach is a master's degree study carried out by Winifrida Kambona, a graduate student of the Department of Psychology of the University of Dodoma, Tanzania, under my supervision. The study was entitled: The Challenge of Educating the AIDS Orphans in Tanzania: A Case Study of the Dodoma Village of Hope Centre in Dodoma Municipality. It was concerned with the study of the objectives, history and development, and initial constraints and present successes of the Village of Hope (VoH).

To gather data to respond to the study's goals and questions, a triangulation of people and data collection methods, involving multiple sources of information (observations, interviews, documents, and audiovisual material, such as photographs of key officials, buildings and classrooms) were used. At the end, the researcher came out with findings which revealed an interesting approach to educating the AIDS orphans at the VoH, with practices rich in deep psychological relevance.

For instance, it was found that the orphan children at the Village of Hope were shared into houses, with each house bearing a religious name; and each house and its occupants being assigned to the care and management of a male and a female teacher, who, together acted in loco parentis, operating as the designated father and mother respectively, of all the children allocated to that house. In that way, the orphans in the VoH are made to grow up used to the critical words of 'mom' and 'dad' in their early lives. From such a study it was concluded that the operational psychology of orphan handling entrenched at the VoH is The Psychology of "As if", credited to Vaihinger (1924): the orphaned children were seen to be living and behaving, relating to their house 'dads' and 'moms' as if these school officials were their true parents (or their actual mothers and fathers).

CONDITIONS FOR THE USE OF A QUALITATIVE METHODOLOGY

Now, there are several issues to take into account when deciding to adopt a qualitative research methodology in one's study.

The first is that qualitative methods are mainly called for when there is need to better understand any phenomenon (such as an individual, or a group, or an institution or a community) about which little is yet known; or to gain new perspectives on things about which much is already known, but the remaining gaps still appear crucial to be addressed. The second point is that qualitative research is often called for when there is need to gain more in-depth information (often through an in-depth interview process) that may be difficult to convey quantitatively, such as in auto-ethnography in which the researcher is at the same time the source of the data for the study

In sum, then, a qualitative research approach is appropriate when a complex, detailed understanding of an issue or an individual or community is required and when quantitative measures and statistical analyses do not fit, or will not be able to do justice to the problem that needed investigation.

CHARACTERISTIC FEATURES OF QUALITATIVE RESEARCH

To further assist a prospective qualitative researcher in Africa in coming to a firm decision on whether or not to choose a qualitative method for his or her study, I wish to summarize below some of the views of several authors and researchers on the characteristics of qualitative, or naturalistic, research in the social sciences. They include the following:

1. Qualitative research uses the natural setting as the source of data. In it, the researcher attempts not to rate or assess, but to observe, describe and interpret settings as they are, or the person under study as s/he is, thinks and or feels; with the researcher maintaining, in doing this, what Patton calls an 'empathic

neutrality' (1990: 55). Thus the operative word in most qualitative research particularly in phenomenological research is the notion of description. Thus in phenomenological research, according to Groenewald (2004: 5) 'the aim of the researcher is to describe as accurately as possible the phenomenon, refraining from any pre-given framework, but remaining true to the facts.' This is the kind of thing that happens in phenomenological case study like the one undertaken by Wambona (2011), earlier cited.

2. In qualitative research the researcher assumes the role of the 'human instrument' of data collection. This means that in qualitative research, unlike in quantitative survey research, the researcher is the vehicle through which data are collected and interpreted; which means that in it, there is a direct contact between the subject of study and the researcher doing the study. This is different from what happens in a survey research, in which a researcher can send his or her questionnaire to a respondent, not directly, but often through posting or by proxy, and the responses returned to him or her without the researcher ever knowing the respondent in person.

3. Qualitative researchers predominantly use inductive data analysis. This means that in qualitative research, there is an attempt to generate new knowledge, or new idea or models or assumptions for understanding the phenomenon under study on the basis of what is found. That is, in qualitative research, there is an effort to go beyond the information given, to draw important conclusions from the data collected. Qualitative researchers appear to engage in this inductive analysis process convinced, in line with the view credited to Coffey & Atkinson (1996: 139) that 'good research is not generated by rigorous data alone, ... (but) 'going beyond' the data to develop idea'. In it too, there is an attempt to detect the

typical within the general. In this way, initial theorizing no matter how small is often a product of qualitative research.

4. Qualitative researchers pay special attention 'to the notion of lives as lived', seeking the uniqueness of each case. Hence, qualitative methodology is a choice research approach for the study of lives (Crossley, 2000). In particular, the adequacy and believability of a qualitative research report is judged using special criteria, different from those applicable for evaluating the adequacy of a quantitative research report. In this regard, the suggestion proposed by Maxwell (2001) appears to be the most interesting of the options available in the literature. According to Maxwell, there are five types of validity processes to be followed in order to enhance the trustworthiness and appropriateness of a qualitative research report. These include (a) the notion of validity as reportage accuracy; (b) interpretive validity; (c) theoretical validity, (d) the notion of validity as generalisability; and (e) evaluative validity which refers to the study's ability to stand the test of evaluative scrutiny, particularly as regards how the study was planned and how the data were collected.

As a complementary perspective to Maxwell's view, Schurink, Schurink and Poggenpoel (1998) propose a number of strategies to achieve truth in qualitative research. Among such strategies are: (a) effort at bracketing one's beliefs and assumptions in order to gather data and to understand the person being studied, with a focus on getting an 'insider perspective' on the case, (b) audio-recordings made of each interview, (c) bracketing oneself during the transcription of the interview process; and (d) sending a copy of the text of the report to the study participants to crosscheck if it accurately portrayed their perspectives regarding the phenomenon investigated.

The above observations imply that in qualitative as much as in quantitative research there is usually a commensurate attempt to ensure and enhance the truth value of the report of the study.

QUALITATIVE RESEARCH DESIGN AND SAMPLING STRATEGIES

What I plan to emphasise under this theme is the fact that the particular design of a qualitative study depends on the purpose of the study, the kind of information needed for the study questions to be adequately answered, and the type of data that will have the most credibility when collected. Hycner (1999:156), in commenting in this regard, points out that 'the phenomenon dictates the method (not vice-versa) including even the type of participants to get into the sample.' This means that in qualitative research, the decisional wisdom is to let the problem under attention dictate the method of study to be used.

On the other hand, in qualitative methodologies, there are no strict criteria for sample size (Patton, 1990). In qualitative research, the sample size can be one, like in situations where an individual is the subject of the study. Concurring, Boyd (2001) regards two or 10 participants or research subjects or respondents as sufficient to reach saturation in some types of qualitative research, and Creswell (1998: 65 & 115) is of the view that 'long interviews with up to 10 people' within the context of a phenomenological study is sufficient to get the typical pattern in a data from the participants on a given theme.

Thus whereas in quantitative research the dominant sampling strategy is probability sampling, which depends on the selection of a random and representative sample from the larger population, by contrast, purposive sampling is the dominant strategy in qualitative research (Maxwell, 1992).

Purposive sampling targets an individual or those persons with the needed data for achieving the goals of the study. However, absence of randomization in sample selection in qualitative research does not imply that issues of sampling and those of representativeness and generalisability where applicable, are not important in qualitative research. But it needs to be mentioned that those concerns are still crucial in both qualitative and quantitative research whenever one wants to draw inferences from the actual persons, events, or activities investigated to other persons, events or situations not covered in the study, or to those at other times and places than when the investigation was conducted.

In qualitative research, snowball sampling is used to trace additional participants or informants for the study. Here, the term snowballing is used to refer to a method of expanding the sample by asking one informant or participant to recommend others for interviewing (Groenewald, 2004; Babbie, 1995; Crabtree & Miller, 1992). In this regard, Groenewald (2004: 9) notes that many authorities like Bailey (1996), Holloway (1997), and Greig and Taylor (1999) refer 'to those through whom entry is gained gatekeepers and those persons who volunteer assistance key actors or key insiders.' Contributing his own view, Neuman (2000) qualifies a gatekeeper in qualitative research as 'someone with the formal or informal authority to control access to a site' (p.352); that is, a person from whom permission is required for the study. In this way, according to him, key insiders often adopt the researcher, by accepting to give time and attention to share their views with the researcher on the phenomenon being studied.

Now a crucial point about the problem of design in qualitative research concerns the issue of promoting acceptable ethical practice in such researches. And, according to Holloway (1997) and Kvale (1996) what this entails is procurement of informed consent from each research participant. To achieve this objective, there is need to develop a specific informed consent 'agreement', form specifying the following: (1) That they are participating in research; (2) The purpose of the research (without stating the central research question); (3) The procedures of the research; (4) The risk and benefits of participating in the study; (5) That participation in the research is voluntary; (6) That each participant has right to stop the research or their participation in the study at any time; and (7) Safe guards that have been made to ensure and protect participants' anonymity and confidentiality (Arksey & Knight, 1999; Bless & Higson-Smith, 2000; Kvale, 1996; Street, 1998).

Bailey (1996) emphasizes that apart from the need to secure participants' informed consent, there is also need to prevent any possibility of deception in qualitative research as its occurrence might prevent insights, whereas honesty coupled with confidentiality reduces suspicion and promotes sincere response from participants. Consequently, to avoid inciting suspicion in the minds of qualitative study participants, the 'informed consent agreement' form must be explained to the participants before the start of each interview.

DATA COLLECTION TECHNIQUES IN QUALITATIVE RESEARCH

There are so many possible data collection techniques in qualitative research, including interview, observation, focus group, audiovisuals, diary and document analysis. But the most prevailing forms of data collection associated with qualitative research are interviews and observation and document analysis. On account of their relative importance in this regard, some few more words will be said on each of them below.

(a) Interviews

Qualitative interviews may be used either as the primary strategy for data collection, or in conjunction with observation, focus group, document analysis, or other techniques (Bogdan and Biklen, 2003). Qualitative interviewing utilizes open-ended questions that allow for individual variations. In most interview-based studies, the development of an interview guide (or schedule) is usually recommended. It contains a list of questions or general topics that the interviewer wants to explore during each interview. Qualitative researchers agree that interview guides are useful in that (a) they ensure good use of limited interview time; (b) they make interviewing multiple subjects more systematic and comprehensive; and (c) they help to keep interactions focused.

However, an important decision to make before going ahead with the interview process is how to record the interview data. Some researchers prefer written notes. Others prefer the use of a tape recorder instead. The critical issue is that whichever mode is preferred must be justified for its use.

Furthermore, in qualitative research interview it is usually an accepted practice to believe that the topic under discussion has been exhausted or saturated, when the interviewees (subjects or participants or informants) do not introduce any new more perspectives on the topic. Also, it is important to draw attention to the point made by Kvale (1996) to the effect that any qualitative researcher must recognise that there is usually a distinction between the research question and the interview question, the former being the foundation for, or source of, and fewer in number, than the latter. And the interview question is reciprocal: both researcher and research subject are engaged in the dialogue. In this way the duration of the interview and the number of questions vary from one participant to the other.

(b) Observations

Most qualitative researchers would agree that the most fundamental form of data collection in qualitative research is observation of participants in the context of a natural setting. In case studies of places and institutions and their rituals and ceremonies, for example, observational data are used for the purpose of description of settings, activities, people, and the meanings of what is observed from the perspective of the participants. According to Patton (1990) observation can lead to deeper understandings than interviews alone, because it provides knowledge of the context in which events occur, and may enable the researcher to see things that participants themselves are not aware of, may not see, are not able or are unwilling to discuss.

However, researchers do not just observe events or settings. They make field notes, which are running descriptions of settings, people, activities, and sounds observed. In some psychological studies, such field notes may include drawings or maps. In addition, Miles & Huberman (1984: 69) draw attention to the importance of 'memoing' as another instrument of data collection in qualitative research. Concurring, Groenewald (2004: 13) observes that memoing is an aspect of the researcher's field notes, 'recording what the researcher hears, sees, experiences and thinks in the course of collecting the data and reflecting on the process.' In this regard, the importance of memoing during the process of data collection in qualitative research lies in the fact that usually researchers are easily absorbed in the data-collection process and may fail to reflect on what they are seeing or what is happening within the setting of the research. On the other hand, through memoing, the researcher is able to introduce and maintain a balance between descriptive notes and reflective notes, such as hunches, impressions, feelings, and so on. To make the best use of it, Miles and Huberman (1984) recommend that memos must be dated in order to enable the researcher to track or correlate them with the data. The same authorities (Miles and Huberman, 1984) suggest the need for fleshing out these memos as soon after observation as possible, preferably the same day.

Underlining a similar point, Groenewald (2004) proposes that for the field notes to be useful, the researcher must be disciplined to record, subsequent to each interview, as comprehensively as possible, but without judgmental evaluation, for example: 'what happened and what was involved? Who was involved? Where did the activities occur? Why did an incident take place and how did it actually happen?'(p. 15). Also as emphasized by Lofland and Lofland (1999: 5), field notes 'should be written no later than the morning after'.

In particular, according to Leonard Schatzman and Anselm Strauss in line with the view credited to Robert Burgess as cited by Groenewald (2004) there are four types of fields notes, namely: First, observational notes (ON), or 'what happened notes' deemed important enough to the researcher to make. Second, theoretical notes (TN), consisting of 'attempts to derive meaning', or to see the typical in the general, as the researcher thinks or reflects on experiences understudy. Third, methodological notes (MN), which carry 'reminders, instructions or critique' to oneself on issues understudy. And, fourth, analytical memos (AM), which consists of end-of-a-field-day summary or progress reviews. In commenting in this regard, Morgan (1997: 57-58) observes that because field notes involve interpretation, they are, properly speaking, 'part of the analysis rather than the data collection'.

Now, apart from the use of field notes/memoing, qualitative researchers may use, where available, photographs, videotapes, and audio tapes as means of accurately capturing a setting and events under study (see Winifrida's case study above), and most of these instruments like video-tapes and audio tapes serve, too, as important data-storing methods. But for better results, where they are used, the interview setting must be as free from background noise as possible.

Furthermore, some researchers may require their participants to engage in short essay writing, where they are expected to state their viewpoint, perspectives or feelings on a given issue understudy. In such an essay request, the participants are assured that what is import is not grammar or spelling accuracy but their true views or opinions on the issue being studied. To promote confidentiality, they are also told that they are not expected to put down their names in the answer sheet containing their essay.

(c) Analysis of documents in qualitative research

Another source of information that can be invaluable to qualitative researchers particularly those involved with the study of lives as lived, essential in psycho-biographical studies is analysis of documents. Such documents might include official records, letters, newspaper accounts, autobiographies, diaries, novels, and reports, as well as the published data used in a review of literature.

A pertinent point to emphasise at this juncture is that there are some specialized forms of qualitative research which rely solely on analysis of documents. For example, a doctoral study that was based on the document analysis methodology is the one carried out by Andrew Gilbert (1986) of Rhodes University in South Africa, entitled: "Psychology and social change in the Third World: A cognitive perspective." The study was conducted at the University of South Africa, Pretoria. In it, Achebe's first novel, Things fall Apart (1958), was used as a foil to answer some questions of interest to the study, whose goal was to construct a social psychological theory of the relationship that exists between individual and social change; an area which, according to Gilbert, has remained under-theorized even in cross-cultural psychology.

A similar study is the one credited to Willem Jacobus Smit (2009), entitled: Becoming the Third Generation: Negotiating Modern Selves in Nigerian Bildungsromane of the 21st Century. It was a Master's degree study conducted at Stellenbosch University, South Africa. It entailed an in-depth examination of three 21st-century novels – Chimamanda Nogzi Adichie's Purple Hibiscus (2004), Sefi Atta's Everything Good Will Come (2004) and Chris Abani's GraceLand (2005) with the goal of revealing how new avenues of identity-negotiation and formation are being explored in various contemporary Nigerian situations. It tracked the ways in which the Bildungsroman, the novel of self-development, served as a vehicle through which this new identity was articulated. As Smit (2009: v) noted, 'concurrently, the study also grapples with the ways in which the articulation and negotiation of this new identity reshapes the conventions of the classical Bildungsroman genre, thereby establishing a unique and contemporary Nigerian Bildungsroman for the 21st century'.

I draw attention to the above two researches in this presentation to show that most of the African novels written by illustrious African men and women writers pose as underutilized fitting sources on which doctoral researches in the areas of family, child, personality and social-cultural psychology can be built.

TECHNIQUE OF DATA ANALYSIS IN QUALITATIVE RESEARCH

Essentially, qualitative data analysis or data explication begins with identification of the themes emerging from the raw data, a process sometimes referred to as "open coding" (Strauss and Corbin, 1990). Other ways of analyzing the data is to relate the data to the principal themes contained in each study's research questions. Using this process, the researcher will be able to create descriptive, multi-dimensional categories or subthemes which form a preliminary framework for analysis.

As the raw data are broken down into outstanding themes, in the light of research questions investigated, the researcher must also devise an 'audit trail'- that is, a scheme for identifying or tracing these data components according to their speakers or sources and context (where they came from, where they were collected). The particular identifiers developed may or may not be used in the research report, but speakers are typically referred to in a manner that provides a sense of context or the 'multi-voice' (Gergen, & Gergen, 1983). Qualitative research reports are characterized by the use of 'voice' in the text. This refers to participant quotes that illustrate the themes being described and the assurance of originality of data being discussed or presented.

The next stage of analysis involves re-examination of the themes and categories identified to determine how they are linked, a complex process sometimes called "axial coding" (Strauss and Corbin, 1990). In some cases the result of this effort may give rise to a development of an organogram of description, which puts the pattern of events emerging from the study in graphic form (See Nwoye, 2002).

Based on the above procedures, a qualitative research report results in a rich, tightly crafted account that 'closely approximates the reality it represents' (Strauss and Corbin, 1990: 57). In all instances of qualitative data analysis, one fundamental attitude that needs to inhabit the researcher as he or she engages in all the critical processes highlighted above is a deliberate and purposeful opening up into the phenomenon 'in its own right with its own meaning' (Fouche, 1993; Hycner, 1999). This means that while attempting an analysis of data under qualitative research approach there is need to ensure that one's presuppositions or personal meanings are not allowed to influence the direction of the data. In this regard, the researcher must relate to the data emerging from the study in a neutral frame of mind, taking no position either or against the nature of the findings. In this way, the unique experiences of the participants captured in the study would be allowed to stand as they are, unadulterated.

CONCLUSION

The vast increase of global interest in qualitative and other alternative research methodologies in recent years compels the need for a basic understanding of such alternative research approaches by social science researchers in African universities. So far this has not been truly the case given the prevailing hegemonic status enjoyed by quantitative approaches in social science research in most African universities. This chapter represents a challenge to this unwelcome state of affairs. The illustrative sample of categories of qualitative methodologies discussed in the chapter are intended to serve as a means of opening the eyes of our students and scholars to the enormous promise of the qualitative research approach in the field of the social sciences. The core of my argument is that the current over-emphasis on the use of quantitative approaches in social science research in African universities needs to be reconsidered to create space to accommodate alternative research methodologies highlighted in the chapter that were deemed more suited for the study of lives as lived in modern African societies. This, in no way, implies the urge for the total replacement of quantitative methodologies with qualitative approaches. What is recommended instead is the need for the entrenchment of the spirit of inclusivity in the curricula contents of degree programmes intended for the training of psychologists and other social scientists in Africa. That is, in such way that in such programmes students should be offered some equal access to information and education regarding the fundamental possibilities of the two research paradigms in contributing to the promotion of relevant social science research engagements in African universities.

REFERENCES

Abani, C. (2005) Graceland, New York, Picador

Adichie, C. N. (2004) Purple Hibiscus: A Novel, New York, Anchor Books

Arksey, H., & Knight, P. (1999) Interviewing for social scientists, London, Sage

Atta, S. (2004) Everything Good Will Come, Northampton, Interlink Books

Babbie, E. (1995) The practice of social research (7th ed.), Belmont, CA, Wadsworth

Bailey, C.A. (1996) A guide to field research, Thousand Oaks, CA, Pine Forge

Bentz, V. M., & Shapiro, J. J. (1998) Mindful enquiry in social research, Thousand Oaks, CA, Sage

Bless, C., & Higson-Smith, C. (2000) Fundamentals of social research methods, an African perspective (3rd ed.), Lansdowne, South Africa, Juta

Bogdan, R.C. & Biklen, S.K. (2003) Qualitative research for education: An introduction to theories and methods (4th ed), Boston, Allyn and Bacon

Boyd, C.O. (2001) 'Phenomenology the method.' In P.L. Munhall (Ed.), Nursing research: A qualitative perspective (3rd. ed., pp. 93-122), Sudbury, MA, Jones and Bartlett

Coffey, A., & Atkinson, P. (1996) Making sense of qualitative data: Complementary research strategies, Thousand Oaks, CA, Sage

Crabtree, B. F., & Miller, W. L. (eds) (1992) Doing qualitative research: Research methods for primary care (Vol. 3), Newbury Park, CA, Sage

Creswell, J. W. (1998) Qualitative inquiry and research design: Choosing among five

Traditions, Thousand Oaks, CA, Sage

Crossley, M. L. (2000) Introducing narrative psychology: Self, trauma, and the construction of meaning. Buckingham, UK, Open University

Crossley (1999a) 'Making sense of HIV infection: discourse and adaptation to life with an HIV positive diagnosis', Health, 3(1): 95-119

Crossley, M.L. (1998a) 'Women living with a long-term HIV positive diagnosis: problems, concerns and ways of ascribing meaning', Women's Studies International Forum, 21 (5): 521-33

Denzin, N.K., and Lincoln, Y. S. (1998) The Landscape of Qualitative Research. Thousand Oaks, CA, Sage Publishing

Federal Republic of Nigeria, National Universities Commission (1989) Approved Minimum Academic Standards in Social Sciences for All Nigerian Universities, Lagos, NUC

Fouche, F. (1993) 'Phenomenological theory of human science.' in Snyman, J. (ed) Conceptions of social inquiry (pp. 87-112), Pretoria, South Africa, Human Science Research Council

Gergen, Kenneth & Gergen, Mary (1983) 'Narratives of self', in Sarbin, T.R. & Schiebe. K.E. (eds) Studies in Social Identity, New York, Praeg

Gilbert, A. (1989) 'Things fall apart? Psychological theory in the context of rapid social change', South African Journal of Psychology, 19(2): 91-100

Greening, T. (2006) 'Five Basic Postulates of Humanistic Psychology', Journal of Humanistic Psychology, 46: 239

Greig, A., & Taylor, J. (1999) Doing research with children, London, Sage

Groenewald, T. (2004) 'A phenomenological research design illustrated', International Journal of Qualitative Methods, 3(1). Article 4. Retrieved [22/102011] from http://www.ualberta.ca/-iiqm/backissues/3_1/pdf/groenewald.pdf

Holloway, I. (1997) Basic concepts for qualitative research, Oxford, Blackwell Science

Hycner, R. H. (1999) 'Some guidelines for the phenomenological analysis of interview data', in Bryman, A. &. Burgess, R.G. (eds) Qualitative research (Vol. 3, pp. 143-164), London, Sage

Kambona, W. (2011). 'The Challenge of Educating the AIDS Orphans in Tanzania: A Case Study of the Village of Hope Centre in Dodoma Municipality ', Unpublished Master's Thesis, University of Dodoma, Tanzania

Kvale, S. (1996) Interviews: An introduction to qualitative research interviewing, Thousand Oaks, CA, Sage

Lofland, J., & Lofland, L. H. (1999) 'Data logging in observation: Fieldnotes', in A. Bryman, A. & Burgess, R.G. (eds) Qualitative research (Vol. 3), London, Sage

Marshall, C., and Rossman, G.B. (1999) Designing Qualitative Research (3rd ed.), Thousand Oaks, CA, Sage Publishing

Miles, M. B., & Huberman, A. M. (1984) Qualitative data analysis, a sourcebook of new Methods, Newbury Park, CA, Sage

Miller, W. L., & Crabtree, B. F. (1992) 'Primary care research: A multimethod typology and qualitative road map', in Crabtree, B.F. & Miller, W.L. (eds) Doing qualitative research. Research methods for primary care (Vol. 3), Newbury Park, CA, Sage

Morgan, D. L. (1997) Focus groups as qualitative research, Thousand Oaks, CA, Sage

Mouton, J. & Marais, H.C. (1990) Basic concepts in the methodology of the social sciences (Revised ed.), Pretoria, South Africa, Human Sciences Research Council

Neuman, W. L. (2000) Social research methods: Qualitative and quantitative approaches (4th ed.), Boston, Allyn and Bacon

Nicholson, I.A.M. (2009) Inventing Personality: Gordon Allport and the Science of Selfhood, Washington, DC, American Psychological Association

Nwoye, A. (2000) 'Building on the Indigenous: theory and method of marriage therapy in contemporary Eastern and Western Africa', Journal of Family Therapy, 22(4): 347-357

Nwoye, A. (2001) 'History of Family Therapy: African Perspective', Journal of Family Psychotherap, 12(4):61-77

Nwoye, A. (2002a) 'Hope-healing communities in contemporary Africa', Journal of Humanistic Psychology, 42(4):58-81

Nwoye, A. (2002b) 'Visions and Revisions in family therapy in Africa', Australian and New Zealand Journal of family therapy, 23(4):191-195

Nwoye, A. (2003) 'African Approach to Truth and Reconciliation', Human Systems: The Journal of Systemic Consultation and Management, 14(4): 183-198

Nwoye, A. (2004a) 'The Shattered Microcosm: Imperatives for Improved Family Therapy in Africa in the 21st Century', Contemporary Family Therapy, 26(2): 143-164

Nwoye, A. (2004b) 'Decision-making Therapy in HIV/AIDS: The African Experience', Dialectical Anthropology, 28: 377-395

Nwoye, A. (2005) 'Memory Healing Processes and Community Intervention in Grief Work in Africa', Australian and New Zealand Journal of Marital and Family Therapy, 26(3): 147-154

Nwoye, A. (2006a) 'A Narrative Approach to Child and Family Therapy in Africa' Contemporary Family Therapy, 28(1): 1-23

Nwoye, A. (2006b) 'Theory and Method of Marriage Therapy in Contemporary Africa. Contemporary Family Therapy, 28(4): 393-504

Nwoye, A. (2006c) 'Re-mapping the fabric of the African self: A synoptic theory', Dialectical Anthropology, 30: 119-146

Nwoye, A. (2010) 'A Psycho-Cultural History of Psychotherapy in Africa', Psychotherapy and Politics International, 8(1): 26–43

Schurink, W. J., Schurink, E. M. & Poggenpoel, M. (1998) 'Focus group interviewing and audiovisual methodology in qualitative research', in. De Vos, A.S. (ed) Research at grassroots, a primer in care professions, Pretoria, South Africa, Van Schaik

Schwandt, T. A. (1997) Qualitative Inquiry: A Dictionary of Terms, Thousand Oaks, CA, Sage Publishing

Skinner, B.F. (1987) 'Whatever happened to psychology as the science of behavior',American Psychologist, 42(8):780–786

Street, A. (1998) 'In/forming inside nursing: Ethical dilemmas in critical research. in G. Shacklock, G., Smyth, J (eds) Being reflective in critical educational and social research, London, Falmr

Vaihinger, H. (1924) The Philosophy of 'As If': A System of the Theoretical, Practical and Religious Fictions of Mankind, Translated by C. K. Ogden, Barnes and Noble, New York, 1968 (First published in England by Routledge and Kegan Paul, Ltd., 1924)

Welman, J. C., & Kruger, S. J. (1999) Research methodology for the business and administrative sciences, Johannesburg, South Africa, International Thompson

Chapter Six

Re-claiming Schooling and Higher Education in Africa

George J. Sefa Dei

Introduction

This paper follows Molefi Asante's call for us to rethink social science education not only from a neo-liberal capitalist informed project, but also, to offer new ways of doing scholarship on Africa. As an educator my intellectual/academic project and political desire is to suggest ways of reclaiming schooling and higher education in Africa in ways that speak to our lived realities and conditionalities. In such a project, speaking our stories in our own voices is critical. I am making a case for us to think of schooling and education in 'post-colonial' African contexts through decolonization by way of Indigenous philosophies' transgressive pedagogies (Dei 2010a, 2011a). We need to dialogue with counterinsurgent knowledges that embody the civic will of local African peoples to questions of classroom learning as well as the politics of the relevance of local knowledges in the space of the oppressive Eurocentric curricula and pedagogies. From curricula, to pedagogies, to epistemologies, the African academy (e.g., schools, colleges and universities) has been localized to some governing Eurocentric paradigms, well-steeped within colonial specificities of academic imperialism. Yet, importantly, the experience of classroom learning cannot be devoid of the lived experiences of the African learner. Today, within the Global South, social and natural science research produces a mode of alienation (Fanon 1963) through myriad academic disciplines onto the African learner by way of absenting ontological primacy from Euro-Enlightenment epistemologies. Schooling and education in the African contexts must work with the ontological primacy immanent to African learners. I would argue that, for example, African Indigenous proverbs and local stories have the potential to educate the African learner in ways that make for responsible citizenship, community building, respect for Eldership, social responsibility and knowledge that propel action in terms of serving local people's needs, hopes and aspirations.

For example, with the globalization of schooling and education, we should be asking: African education for whom and at what cost? What are the perils when we think of "African Development" through conventional academic disciplines that worship the will of capitalism as its ontological mantra? From global exploitative relations, to the continued production of underdevelopment in the Global South, to the continued destabilization of racialized geographies, Eurocentric academic disciplines continue to bring sustainability to the Western metropolis.

We need a particular type of bridge to broach the lacunae of social science research about African schooling and education and conventional forms of knowledging. Concerning schooling and education in the African context, the issue of the production and positionality of the different Eurocentric epistemes and how they come to be accorded with power, privilege and discursive authority within particular academic disciplines. How does social science research about African schooling and education come to limit possibilities for an Integrative Indigenous framework? What does it mean for Indigeneity to participate in schooling and education without compromise? Key questions: How do we come to recover, reclaim, and recuperate Indigeneity that speaks to the holistic ways of the lived experiences of African peoples? And what are these socio-cultural sites of contestation that make this political process of knowledge dissemination possible?

What then are the consequences for the different voices of the oppressed when the politics of identification, the politics of knowledge-legitimation, the politics of representation, work to dissipate the collective oppressed voice of African peoples within academic spaces?

AN AFRICAN-CENTRED DISCURSIVE FRAMEWORK

The African-centred paradigm provides a space for African peoples to interpret their own experiences on their own terms, worldviews and understandings rather than being forced through a Eurocentric lens. An African-centred perspective is about developing an African worldview. This worldview borrows from the Afrocentric perspective as a system of thought. It is shaped by the lens of Africology stressing the centrality of culture, agency, history, identity and experience. Consequently, African-centred, like Afrocentric educa-tion, stresses notion of culture, centring learners' histories, identi-ties and experiences, focusing on the learner's agency to bring about change in personal and community lives. It is argued that we need to work with the notion of 'centredness' of the learner in her or his own learning in order to engage knowledge. Such that African/ indigenous learners becomes subjects of their own histories and stories and experiences (see Asante 1991, 2003; Mazama 2001; van Dyk 1996; Ziegler 1996). Bringing an anti-colonial reading to Af-rican-centred knowing and knowledge base contributes to sharpen the politics of intellectual engagement for African peoples. Among the theoretical suppositions of anti-colonialism is the insistence that the transformation of Africa/n realities must start with the issue of re-conceptualizing education, e.g., asking new questions about the what, how, and why of education. Current schooling and education is essentially a colonizing and oppressive experience and any attempt at transforming African educational systems calls for taking an unequivocal anti-colonial stance.

African learners, in particular, have a responsibility to always represent excellence in scholarship by developing an intellectual perspective that foremost speaks to our lived realities. The question of how to advance African culture, history and knowledge is criti-cal. Molefi Asante (2003) has long maintained that African peoples have knowledge, comments and opinions of world affairs and events and can proceed to offer their insights from a centredness of their cultures and places in history. That, how others have viewed Africa is fundamentally different from how Africans have viewed them-selves, and that as African learners we must tell "African stories" from the standpoint of our centrality in the historical moments and specificities that these stories and events occur.

African learners must certainly look beyond the confines of Africa as a geographical space. We must uphold the idea of the construction of our Africanness [or for that matter, Blackness] in all its complexities and tensions. But, in that, we must consider that this exercise is only meaningful if it helps us as African peoples to connect us to our shared histories, challenges and struggles. In African knowledge production [as well as other forms of knowledge production] the question of social transformation is relevant. Thus, when we come into any space, we cannot just be there/here. There is a moral, intellectual and political imperative–'Don't just be There/Here" in knowledge production. What we need are deep thinking African learners/scholars [as scholar activists] who can help lead the way for us to take our communities back. We must transcend our luminal boundaries and the theatricality of our performances as trained pseudo "Euro-scholars" (I use the qualifier 'psuedo' here to amplify that in the realm of Euro-scholarship, we, as scholars of African descent are always having to defend our scholarship). Culture is the basis of all our ideas. As Karenga (2011) exhorts, as African scholars we must keep open and develop a flexibility of knowledge and seek to interpret African humanity in its most profound and ethical forms. Critical education and social research is needed to recover/ uncover and reclaim our past, histories and traditions, as well as cultural mythologies and their embedded meanings.

PRE-COLONIAL EDUCATION IN AFRICA

At this juncture, some points are worthy of note in discussing pre-colonial African education. Contrary to conventional Eurocentric thinking education was NOT introduced to Africa by European missionaries or colonial authorities. What colonialists introduced was a particular form of defined and restricted "school education" (see Nukunya 1992). For one thing in Western Africa we know that the City of Timbuktu even before the coming of Europeans was a hub for Islamic intellectualism in the 15th Century, with its famous Sankore University and other Madrasa attracting scholars from all over the world to the Mali Empire, especially during the reign of Mansa Musa (see also Mensah 2006; Williams 1987; Kryza 2006).

The fact, however, is that pre-colonial Africa was largely characterized by an Indigenous education in which knowledge production, interrogation, validation and dissemination [including teaching and learning] utilized what was available, what people know and sought to know (Abbam 1992; Wiredu 1995). Education therefore defined/determined ways, practices, strategies, means and options through which African peoples themselves came to know, understand and interpret their worlds [social, physical and metaphysical] and acted within such worlds for effective social existence (Okrah 2003; Boateng 1990). Education was teaching and learning about the past, present and future continuum emphasizing the place of local culture, traditions and history and making the individual subject a whole being belonging to a community and with societal responsibilities (Boateng 1990).

The focus of education was on teaching, learning and acting from the everyday and not strictly obtaining formal schooling in a four-walled classroom as such. This education was defined broadly as more than going to school. It was learning about family, community, nature and society interconnections through everyday practice and social activity. Pre-colonial education was largely informal (see also Fafunwa 1974, 1982: Fafunwa and Aisiku 1982; Sifuna 1990, 1992) as linked to traditions and cultural education. Education started in the early years of an individual's life and was approached through a culturalized medium of instruction, such as story sharing fables, folktales, songs, proverbs, apprenticeship, arts and crafts, vocations, trades, and other forms of folkloric productions (Abbam 1994; Wiredu and Gyekye 1992 Yankah 1989; Miruka 1994; Okrah 2003).

The educational site was not the 'school' but within and throughout communities, homes and families. The medium of instruction was through the local vernacular. Pre-colonial education as understood by local communities would make a distinction between 'wisdom' and 'knowledge' acquisition by insisting that an educated person is one who understands herself/himself as a whole person—mentally, spiritually, culturally, emotionally, physically and materially — and as continually guided by the mutual obligations to, and interdependence with the wider community (Wiredu and Gyekye 1992; see also Shizha 2005). In effect, pre-colonial African education was to advance African culture, history, traditions and spirituality. The success of such education depended largely on the important roles of parents, family, Elders, cultural custodians and community leaders as teachers of knowledge, wisdom and morality (see also Yankah 1989, 1995; Opoku 1975, 1997). Within local communities there were also other culturally-sanctioned modes and mediums of education (e.g., intergenerational transmission of knowledge through age sets/grades; secret gender societies, rituals) [see also Boateng 1990].

Pre-colonial education did not compartmentalize education into social, cultural, spiritual, political, biological dimensions, nor social and natural science splitting, i.e., the disciplines and the disciplining of knowledge associated with formal schooling. The centrality and interconnections of culture, tradition, language and spiritualities ensured that learning was a life-long activity (Busia 1969; Thairu 1975; Abbam 1994; Dzobo 1973; Okrah 2003). Pre-colonial African education was pursued with a philosophy of 'worldsense', i.e., systems of thought and ontologies speaking to the realities and workings of the cosmos, and the nexus of the nature, society and culture interface. Music, dancing and orality were important modes of communication, including Indigenous stories, songs, fables, tales, myths and mythologies as pedagogies and instruction (e.g., the use of Ananse stories and parables). The idea of mythic science was embedded in Indigenous education as linked to surrounding environments and the forces of Nature (Agyarkwa 1974; Busia 1969; Gyekeye 1987; Wiredu 1995). The whole idea of the uncertainty of knowledge and knowing was cultivated and with it 'not knowing' and/or 'the fear of not knowing' was acceptable and inconsequential. As pre-colonial education became a socialization of knowledge upholding the everyday teachings of culture, spirituality, language, Indigenous songs and traditions, folktales, proverbs and mores, the community was held together. Education focused on lived experiences and was primarily intended for everyday human survival and the search for solutions to practical problems (Okpewho 1990; Uchendu 1993).

Education was about the celebration of African mythoforms and cultural stories of traditions. The story telling tradition of African culture was a means of an Indigenous educational pedagogy and instructional strategy. It was about moral and character development of the learner that moved beyond rights, individuality, self discipline to developing a sense of purpose, meaning in life, social collective, social responsibility and community enhancement. Science and technology was pursued as pragmatic and practical (e.g., vocational and technical training, arts/crafts) (Awoonor 1994; Nyerere 1967; Adaye 1934; Anobil 1955; Akrofi 1958).

COLONIAL AND POST-COLONIAL EDUCATION

Colonial [formal] education took place in established institutional settings called "school"; churches and places which later became formalized as schools, colleges, vocational and technical institutes, and universities. The colonial State and other Christian and private bodies became responsible for the provision of the 'schooling infrastructure'. Schooling in such formal settings removed the learner from her or his community physically, mentally, emotionally and spiritually. The separation of schooling and community was also enforced through the view of teachers as professionals and teaching as a professional activity. Colonial education was primarily intended to provide regimented, regulated and certified basic skills set to the individual learner as separate from the community. Schools and educational institutional settings were sites and sources providing merit badges including certificates, diplomas and accreditations.

With time there came the emergence of the disciplines and further compartmentalization of knowledge. The initial goal of colonial education was the training of a workforce needed top service colonial administration (e.g., office clerks, secretarial staff, and an industrial labor force) tied to the exploitation of Africa's resources and the subjugation of her peoples, either directly or through divide and rule tactics. Colonial education created a seg-mented work force and vocational and technical training was priv-ileged through the teaching of an abstract science and technology. Schooling was about acculturation and assimilation through the devaluation, negation and delegitimization of local culture, tradi-tions, religion and language.

The current direction of post-colonial education in Africa must be fully understood as a huge part of the problem of edu-cation in Africa. There are some challenges of colonial and post-colonial education that we can briefly point to. For example, there is the assumed link of African education with the question of African Development. As noted elsewhere (Dei 2010a) this link is often assumed but not theorized. Questions about the type of education, the model of development to be pursued, and the place of local cultural resource knowledge are legitimate and need to be asked. We also need to have debates about how nation states are prioritizing education in the face of competing claims on national educational budgets. Similarly there are ensuing tensions between internationally supported calls for Free and Compulsory Universal Primary Education and the push for more resources to tertiary education. Maikish& Gershberg 2009; Caffentzis & Federici's (1992) work shows the national initiative in Ghana in 2004 regarding the implementation of the Free Compulsory Universal Basic Education [FCUBE] recognized under the title of the Capitation Grant Scheme. While the evidence suggest increased enrolment , especially in female enrolment and school dropouts returning to school, the assessment also found that many classrooms were overcrowded and rundown, compromising an effective implementation of the Capitation Grant policy and was disheartening to some parents preventing them from enrolling their children in school.

A neo-liberal educational agenda in which African education is promoted primarily to serve the needs of the labor market and the global economy, trends towards the 'marketization of school education' (Kenway & Epstein 1996) and "standardization recipes" (Lewin 2008) are all too common in many African countries today (see also, Crewe & Harrison 1998). Education is approached as an investment sector, "a sector dealing with human capital" (Brock-Utne 2000, p. 12) Therefore there is push for primary education, as it has been calculated to have the highest rates of return. Furthermore, the World Bank does not function as a donor but as a bank, therefore investments must yield returns, yet this method of "lending" has set the stage for the donor relations reflecting a human capital approach to education reform (Brock-Utne 2000). Furthermore, the Bank's approach continues to model a "top-down expert-led depoliticized model of change clearly at odds with the realities of implementing educational reform" (Mundy 1998, p.475. The impact of globalization on education through SAPs, MDGs and reform are old ideas wrapped up in new packaging. Colonial and neo-modernization policies are grounded in "free market ideology and economics and international policitics" (Geo-Jaja & Zajda 2005, p.110).

Recent development only gives voice to long-standing concerns about curricular, pedagogic and instructional relevance of colonial and post-colonial African education. There are also the questions of curriculum development, not only considering what local cultural and Indigenous knowledges are taken up, but also who is taken them up and in what ways in the production of knowledge about Africa. The neo-liberal educational policies have ushered their own problems. For example, in the areas of educational resourcing to do with curriculum, texts and physical staffing the issues of staff retention, brain flight, teacher professionalism or professional and in-service training for educators, payment of salaries/renumeration, local teachers/faculty attraction to private employment in private sectors, NGOs, government sectors etc., where salaries are competitive are all too real. There is the problem of retiring renowned scholars even before younger replacements have been found and official corruption and embezzlement of public education funds, administrative bottlenecks; duplication of educational services, lack of jobs for trained school leavers. Physical infrastructural development is lacking in many cases and the expressed commitment to science education and to resource vocational training is lip service at best. While equity has been under consideration, its definition has been limited to the question of access [usually gender, class and resource allocation to sectors (see also Gifford-Lindsay 2008; Inoue & Oketch 2008). The under-researched and theorized aspect of equity in African education is social difference in pluralistic contexts in relation to schooling experiences and the impact of educational outcomes (see Yusuf Sayed's work for exception; see also Dei et al. 2006). Again as noted elsewhere (Dei 2010a), historically, education has been approached in terms of its fundamental contribution to national development. But, in emphasizing the goal of national integration, post-independence, 'post-colonial' education in Africa has denied heterogeneity in local populations, as if difference itself was a problem. With this orientation, education has undoubtedly helped create and maintain the glaring disparities and inequities, organized along lines of ethnicity, culture, language, religion, gender and class, which persist and grow. So we must contemplate on how research on African education would acknowledge difference and diversity while, at the same time, highlighting commonalities, even among peoples with conflicting interests is critical. There is a need to connect the questions and issues of access, equity, quality and relevance. As Ward et al. (2003) long noted, in most sub-Saharan African (SSA) countries, the key challenges in the education sector remain access, equity, quality and relevance. The effects of neo-liberal policies driven by the World Bank and emphasis on internationalization of curriculum and marketization of higher education rendering, questions of ethnicity, language, religion, disability and other forms of social difference rendered students invisible in education circles.

There is a need for us to rethink who is included and who is excluded in schooling processes; access, curriculum design and pedagogy. We must also ask: How do African schools, colleges and universities deal with difference and diversity among the student populations? How does schooling connect issues of identity and knowledge production? What particular pedagogic and instructional and curricular practices address difference? And how educators integrate African-centred teachings and materials in classroom practices? We also need to fully understand gender and schooling in African contexts.

There are a couple of problems regarding the way gender education is pursued. There is the lip service to gender, schooling and education as an equity issue. We also have Eurocentric constructions of gender and gendered relations provide the basis of a critique of gender and schooling in Africa. Understandings of gender are usually informed by externally-imposed Eurocentric constructions. Well-worn narratives are paraded as fact or observation without any regard to whose truth they compromise or whose lens is used for observation. An examination of "gender" in African Indigenous ways of knowing would permit us to simultaneously examine boys and girls in relational terms. Similarly, there are complexities and contradictions in the function of schools as gender socializing agents. African schools have become 'masculinizing agencies' through official policies and practices (curriculum, pedagogy and instruction). And yet, there is a failure to examine how these reinforce particular notions of what it means to be a male/female. Colonial/post-colonial forces, including globalization have, and continue to, impact[ed] everyday social constructions and practices of masculinity in the African schooling setting. Much research on gender and schooling in Africa has excluded boys' experiences and how they are implicated in unequal and unjust gender relations. Often within African schooling and education questions and concerns about [African/Black] masculinity are reduced to questions of identity, identifications, and sociocultural differences, thereby eroding in a sense the question of community (see Masinere 2011).

On the global scale initiatives around Education For All [EFA] may have lofty goals and objectives such as expanding early childhood education, pursuit of Free universal access to basic education, identifying educational equity as a priority, and working for a 50% improvement in literacy and the elimination of gender disparities in education. The links of education to a poverty reduction strategy framework is simply rhetorical; (see also United Nations Millennium Project 2004; Watkins 2009; Mundy 2007).

Notwithstanding the above initiatives there is a continuing deterioration in access to education in the C21st. The rise of street children, child labourers, child soldiers, children from poor house-holds, children living in rural, remote and marginalized areas, and children orphaned by or affected/infected with HIV and AIDS. This calls for a search for genuine educational options for African education.

GOING FORWARD: TOWARDS A COUNTER RE-VISIONING OF AFRICAN SCHOOLING AND HIGHER EDUCATION

A major problem with 'post-colonial' African schooling and higher education is that, notwithstanding genuine intentions, most educational initiatives are steeped in vestiges of colonial education. There is an on-going disturbing failure to ask the most relevant and critical questions such as: Who and what is shaping educational policy directions in Africa? What is the assumed and preserved role of the donors and international agencies in this process? How do we account for and implicate the role of the World Bank and its conditions promoting the neo-liberal development agenda (see Brock-Utne, 2003)? How are recent policy frameworks to African education outside of the historic critique of Western colonial education as "cultural imperialism? How has post-colonial education succeeded in exposing the cultural dimensions of neo-colonialism? How have African philosophies and Indigenous knowledge forms been taken up as counter/ alternatives to Western approaches to schooling, learning and education? Where are the local voices in the educational policy prescriptions? How is inclusion understood in contemporary African educational contexts? Where is social difference in the accounting for schooling and educational change? How are questions of gender, race, ethnicity, class accounted for in the policy analysis on African education? How do these "standardized recipes" of educational reforms taken into account differences at local, regional and national levels?

In re-visioning schooling and higher education in Africa I will concentrate on the areas of contextualized teaching and learning, the use of local environment in curriculum and pedagogical practice, the question of applied Indigenous technologies and sciences in the context of the significance of local/Indigenous African knowledges and languages. We need a bottom-up approach to schooling that challenges the top-down delivery of education to "consumers and actors'. We need to serve education as giving back African agency, historicity and subjectivity.

A rethinking of schooling and higher education has to take us back to our roots to examine our histories and cultural traditions of knowledge production, dissemination and use. We must focus on the capacity of the continent to know itself (Mkandawire 2010). We need to look at education from this source in terms of its connections with family life, community and social relevance. This means drawing from the lessons of how knowledge is impacted through early socialization practices, child rearing practices, teaching and learning responsibilities of community membership, and the application of knowledge to solve everyday practical problems within one's backyard and beyond. What comes to mind is contextualized teaching and learning as part of responsible and relevant education. Much of what is lost can be encapsulated in the neglect of these fundamental bases of education. A re-visioned African schooling and education must address the cultural, social, spiritual and political alienation of the contemporary learner.

African schooling and higher education must prepare learners to be able to use their knowledge to satisfy locally-defined needs and aspirations through cultural affirmation, self-dependence and autonomy over one's resources. A socio-ecologically sound education that is pursued through social justice, equity and respect for local peoples' freedoms and rights of peoples. Such education prepares Africans to view development as more than economic and technological; it challenges Eurocentric understandings of what it means to be 'developed' or 'developing'. In this way, education is fundamentally about social, cultural and spiritual improvements in peoples' lives and developing an appreciation of the workings of the culture, society and nature nexus. In other words, education that has local social relevance and is conceived, planned and executed for African people's benefit and not in the service of neo-colonial agenda or simply a global capital market. Education must assist African peoples in a cultural rebirth, cultural empowerment, reclamation of past, history and lessons for present and future...and not education that promotes alienation and entanglement. Such education acknowledges a role for local science and technology and a people's knowledge base. It is education that will challenge current neo-classical and neo-liberal assumptions of capital accumulation processes as engine for development. It will focus on local knowledge capabilities and a people's humanness, building on what people know and what they have come to know through time. It will work with what is already there in terms of local endowments, capabilities and existing resources in the surrounding environments.

Re-visioning African schooling and education will call for African peoples and governments to make significant investments in local/traditional and Indigenous knowledges, that is research development, intellectual capacity building, protection and use of local knowledges. African peoples cannot trade our culture for someone else's; we need an education that helps Africans to challenge racist and Eurocentric discourses about the backwardness of our culture/traditions and the powerful allegory and ridiculous imagery of the tradition/modernity split (Lauer 2007). As Prah (2011) notes, African Indigenous knowledges constitute our cultural inheritance, a fund of knowledge as well as a process of knowledge construction, and as such must be investigated.

Prah (2011) in a revealing article notes that "few features of African education at the university level are as revealing as the notion of African Studies in Africa!" He notes, for example, studies concerning Africa are all shifted into one Department or Institute in the university. Hence he questions: If studies concerning Africa are shifted to into one Department or Institute in the university then which societies are all the other studies pursued in the university about? Are they not about the societies in which the universities are located? What are all the other studies in the university focused on? Do they focus outside Africa? Are all the students being trained to live elsewhere? Why is this so? (Prah 2011, p. 8).

The continued production of colonizing and imperial knowledges only serves the interests of dominant intellectual traditions. We must relate our education to the local environments. This is the beauty of contextualized teaching. The practice of de-contextualized education only serves to alienate African learners from the prevailing processes of educational delivery. A critical evaluation of the form, content and delivery of such school/academic knowledges to ensure that school pedagogies, texts, curricula and instructional materials employed in schools utilize local and Indigenous knowledge and languages (see some contemporary writings on Indigenous languages and African education in Brock-Utne & Skattum 2009).

Writing on the African context, Lebakeng (2010) poignantly asks: how is knowledge production in African institutions of higher learning producing relevant Indigenous African knowledges, and "what are the epistemological paradigms undergirding university curricula?" (p. 27). What we teach and offer to our students as curriculum and methods of learning African schooling, and higher education as a whole, cannot continue to operate as mere extensions of the colonial order/power' even in a supposedly decolonized Africa. Surface remedies are not the answer for curing a 'sick' system. There is a particular responsibility for our institutions/centres of excellence to break this colonial dependency and help provide the necessary conditions for young learners to cultivate, affirm and propagate our Indigenous science knowledge for humanity in general. A failure to embark on such intellectual journeys holds serious ramifications and implications for the continent. True development will only emerge in a context where people are able to critically evaluate the knowledge systems embedded in their histories, cultures and identities to offer counter and alternative readings of our worlds and how we comprehend human challenges and design futures (see also Asabere-Ameyaw, Dei & Raheem 2012),

Higher education in African must lead the charge in the

re-thinking of education and development in African contexts away from the overemphasis on a "capital/resource-based" to a "local culture and science knowledge-base" approach that nurtures Indigenous creativity and resourcefulness. Within all African institutions of higher learning we must create "Indigenous Knowledge and Language Research Centres" that will pay serious attention to African human capacity building for endogenous development. Such centres can generate knowledge to help shape our thinking of African development from the unquestioned faith in the power and efficacy of intensive foreign capital investment/ infusion to the examination of Indigenous knowledge systems dealing with local science, technology and culture local economies. African education can help fashion our own development proceeding with innovations in Indigenous science, technology and culture through the establishment of such centres devoted to the cause of African development. These will be 'Centres for Excellence' whose work will emphasize 'appropriate-science/technology innovations', 'African human cultural development' and 'Indigenous resource applications' for development. The model of development being advocated will require a strong interaction among institutions of higher learning for human capacity building through sustained research and applied knowledge of Indigenous science, technology and culture (see also Etzkowits & Dzisah 2007). State funding will be purposely directed to research innovations and excellence in Indigenous systems of thought as catalyst for scientific, industrial and technological accomplishments in the coming years (see also Etzkowits & Dzisah 2008; Dei 2011b). In such context a revitalization and use of African Indigenous knowledges as mediums of instruction in schools is going to be critical, content cannot be divorced from pedagogy. Schooling and education in Africa cannot move forward to offer genuine educational and development options for local peoples without such education being steeped in our Indigenous African languages and methodologies (see Prah 2011).

I agree with African scholar, Thandika Mkandawire that any 'crisis' of development in Africa is related to the "crisis" of the African university as a colonial vestige (Mkandawire 2010). In effect, I see an important role of the African University today as we move forward. African universities should produce their national 'experts' [not imported nor foreign-trained] on development well-versed in Indigenous knowledge systems for local science, culture and industry development and for government policy making in these areas. The University will engage in a conscious attempt to circulate such Indigenous-informed 'experts' in a working partnerships of university-local industry-government [see also Etzkowits & Dzisah (2010) in a different context]. Local human capacity building and institutional development will involve universities as intensive research centres, as incubators for the development and promotion of Indigenous knowledge, African science and technology. The work of such Indigenous scholars will challenge existing dominant epistemological paradigms and re-conceptualize 'African development' from anti-colonial and locally-centred perspectives and will embrace a model of development built on the interface of Indigenous science, technology and culture. This model of development must fully engage cultural and local knowledge as critical dimensions of any linkage between academic/university, industry and government.

Transformation of such education is not only in the social

sciences, arts and humanities. The natural and applied sciences are implicated. All these subject areas must be decolonized through research, teaching, curriculum content and pedagogical practices. The Indigenous worldview prioritizes the connections between knowledges and disciplines, re-articulating the demarcations and divisions of Eurocentric knowledge. As we have argued (Asabere-Ameyaw, Dei & Raheem 2012) we need all African teachers to be properly trained in Indigenous knowledges and sciences. We also need to create spaces in our schools, colleges and universities for parents, Elders, families and cultural custodians to come in as teachers to work on a daily basis to complement the work of professionally trained educators. Students must be firmly grounded in their local communities and a practical component of every classroom teaching must see students located in their communities to implement their classroom ideas and also engage community knowledge. Knowledge production and dissemination cannot be a one-way avenue from the school to the community; it must be reciprocal, a revaluing of community produced knowledge. We have to go back to the days when the separation of school and community was non-existent and was practiced in every sense of the link.

Similarly, the curriculum for the arts, vocational and technical subjects must be transformed to incorporate knowledge and teaching methods of local artisans, craftsmen and women, cultural custodians of fables, folktales, songs, proverbs and story forms, etc. as part of science education. The writing of curriculum must engage the expert knowledge of local artisans and craftsmen and key partners rather than being shaped at the prerogative of intellectuals sitting in offices. In the African contexts, teaching Indigenous science will also have to recognize the social-political and spiritual contexts of the ways of knowledge production, inter-rogation, validation and dissemination. School and community relations have to be restructured in such a way that places school-ing within communities, and also allow communities to have easy access and voice in schools in all the aspects of teaching, learn-ing and administration of education. There are differential roles and responsibilities that can be performed all in the service of joint partnership in the provision of education (see also Asabere-Ameyaw, Dei & Raheem 2012).

The pursuit of social sciences, arts, humanities and science [natural/physical/biological] education in the classroom must be viewed as everyday practice and activity for the African learner. The method and methodology of social sciences, arts, humani-ties and natural/physical/biological sciences' education must be broad enough to engage communal and communities' ances-tral, cultural, historic and experiential knowings. Africans have Indigenous conceptions of mathematics, science of the body and the physical universe, arts, humanities and technology educa-tion, including understandings of the laws of nature, geography, physics, biology, and nature. We have systems of mathematical thought, social processes of understanding the human body and its place in nature, the spiritual and metaphysical realms of every-day existence. Infusing such knowledges in [natural and social] science education offers a more comprehensive knowledge base and grounding for the contemporary African learner.

The counter-visioning of African schooling and education must focus on developing local human capacity and the endowed natural resources informed by the needs and challenges of today's knowledge-based society. Africa's development will take off with

Indigenous science and technology initiatives and innovations. It will require that we have an endogenous educational system that cultivates local technological-industrial sector producing local goods and services to serve local needs. Investments in relevant youth education, the development of local skills and infrastructure will empower local communities to think through solutions to their own problems. We need to create a society of creative and critical thinkers, innovators and social entrepreneurs engaged in a genuine African-centred development practice. School curriculum must equip young learners with the knowledge, skills and values necessary for functioning in interdependent communities.

Increasingly, initiatives in local scientific, technical and vocational education are seen as a vital aspect of the educational process. It is an important source and engine for an endogenous scientific and technological development. Such education that is directed towards "the acquisition of practical skills, attitudes, understanding and knowledge relating to occupations in various sectors of local economic, social, [technological and political] life" (Richards 2011, p. 103) is highly welcome. Too often references are made to the development achievements of the countries of the Pacific Rim–Japan, Singapore, Taiwan etc.–which have emerged as dominant international competitors in the production of high-tech goods. It is noted that these countries have successfully embarked upon the educational changes necessary and relevant to national development moving from "standardized mass production to flexible customized production in keeping with dynamic global market forces" (Richards 2011, p. 33). What are the important lessons to be learned?

While I would urge for taking endogenous education in

science, technical and vocational fields, I also want to sound a caution on how this is pursued. In looking at current trends in vocational and technical education, questions of which bodies are being 'streamed' into vocational training and why are important. Is Africa again being shaped to provide cheap, exploitable labor for the global economy? African countries would need a cultural and paradigmatic shift and avoid the privileging of Cartesian reasoning and 'intellect' over body, such that vocational training is seen as less desirable and more suited for lesser intellects, often meaning poor and working class classed bodies. We know that vocational training often forces this separation of intellect from body, skill from reason–which, if we approach the critique with an Indigenous framework in mind is a false demarcation, knowledge is more integrated and organic than this. Because of this demarcation vocational schools often receive less funding, struggle to attract top teachers, etc. and the subsequent social stigmatization of the students, affects their self-worth. A re-visioned education will have to change this mindset of vocational training while simultaneously challenging the Western privileging of 'academic' pursuits which is the other side of the false separation of knowledge. Intellect and activity must be envisioned as complementary and not as part of an either/or model that ranks knowledge for the purpose of exploiting it.

In my most recent work on Indigenous African philosophies (Dei 2010b, 2012) I have began to appreciate local proverbs, folktales and songs as having powerful instructional, pedagogic and communicative relevance for teaching young learners (see some of the extensive literature on African proverbs in such works as Yankah 1989, 1995; Opoku 1975, 1997). These constitute parts of Indigenous ways of knowing. They are knowledges that present a philosophy of life, a wise sayings used in teaching about the meaning of collective social existence and responsibility, self discipline, identity and social sense of worth and purpose in life, respect for Eldership and authority, character and moral development of the learner. Educating about Indigenous proverbs and the meanings of Indigenous songs and folktales, myths and mythologies present forms of knowledge as about tradition and power. African proverbs and traditional stories are told to the young to allow them to grow mentally, spiritually, morally into adulthood. They are a form of customary teachings and wise sayings that guide social conduct for all including adults and Elders as cultural custodians. Elders and cultural custodians are generally seen as having a particular responsibility to teach and lead by example. The individual grows up responsibly through advice contained in proverbs and riddles. As a form of communication proverbs and riddles provided forums of socialization around the genders. They helped keep communities and peoples together. Individuals learn from examples. Social gatherings provided avenues for teaching the young. Embedded in African proverbs and riddles are the bonds of African hospitality, generosity and communionship. In a world so much characterized by rugged individualism, competitiveness and hierarchies of thought and social practice, teaching young learners some of the ideals of African proverbs will contribute to the task of African education preparing the youth to be future leaders.

Re-visioning transformative education for Africa is also about reclaiming the language of Africanness. Here, I add my voice to the ongoing call for Africans to re-claim their indigenous languages to the centre of knowledge production (see Wa Thiong'O 1986) Ngugi wa Thiong'o, saw the relevance of language to the psychological, intellectual, and emotional equilibrium among members of a community. Language performs a relevant process in the identity formation and development of the psychological, spiritual, mental and cognitive abilities. Kirkness (1997), a strong advocate for Aboriginal language in Canada asks; what do we lose when we lose a language? The short answer is we lose everything. Individuals' culture lies in their language. When a community loses their language, they also lose their ways of greeting, praising and cursing. They lose their laws, literature (legends), songs, proverbs, curative powers, wisdom, prayers and basically their whole sense of being and identity (see Fisherman 1972). Language is deeper than the lexicon. Language is epistemic because it is a vehicle through which one can make sense of his or her reality. Walker (1984, p.185) argues that in looking at international relations we must start with the assumptions that "social and political change is both reflected and constituted by language." Similarly, Bernard-Donals and Glejzer (1998, p. 4) note that language has the "capacity to exert power in observable (and reproducible) ways that as a form of praxis it can produce real social change." The challenge is that when one's language is distorted, one's reality can become equally distorted. This is especially pertinent to higher education in Africa. While Indigenous languages have gained some traction in primary schooling, there is still the colonial assumption that these languages are not 'developed' enough to carry the high level concepts of higher education (Bgoya 2001).

I argue that the challenge of "development" within an African context is the challenge of language. In the situation where the language of development is steeped in Euro-Modernized sense of what a society lacks or is expected to become, human centered development, which is what Africans need most, will be lost. Surely, one cannot look at the current face of development in Africa and not think that all is not well. In fact, one does not require any intellectual imagination to realize that the euphoria of international development has worn thin in the minds of many Africans, partly, because the so-called development paradigm in Africa has come at high human, ecological, political, and ethical costs to Africans (See Adjei & Dei, 2008). As Kwapong (1992) warned more than a decade ago that:

Until and unless we Africans are able to confront realistically in Africa the major issue of language, the essential gateway to any cultural self-expression and authenticity, we will continue to suffer from a severe debilitating human handicap-the handicap of cultural alienation, which bedevils any human development. Africa's modernization must be firmly rooted in Africa's cultural authenticity, and true self-expression. This is primarily an educational challenge, and the issue of language is an essential dimension of this challenge (p.40).

Therefore, the way forward for African development is reclaiming the language of development. Fanon (1963) called on African educators to re-imagine a new development paradigm that completely shifts away from Euro-Modernity:

So comrades, let us not pay tribute to Europe by creating states, institutions, and societies that draw their inspiration from it. Humanity expects other things from us than this grotesque and generally obscene emulation. ... Moreover, if we want to respond to the expectations of the Europeans we must not send them back a reflection, however ideal, of their society and their thought that periodically sickens even them. For Europe, for ourselves and for humanity, comrades, we must make a new start, develop a new way of thinking, and endeavor to create a new man and woman. (Fanon 1963, p.315)

For Frantz Fanon, the re-imagining of a new development paradigm is not a question of choice. It is urgent and necessary because the rest of humankinds are relying on Africa to lead a new path outside that which has been created by Europe. But this new path must begin in a new language; the language of humanity; the language of justice and social equity. This new language must be grounded in Indigenous African axiology and ontology. The new language is the language of humanity as Frantz Fanon postulated (Fanon 1963). Mahatma Gandhi once noted that one can attest to a country's civilization base in the way that country treats its marginalized and disadvantaged groups. The new language for African development must be a language that brings a human face to development. It will not be a language that is built on individualism but a language of the collective. It acknowledges that all cannot be well when one is not well. One person's pain is the pain of everybody. In the new language that has to be imagined in African development, the African sense of Obuntu (I am because We are; and because We are; therefore, I am) is a key place to start.

There are pedagogical implications in centering indigenous knowledges in the classroom. Both teachers and learners have responsibilities in ensuring that the historic inferiorization of indigenous experiences, rich histories and cultures are challenged and deconstructed in the classroom. As Prah (1997 p.21) opines that the process of decolonization requires that indigenous peoples confront the "insulting idea that others know and understand them better than they understand themselves." The classroom space should be a site where both learners and teachers engage in critical discussion. Things should not be taken on face value because they are emerging from a text or a teacher; rather, they should be analyzed within the context of local realities. It is only when these knowledges make sense within local contexts and realities that learners should be prepared to work with it. The pedagogic, instructional and communicative approach to synthesizing different knowledge in the classroom must first allow Indigenous peoples to produce and control knowledge about themselves, their communities and their societies. Teachers must utilize and where necessary build on local knowledge/resources to address local needs. Scientific research needs to commit more resources and times to devise ways in which local material could be used to address local needs.

Finally, schools in Africa need to avoid the past domination of colonial and neo-colonial education. They have to pose this question; what is(are) the purpose(s) of education? The answers may be multiple but relevant in pushing schooling and education forward in Africa. According to Kwadwo Okrah (2003), African educators must inquire into the meanings inherent in indigenous educational practices in order to avoid any imposition of colonial interest. Once these meanings are determined, schools should find ways they can use such knowledge to avoid or challenge any hegemonic influence. This means that African educators need to seek more than "knowledge" of subject matter and practical teaching experience before they enter the classroom (Lucas 1969). Teachers need knowledge about what they are teaching, its effects on learners and how they relate to life in general. Teachers should have insightful knowledge about their purpose as teachers, why they are teaching, what they are teaching and how these purposes relate to the institutional setting of the school and the values of the local community and society at large. It is at this stage that schooling and education become meaningful to the learner, local community and society at large.

REFERENCES

Abbam, C. M. (1994) Developing Education. *West Africa, October*

Adaye, J. J. (1947) *Twi Mmebusem Ahannum Mmoano*, Kumasi, Presbyterian Book Depot

Adjei P. B. and Dei, G. (2008) 'Sankofa: In search for alternative development paradigm for Africa', in Abdi, A & Richardson, G (eds) *Decolonizing Democratic Education: Trans-disciplinary Dialogues,* Rotterdam/ Taipei, Sense publishers

Agyarkwa, K. A. (1974) 'Akan Epistemology and Western thought: A philosophical approach to the problem of educational modernization in Ghana', Ph.D Dissertation.Unpublished manuscript, New York, Columbia Univeristy

Akrofi, C. A. (1958) *Twi Mmebusem (Twi Proverbs)*, Kumasi, Presbyterian Book Depot

Annobil, J. A. (1955) *Mbebusem Nyerekyeremu*, Cape Coast, Methodist Book Depot

Asabere-Ameyaw, A., Dei, G. J. S., and Raheem, K. (eds) (2012) *Contemporary Issues in African Sciences and School Science Education*, Rotterdam/ Taipei, Sense Publishers. (In print).

Asante, M. (1991) 'The Afrocentric Idea in Education', *Journal of Negro Education*, 60 (2): 170-180

Asante. M. K. (2003) *Afrocentricity: The Theory of Social Change,* Chicago, African American Images

Awoonor, K. (1994) 'Enhancing the African's dignity:Keynote address',paper presented at the Panafest, Cape Coast, Ghana, February 6-12.

Bernard-Donals M. and Glejzer, R. R. (eds) (1998) *Rhetoric in an Antifoundational World: Language, culture and pedagogy*, New haven and London, Yale University Press

Birdsall, N., Ibrahim, A. J. and Gupta, G.R. (2004) Task Force 3 Interim Report on Primary Education, New York, UNDP, http://www.unmillenniumproject.org/documents/tf3edinterim.pdf, accessed September 10, 2004

Bgoya, W. (2001) 'The effect of globalisation in Africa and the choice of language in publishing', *International Review of Education*, 47(3-4): 283-292

Boateng, F. (1990) 'African Traditional Education: A Tool for Intergenerational

Communication' in. Asante, M.K., and Asante, K.W. (eds) *African Culture: The Rhythms of Unity*, Trenton, African World Press

Brock-Utne, B. (2003) 'Formulating Higher Education Policies in Africa- the Pressure from External Forces and the Neoliberal Agenda' http://www. netreed.uio.no/articles/high.ed_BBU.pdf, accessed October 2, 2010.

Brock-Utne, B. (2000) *Whose Education for All: The Recolonization of the African Mind*, New York, Falmer Press

Brock-Utne, B. and Skattum, I (eds) (2009) *Language and Education in Africa: a comparative and transdisciplinary analysis*, Oxford, Cambridge University Press

Busia, K. A. (1969) *Purposeful Education for Africa*, The Hague, MoutonCaffentizis, G and Federici, S. (1992) 'The World Bank and Education in Africa', *Race and Class*, 34(1):51-60

Crewe, E and Harrison, E. (1998) *Whose Development*, Zed Books, New York.

Dei, G. J. S. (2010a), *Teaching Africa: Towards a Transgressive Pedagogy*, New York, Springer Publishing

Dei, G. J. S. (2010b) 'Reclaiming Indigenous Knowledge Through Character Education: Implications for Addressing and Preventing Youth Violence', A Final Report submitted the Literacy and Numeracy Secretariat (LNS), Ministry of Education, Ontario. [with the assistance of Jagjeet Gill, Camille Logan Dr. Meredith Lordan, Marlon Simmons and Lindsay Kerr]

Dei, G. J. S. (ed) (2011a) *Indigenous Philosophies and Critical Education*, New York, Peter Lang

Dei, G. J. S. (2011b) 'Reframing 'Development': Situating Indigenity and Indigenous Knowledges', Keynote Address at the 2nd Africa Regional Conference on 'Endogenous Development'. University for Development Studies (UDS), Tamale, Ghana, August 18-19

Dei, G. J. S. (2012) 'Culture, Identity and Science in African Education: The Relevance of Local Cultural Resource Knowledge', in Akwasi Asabere-Ameyaw, A., Dei, G. J. S & Raheem, K. (eds) *Contemporary Issues in African Science Education*, Sense Publishers. [In print]

Dei, G. J. S., Asgharzadeh, A., Eblaghie-Bahador,S . and Shahjahan. R. (2006) *Schooling and Difference in Africa: Democratic Challenges in a Contemporary Context*, Toronto, University of Toronto Press.

Dzobo, N. K. (1973) *African proverbs: A guide to conduct*, Cape Coast, Ghana University Press

Etzkowitz, H. and Dzisah, J. (2007) 'The Triple Helix of Innovation: Towards a University-led Development Strategy for Africa', *Africa Technology Development Forum (AFDT) Journal,* 4(2): 3-10.

Etzkowitz, H.and Dzisah, J. (2008) 'Rethinking Development: Circulation in the Triple Helix', *Technology Analysis and Strategic Management,* 20(6): 653-666

Etzkowits, H. and Dzisah, J. (2010) 'Who Influences Whom? The transformation of University-Industry-Government Relations', *Critical Sociology,* 36(4): 491-501.

Fafunwa, A. B. (1974), *History of Education in Nigeria,* London,Allen and Unwin

Fafunwa, A. B. (1982), 'African Education in Perspective', inFafunwa, A.B. and Aisiku, J. (eds) Education in Africa: A Comparative Study. London: George Allen & Unwin

Fafunwa, A. B. and Aisiku, J. (eds) (1982) *Education in Africa: A Comparative Study,* London/Boston, George Allen & Unwin

Fanon, F. (1963) *The Wretched of the Earth,* New York, Grove Press

Fishman, J. A. (1972) 'Domain and the relationship between micro and macro sociolinguistics', in Gumperez, J.J. and Hymes, D.H. (ed) *Direction in Sociolinguistics,* New York, Holt, Rinehart and Winston.

Geo-Jaja, M. and Zajda, J. (2005)'Rethinking Globalization and the Future of Education', in Zajda, J.(ed) *International Handbook on Globalisation, Education and Policy Research,* Netherlands, Springer

Gifford-Lindsay, K. (2008) 'Poverty Reduction Strategies and Governance, with Equity,

For Education: Four Case studies: Cambodia, Ethiopia, Ghana and Nepal', Paper commissioned for the EFA Global Monitoring Report 2009, Overcoming Inequality: why governance matters?

Gyekye, K. (1987) *An essay on African philosophical thought: The Akan conceptual scheme,* Cambridge, Cambridge University Press

Inoue, K. and Oketch, M. (2008) 'Implementing free primary education policy in Malawi and Ghana: Equity and Efficiency Analysis', *Peabody Journal of Education,* 83 (1): 41-70

Karenga, M. (2011) 'Malcolm X, History and Cultural Memory: Maatian Reflections on Rightful Remembrance', Keynote Address, 23rd Annual Cheikh Anta Diop International Conference, Holiday Inn, Historic District, Philadelphia,. October 7-8.

Kenway, J. and Epstein,D (1996). 'Introduction: The Marketisation of School Education: Feminist Studies and Perspectives', *Discourse: Studies in the Cultural Politics of Education,* 17 (3): 301-314.

Kirkness, V. J. (1997). 'Sharing through language : Pipe dream or Reality?', November, *The First Perspective.*

Kryza, F. T. (2006) *The Race for Timbuktu: In Search of Africa's City of Gold,* New York, HaperCollins Publishers

Kwapong, A. (1992) 'Capacity Building for People-Centered Development, With Special Reference to Africa', paper presented at the British Columbia Council for Internal Cooperation, Vancouver B.C., February 1.

Lauer, H. (2007) 'Depreciating African Political Culture', *Journal of Black Studies,* 38(2): 288-307.

Lewin, K. M. (2008), 'Strategies for Sustainable Financing of Secondary Education in Sub-Saharan Africa'. Human Development Series World Bank Working Paper No. 136. Washington D.C. World Bank

Lucas, C. (1969) *What is philosophy of Education?,* Toronto, Canada, Macmillan Company Limited

Maikish, A. and Gershberg, A. I. (2009) 'Targeting Education Funding to the Poor: Universal Primary Education, Education Decentralization and Local Level Outcomes in Ghana', Paper commissioned for the EFA Global Monitoring Report 2009, Overcoming Inequality: why governance matters

Masinere, A. (2011) 'Interplay of Masculinity and Schooling in Rural Zimbabwe', Unpublished PhD. Dissertation, Faculty of Education, School of Graduate and Postdoctoral Studies University of Western Ontario, London, Ontario, October 6

Mazama, A. (2001) 'The Afrocentric Paradigm: Contours and Definitions', *Journal of Black Studies,* 31(4): 387-405

Mensah, J. (2006) 'West Africa: History and Economic Development', in Leonard, T.M. (ed) *Encyclopaedia of the Developing World,* New York, Routledge

Miruka, O. (1994) *Encounter with oral literature.* Nairobi, East African Educational publishers.

Mkandawire, T. (2010) 'Running While Others walk: Knowledge and the Challenge of African Development', Inauguaral lecture, London, April 20

Mundy, K. (1998) 'Educational Multilateralism and World (Dis)Order', *Comparative Education Review*, 42(4): 448-478.

Mundy, K. (2007). 'Education for All: Paradoxes and Prospects of a Global Response', *International Perspectives on Education and Society*, 8: 1-30.

Mundy, K., Cherry, S., Haggerty, M.,Maclure, R. and Sivasubramaniam, M. (2008), 'Basic Education, Civil Society Participation and the New Aid Architecture: Lessons from Burkina Faso, Kenya, Mali and Tanzania', Report of research was sponsored by OISE-UT, the University of Ottawa, the Canadian International Development Agency and the International Development Research

Nukunya, G. K. (1992) *Tradition and Change in Ghana: An introduction to Sociology*, Accra, Universities Press

Nyerere, J. K. (1967), *Education for self-Reliance*. Dar-Es-Salaam, Information Services Division, Ministry of Information and Tourism

Okpewho, I. (1990) *The Oral Performance in Africa*. New York, Columbia University press

Okrah, K. A. (2003) *Nyansapo (The Wisdom Knot): Towards an African philosophy of Education*, New York & London, Routledge

Opoku, K. A. (1975) *Speak to the Winds: Proverbs from Africa*, New York,Northrop, Lee & Shepard Co

Opoku, K. A. (1997) *Hearing and Keeping. Akan Proverbs*, Accra, Asempa Publishers.

Prah, K. (1997). 'Accusing the victims–Review of in My Father's House by Kwame Anthony Appiah', *Codesria Bulletin*, 1, 14-22.

Prah, K.(2011) 'Betting on Our Strength: Endogenous Development, Research, Education in Higher Education Institutions in Africa: Prospects, Challenges and the Way Forward', Paper presented at the 2nd Africa Regional Conference on: 'Endogenous Development'. University for Development Studies (UDS), Tamale, Ghana, August 18-19

Richards, F. A. (2011) 'A Review of Technical and Vocational Education in Trinidad and Tobago'. Unpublished MPhil dissertation, Office of Graduate Studies and Research, The University of West Indies, St Augustine, Trinidad and Tobago

Shizha, E. (2005) 'Reclaiming Our Memories: The Education Dilemma in Postcolonial African School Curricula' in Abdi, A. and Cleghorn, A. (eds) *Issues in African Education: Sociological Perspectives*, New York, Palgrave Macmillan

Sifuna, D. N. (1990) *Development of Education in Africa: The Kenyan Experience,* Nairobi, Initiatives

Sifuna, D. N. (1992) 'Diversifying the Secondary School Curriculum: The African Experience', *International Review of Education,* 38(1): 5-20.

Thairu, K. (1975) *The African civilization (Utamanduni Wa kiafrika),* Nairobi, East African Literature Bureau.

Uchendu, P. K. (1993) *Perspectives in Nigerian education.* Enugu, Fourth Dimension Publishing

UNESCO (2009) *Overcoming Inequality: Why Governance Matters,* Oxford, Oxford University Press

van Dyk, S. (1996)'Toward an Afrocentric Perspective: The Significance of Afrocentricity' In Ziegler, D (ed) *Molefi Kete Asante and Afrocentricity,* Nasville, James Winston.

Ward, M., Bourne, J.,Penny, A. and Poston, M (2003) 'Why Do EducationPolicies in East Africa Fail? What's Changing?', *Journal of Education, 30,* 127-148

Williams, C. (1987) *The destruction of black civilization: Great issues of a race from 4500B.C. to 2000A.D.*, Chicago,Third World Press

Wiredu, K. (1995) 'Custom and Morality: A comparative Analysis of Some African and Western Conceptions of Morals', in Mosley, A.G. (ed) *African philosophy: selected readings,* Englewood Cliffs, Prentice Hall

Wiredu K and Gyekye, K. (1992) *Person and community: Ghanaian philo-sophical series* Washington, DC, The Council for Research in Values and Philosophy

World Bank. (1995) *Priorities and Strategies for Education,* Washington, DC,World Bank

Yankah, K. (1989) *The Proverb in the Content of Akan Rhetoric: a Theory Proverb Praxis,* Bern, Frankfurt au Main, Peter Lang.

Yankah, K. (1995) *Speaking for the Chief: Okyeame and the Politics of Akan Oratory.* Bloomington & Indianapolis,Indiana University Press

Sayed, Y., Subrahmanian,R., Soudien,C., Carrim, N with Balgopalan, S., Nekhwevha, F. and Samuel, M. (2007) *Educational Resources in the Commonwealth and Education Exclusion and Inclusion: Policy and Implementation in South Africa and India,* London, DFID   http://www.dfid.gov.uk/r4d/PDF/Outputs/impAccess/ ResearchingtheIssuesNo72.pdf, accessed April 1, 2009.

Ziegler, D. (ed) (1996) *Molefi Kete Asante and Afrocentricity*. Nasville, James Winston.

CHAPTER SEVEN

Western Media Stereotypes and Portrayal of Africa

Nnamdi T. Ekeanyanwu

INTRODUCTION

This chapter presents the Eurocentric, especially the Western portrayal of Africa as part of the media typecasting of the African situation which was primarily meant to twist the rich African history and mangle her voice. The chapter partly reviews Miike Yoshitaka's "An Anatomy of Eurocentrism in Communication Scholarship" and media framing as literature and theoretical basis for the call for Afrocentrism in retooling the true African story. To discuss the African narrative as portrayed in Eurocentric circles outside of the broader context of political and socio-economic relations between Africa and the rest of the west is to be part of an odious accord to cover up for the real reasons why

Africa was invaded, harassed, bounded, raped, caged and her story twisted. This is supported by Carragee and Roef (2006) who are of the view that a major problem with framing studies (which the present paper falls into) is for scholars to neglect the relationship between media frames and the deeper issues of political and social power relations that are usually at the root of media typecasting. They therefore conclude that media framing or stereotyping must be tied to the political and social questions of power relations significant to media hegemony discourse and scholarship.

Based on this understanding, this paper first dissects the deeper issues of news flow and how the west and her allies came about reporting Africa in such negative and debasing manner. The section on background to media typecasting directly leads to Miike Yoshitaka's (2010) article that sets the stage as literature basis for the current paper. Media framing is later discussed as a theoretical support for the argument propounded here that the west merely reports Africa in debasing manner fundamentally for her selfish interest. This was empirically documented in most of the studies reported here. The author also used the most recent alleged terrorist attempt by Abdulmutallab on the so-called United States interest where researchers found stereotypical coverage in the west's analysis of the situation as against the Middle East version of that reality, to further buttress its point that the west is still stereotypical in her coverage of Africa and African issues. The various forms and ways, including the actual text and language of the west portrayal of Africa is chronicled next and the author concludes by advocating for post-modern Afrocentrism in communication scholarship as a viable counter to the negative and abusive portrayal by Western media agents and institutions.

BACKGROUND TO MEDIA STEREOTYPING OF AFRICA BY THE WEST

The News Flow Controversy (NFC) is one of the outcomes of the west's many years of maligning, misreporting and misrepresenting Africa before the global community. The Controversy led to the call for a New World Information and Communication Order (NWICO) which was frustrated by the same west.

The history of the debate on the New World Information and Communication Order is traceable to about hundred years ago when the present industrialized nations of Western Europe arrived on the shores of the African continent, Latin America, Asia etc. to colonize them. Colonization of the African continent according to Lawal (1997:8 cited in Ekeanyanwu, 2008) was, however, preceded by imperialism, which as a concept of political economy is a combination of political and economic structures and relations in Africa and other continents between 1880s and 1906. In Marxist philosophy, imperialism represented a stage of capitalist development that spanned over one hundred years. According to Lenin (1975:104-5), imperialism was a means adopted by European nation-states to create colonies and privileged positions in foreign markets; to monopolize protected sources of materials and opportunities for profitable exploitation of labour. Brown (1976: 22) also says that imperialism involves an idea of one nation or people seeking to dominate another for exploitation. In the process, the dominant party accumulates capital at the expense of the exploited party.

After the collapse of imperialism in 1900, colonialism was adopted as a concept that described the resultant complex of political and economic controls imposed on dependencies.

Notwithstanding the change of concept and method, the objective of exploitation and underdevelopment was vigorously adhered to. Colonialism, therefore, is the policy and principle of having, maintaining and retaining colonies, especially of keeping them perpetually dependent on the colonising force for resource exploitation (Ekeanyanwu, 2008).

To perpetuate the colonial heinous agenda, Africa was carved into colonies and protectorates through forces of arms with definite boundaries that separated various ethnic groups. Thus, African kingdoms, empires and peoples were deprived of their freedom and independence. Henceforth, the colonial authorities decided how Africa would be ruled, how their society would be organized and their economic resources exploited. Each State was given a common central government, a common national capital city, a common national name, a common official language, currency and other common institutions that did not reflect or recognise the uniqueness of the people that make up such arrangements. These served as the basis for citizenship and the subsequent economic exploitation of the colonies.

There is no doubt that African economies were radically transformed from basic subsistence stage to the market economy especially through the gradual process of integration into the world market controlled by the west. Essentially, cash crop farming was encouraged by propaganda, offer of good prices and provision of transport facilities. However, it must be noted that the construction of infrastructure, which attracted European capital and technology, were not primarily for the development of the colonies, but for the promotion of western capitalism (Rodney, 1972:21).

Thus, by such transport facilities, European traders were able to reach the interior of each colony to procure available agricultural, mineral and forest resources. These were shipped to Europe and North America to feed their factories to manufacture various consumable items, which were brought into the colonies for sale. The cost of these imports were, however, far higher than what the Europeans paid for the raw materials from African producers. Hence, the terms of trade were unfavourable to the colonies, as they were unable to bargain or negotiate prices with the European firms. To a very large extent, the inflexible policies of unequal exchange and international division of labour and the subsequent trade in human beings known as the slave trade – which also epitomized the world order of that period, consistently promoted the industrial development of North America and Europe at the expense of Africa.

Colonization of African countries also offered people the opportunity to acquire western education. However, Ake (1981:72-4) states that the type of education that Africans received was inferior to the type in Europe. Akintoye (1976:11) captures this vividly when he states thus:

> Africans were not taught the sciences, philosophy, law and medical sciences. Instead, the approved curricula consisted of sewing, needlework, carpentry, arithmetic, health sciences, civic and religious studies. The African, rather than being skilled or semiskilled, remained unskilled.

This created further disadvantages for the African to emancipate herself and her people. This also helped to create a wide gulf between the African and the European in all facets of life. From the foregoing, the colonial powers in concert devised various means of exploiting their respective African colonies to sustain the economic growth and development of their own countries. Agba (2002:258) vividly captures the scenario thus:

> One of the major consequences of the colonization of the Third World is the yawning gap in the levels of development between the developing and developed worlds. Countries of the North (the Western countries of Europe and North America) carted away much of human and natural resources of the countries of the South. Consequently, while the industrialized world used the ill-gotten resources it siphoned from the developing world to build up wealth and boost development in its areas, the developing countries were left to rust with abject poverty and economic retrogression. In other words, while countries in the Northern hemisphere were feeding their economies with the loot from the southern hemisphere, those countries of the South were made to depend on the North for their survival.

This scenario continued until around the middle of the 20th century when decolonization started. Notwithstanding the political decolonization of Africa, the emergent independent African states still remained economically dependent on the former colonial powers. Agba (2002:258) further observes that:

> Even after the colonialist had relinquished, though, partially, their hold of the colonies by way of granting them political independence, the colonial powers further created a relationship whereby they still had an exploitative influence over their former colonies. This amounts to a dangerous but subtle form of colonization described as neo-colonialism.

Neo-colonialism as a concept connotes a complex device or method of indirect and subtle form of domination by political, economic, social, military or technical forces within and outside each African state. The economic forces included continuing economic dependence on the former colonial powers, integration into former colonial economic blocs; economic infiltration of agents of former colonial powers through capital investment, loans, aid, unequal concessions and finances directly controlled by former colonial powers. These situations have made Africa to continuously suffer the colossal disadvantages of unequal exchange and world division of labour and also, remain perpetually dependent on the North.

Furthermore it is believed that the level of economic development of a country largely determines the level of development in other spheres of politics, defense, science and technology. Consequently, the economic empowerment of the countries of the North has, therefore been seen as responsible for their advancement in all facets of life including information and communication. Armed with their various communication technologies, the industrial world controls the international flow of news and information. News is slanted in favour of the Western countries in both qualitative and quantitative terms.

As noted earlier, the NFC is one of the debates in the New World Information and Communication Order (NWICO). One may ask therefore, what is this NWICO all about? According to Traber (1985 cited in Ekeanyanwu 2008), one of the starting points in the demand for NWICO was the right of nations to participate in a multidirectional flow of information on the basis of equality. At the commencement of the NWICO debate, this

equality was completely lacking in the international communication system which was some or less a one-way flow of media
materials from the developed capitalist and information rich
nations of the North to the developing, information poor nations
of the South. To this end, according to Okunna (1993:93-4),
"the demand for NWICO is a demand for the establishment of
a free and balanced flow of communication and a rejection of any
attempt at cultural domination".

Okigbo (1996) puts this into proper perspective when he
opines that in the closing years of 29th century the concerns
of international scholarship were the management of world
resources and the equitable redistribution of the collective wealth
of nations. The most obvious fact is that some nations have enormous resources while others do not. Those that are rich in the
world resources are also rich in communication and information
development while those nations that are poor in resources are
seriously disadvantaged. It is not surprising therefore, that the
prevailing intellectual concerns for equity in global resource management and redistribution have lent much weight to the controversy about international communication imbalance.

The global News Flow Controversy is also traceable to the
monopolistic grip which the "Big Four" transnational news agencies – Reuters, United Press International, Associated Press and
Agence France Presse, all in the West, have on information sourc-
ing and distribution globally. They have various technological and
economic resources with which to gather all kinds of information and news from all nook and crannies of the globe and distribute them globally almost instantaneously at a very minimal
cost (Agba, 2000). Thus, only the advanced countries have the

means for conveniently collecting global information, even from the shores of the developing nations, repackaging it and relaying to all parts of the globe. Since the resources of the developing countries especially of African descent were stolen and plundered by the Western Europe and so cannot afford the floating of such domineering transnational news agencies of their own, they have no options but to accept what they get from these powerful transnational news agencies and their new technology of satellite transmission that serves as agents to the western world to exercise unchallenged and unholy control of global informational and environmental surveillance. This was the root cause of the negative portrayals so that the truth will remain controversial.

REVIEW OF YOSHITAKA MIIKE'S (2010) "AN ANATOMY OF EUROCENTRISM IN COMMUNICATION SCHOLARSHIP" AND IT'S IMPLICATIONS FOR AFROCENTRISM

This section focuses on Miike's problematisation of Eurocentrism as ideologies of totalisation and trivialisation and the present author's analysis of the implication of his argument for Afrocentricity.

Miike titles this section in his article "Eurocentrism as Ideologies of Totalisation and Trivialisation". He begins by analyzing Rogers (1982, 1999) arguments that the discipline of communication has suffered two long-standing divisions that frustrate theoretical advances thus:

1. First, is the divide between interpersonal and media studies and
2. Second is the divide between the empirical and the critical schools in communication scholarship.

According to Miike's arguments, the debates about these divides remains fluid, thus, scholars of different theoretical orientations all agree on the hegemony of Eurocentrism and are therefore putting a common front in their efforts to de-westernize theory and research.

From the perspective of Syed Farid Alatas (2002) as cited by Miike (2010), "Eurocentrism refers to values, attitudes, ideas and ideological orientations that are informed by the notion of European uniqueness and superiority". To put this perspective into proper context, Alatas (2002) as quoted in Miike (2010) says the doctrine of Eurocentrism involves "the tendency to understand non-European history and society in terms of the models, categories and concepts derived from European Experiences". Miike (2010) also anchors his perspective of Eurocentrism on the insightful definition offered by Manlana Karenga (2002: 46-47) thus:

> Eurocentrism is an ideology and practice of domination and exclusion based on the fundamental assumption that all relevance and value are centred in European culture and peoples and that all other cultures and peoples are at best marginal and at worse irrelevant.

In his attempt to further clarify his perspective of Eurocentricity in this article, Miike (2010) draws a distinction between Eurocentrism and Eurocentricity thus:

> Eurocentrism as a Universalist ideology is an ethnocentric approach to non-western worlds and people of non-Western heritage, whereas Eurocentricity as a particularist position is a legitimate culture-centric approach to cultural Europe and people of European decent.

From the perspective of Asante (2006) and Miike (2008a); Miike (2010), however, notes that Eurocentricity becomes Eurocentrism "when the provincial masquerades as the universal degrading other non-western approaches". He, however, cautions that Eurocentrism is not restricted to the Western World alone. He and many other reflective scholars have shown their discontent to the over-reliance on European, particularly U.S. Eurocentric theoretical development and research collaboration by academics of non-western societies. This, most of the reflective scholars note, has very disastrous implications on academic authenticity of the non-western intellectual.

Another outcome of Miike's article (as earlier reflected in Wang and Shen, 2000) is their assertion that "globalization has forced people to come face to face with not only 'others' but also with themselves: who they are, what 'place' they have in this community, and where they are heading", is the fact that most Asian or even African communication scholars and researchers may not necessarily have a deep enough understanding of the philosophies and traditions in their culture to know 'who they are', let alone how these philosophies rob off on communication studies and sound scholarship.

This assertion has been the bane of Afrocentricity and African intellectualism. The African scholar is trained in Europe or North America and when he is trained at 'home', the curricula will have been the one adopted from the West from colonial and post-colonial times without amendments or any form of national or regional impact assessment. To be accepted "internationally", they follow western academic traditions and strive to use western voices to tell their stories. So, they are forced or coerced into distorting the facts of the stories if they wish to use the western (and by their standards)

the so-called global and highly rated media outlets, books and journals to publish even their views of Africa. So, the editors of Western
based Journals insist on their own standards, formats, content etc
before they accept manuscripts from the so-called African intellectual. So, even when the author is African, every other issue around
that story is western or Eurocentric. This is the major problem
facing Afrocentricity in the area of communication scholarship.

This may have influenced Miike (2010:3) analysis of
Eurocentric scholarship as presenting two fundamental problems:

> First, the Eurocentric paradigm often proclaims itself the
> human paradigm without recognizing and incorporating
> non-Eurocentric counterparts. The crux of the issue here
> is not its theoretical propositions themselves, but its one-
> sidedly presumed universality and totalising tendency.
> Eurocentrism practiced in this sense "essentialises" human
> experiences as if all humans were of European decent, and
> as if they were struggling to live in the margins of European
> historical trajectories. Second, the Eurocentric paradigm
> favours some phenomena over others due to their cultural
> origins and orientations. Consequently, it disregards, down
> plays or overshadows certain values and elements that have
> been historically embraced in non-western cultures. In any
> case, Eurocentric scholarship does not theorize from non-
> western cultural and communication particularities about
> non-western visions and versions of humanity.

This article by Miike, especially the evaluation of Eurocentrism
as ideologies of Totalisation and Trivialisation contextualizes
the background of how Africa is portrayed in the media of the

Western world. It is also at the root of the call for Afrocentrism in African intellectualism.

MEDIAL FRAMING: A CASE STUDY

This section of the chapter presents a typical case study of how the western media frame happenings in the African context to suit their own agenda of controlling the discourse and thereby maintain the dominant voice on all the alternatives to the story. The section also forms the basis of the theoretical argument to support the voice being put out.

News is often regarded as a cultural construct that often has frames embedded in it. This is supported by Garyantes and Murphy (2010) who observe that despite the claims of objectivity, completeness, precision and clarity, news organisations are often swayed by ideology and other non news evaluation parameters in their news judgement, thus, frames are embedded in the news text. Harcup and O'neil (2001) are also of the same view that news is a construction of reality. One may ask; whose reality? Out of a million of events that happen every day, only a few that "meets" journalists' subjective opinion get mentioned. This according to Harcup and O'neil (2001:261) is guided by a set of ground rules:

> Such ground rules may not be written down or codified by news organizations, but they exist in daily practice and in knowledge gained on the job, albeit mediated by subjectivity on the part of individual journalists.

But who sets these ground rules and for who, what and when contexts? Again, this is where Eurocentrism as complained by Miike (2010) comes to meaning.

Framing as a theory of media effect is a loose concept with diverse perspectives to its meaning. However, Entman's (1993) description is every apt for our discussion in this chapter. According to him:

> Frames essentially involve selection and salience. To frame is to select some aspects of a perceived reality and make them more salient in a communicating text, in such a way as to promote a particular problem definition, causal interpretation, moral evaluation and/or treatment recommendation for the item described.

This definition by Entman (1993) seems to have been generally accepted. No wonder McQuail (1994) categorically calls news a construction of reality. Harcup and O'neil (2001: 265) citing Vasterman (n.d.) expanded on this definition when they note "news is not out there, journalists do not report news; they produce news. They construct it, they construct facts, they construct statements and they construct a context in which these facts make sense". McNair (2006:60) statement further gives credence to news as frame:

> No matter how live the news is, regardless of how raw and visceral the account of events being brought into our living rooms appears to be, it is still a mediated version of reality.

Herbert (2001:5) backs this up with his emphatic assertion that "sometimes, newspapers decide the angle, headline and tone before the facts are gathered. The global reporter's job is often to make the facts fit the headline". Unfortunately, this is the platform and basis of Western media coverage/reportage Africa and African affairs!

Tomi Oladepo's (2010) study of how the global media framed the Abdulmutallab attempted terrorist act against the U.S. interest is a typical and current example of how stereotypical the west has been in its portrayal of Africa. She used CNN, BBC and Aljazeera's coverage of the event to test for frames in the text used to convey the message. She also evaluated or used language of the reports to reach her conclusion. Oladepo (2010) applied Critical Discourse Analysis (CDA) and Centring Resonance Analysis (CRA) as two main theoretical and methodological approaches to analyse the selected media handling of the event. She hypothesized that:

> News is a frame and frames are closely knit with political and social questions of power, that are of significance to the media hegemony discourse. Therefore, Aljazeera as a global channel with roots in the Middle East will cover the Abdulmutallab terrorist attempt differently from CNN and BBC (*which are Western in origin*). Emphasis and addition in the bracket is mine.

Oladepo (2010) found cultural, stereotypical and socio-political power undertones in the three media organizations' coverage of the event. Her result revealed that Aljazeera, a non-western channel, framed the event differently from BBC and CNN which are Western channels. This validated her hypothesis thus:

> This paper found the BBC frames (and their underlying themes) to be quite stereotypical based on the result of the CDA analysis and the top influential words yielded by the CDA Map. Where a word like 'Muslim' for instance, makes it into the BBC list, with the name of the suspect

and his nationality at the top potion, there is little room for argument compared to the other counterparts. The themes running across the CNN frames were less stereotypical and more nationalist. CNN theme revolved around the state of American's security. Aljazeera had frames that were not at all stereotypical. The frames were highly nationalistic, in terms of focusing on the Middle East, and even somewhat diplomatic-in terms of managing the relationship between Yemen and the U.S.

MEDIA STEREOTYPES AND THE WESTERN MEDIA PORTRAYAL OF AFRICA

Africa has been and remained a victim of the developed world's typecasting and negative portrayals. Stories from Africa only make news when the bizarre, conflicts, wars, hunger, pandemic, epidemics, diseases, scandals etc happen. Otherwise Africa is the "Dark Continent" and is not news at all. This was the story of Makunike Ezekiel (n.d.:1-2) when he went to the U.S. for graduate studies thus:

> I was increasingly dismayed at the near-total lack of news from any part of Africa being presented to Syracuse readers. I also soon discovered that the little African news that occasionally found the light of day and trickled into the *Syracuse Herald and Journal* was almost always negative. This inspired me to spend some of my free time embarking on a more serious investigation of news selection. I requested permission from the news departments of those two daily newspapers to glean through their wastepaper baskets for

telex sheets from wire services containing stories transmitted from Africa. I conducted this search for most of an entire week. While indeed not much was offered by the news services, I was nevertheless surprised to find that much of the little that came in was either "killed" or simply spiked for a more suitable publication date that never came. When I asked an editor to explain these decisions, he told me that stories on Africa are routinely ignored because of a presumed lack of reader interest. "You see," he said, "America does not know Africa well. It never had a colony on that continent. Thus, unless the story has a strong human interest potential, there is no point using it, since no one will read it."

To corroborate this story, Chavis (1998:4) states thus:

How do the media justify perpetrating disparities, circumvention of objectivity, and sometimes questionable journalistic and professional ethics in reporting critical newsworthy African events for domestic and global consumption? Why is it "ethnicity" in Bosnia or Kosovo and "tribe" in Africa? Why are certain African cultural groups, residing in "jungles" designated pygmies while northern, caribou herding Europeans of similar physical stature are referred to as Laplanders? Why was the Sans people of South Africa renamed Hottentots? Can one conclude that negative reportage of events in Africa, compared to other reporting and spin tactics, by major news organizations, like racism in America, is systemic? Can the news chroniclers, wire services, media organizations, and other gatherers of news, find nothing of value to report when Africa is the subject-and a sound byte at that? The media industry practice of consistently practicing the opposite is deeply troubling.

These descriptions by Makunike and Chavis are typical situations most Africans face anywhere in Europe or North America. It shows a total lack of knowledge of Africa by the west yet it goes ahead to distort the African story, her heritage and history through uncorroborated account of supposed events in and about Africa!

Makunike (n.d.) further notes "for Americans readers or viewers to be interested, news out of Africa must be negative. It must conform to the traditional stereotypes in its spotlight on grotesque and sensational events. It must show misery, corruption, mismanagement, starvation, primitive surroundings, chaos and outright anarchy". It was even observed that reporters and editors who have a broader and close-to-the-truth perspective on happenings in Africa run the risk of their stories being tagged 'untrue' and so 'killed' for the other falsified, touched up and sensational stories. This, according to Makunike, "explains why the life of Africa's varied and diverse countries is missing. We hear about famines and coups, but not the rejuvenation of its cities and the cultural vitality of its village life.... about oppression and massacres, but not education, economic self-help and political development... about poaching and habitat destruction, but not ongoing active efforts at conservation, reforestation and environmental awareness".

Makunike's story of the African portrayal is not different from that of Chavis Rod (1998:1) thus:

With the stroke of a journalist's pen, the African, her continent, and her descendants are pejoratively reduced to nothing: a bastion of disease, savagery, animism, pestilence, war, famine, despotism, primitivism, poverty, and ubiquitous images of children, flies in their food and faces, their stomachs distended. These "universal" but powerfully subliminal message units, beamed at global television audiences, connote something not good, perennially problematic unworthiness, deplorability, black, foreboding, loathing, sub humanity, etc. On the other hand, little is said about Africa's strategic importance to so called industrialized nations; her indispensability and relevance to world development, global technology, and the wealth of nations, derived from involuntary African largesse, are not acclaimed in the media.

Since the 1980s, according to De Beer (2010), Africa's news image in the West has been in shambles. Efforts by African Editors' Forum to "tell the African story" in order to counter-balance negative western coverage has not yield positive result. The reason for this is clear – nobody cares! This situation has worried scholars like Chavis since 1998 thus:

Africa's negative and contrived image, promoted in the Western Media, pervades the psyche, pre-empts behaviours, infers worthlessness, disregards African humanity, and devalues the mind, while it attenuates human spirituality and connectivity: key ingredients in equitable planetary wealth sharing. Do media organizations, in the words of Shelly, "have responsibility for their creations"? What level of journalistic professionalism must be achieved in order to obtain balanced, objective, and fair reportage on events

as they occur any place in Africa? Because the modus operandi is so entrenched, so readily applicable to news treatment and for putting a local or provincial spin on news,
newsgathering organizations feel no compunction to do
anything different or right.

CONCLUSION: CALL FOR AFROCENTRICITY IN COMMUNICATION SCHOLARSHIP

Africa is a rich continent whose raw materials helped develop
Western Europe. She is rich in natural resources, culture and
people. Without the support of the natural/raw resources in
Africa, most of the industries in Western Europe will collapse;
yet, Europe still sees noting good in Africa. The African art, grafts
and culture has enriched Europe's so-called artistic collection and
galleries at no profit to the Africans who originally made them.
Africa projects warmth and welcome but for her (Europe) selfish
reasons, European nations still consider Africa as a dark, underdeveloped and will never develop continent. Shame on them!

While wondering over these issues, I am particularly drawn by
the valid questions posed by Chavis (1998:3) thus:

What do negative media images, conveyed by the Western
Media about Africa communicate? What darkness prevails
in the mind of the producer(s)? What gains for whom derive
from journalistic bombast and unmitigated stereotype of a
whole continent? Nouns and adjectives like hut, dark, tribe,
King Kong, tribalism, primitive, nomad, animism, jungle,
cannibal, savage, underdeveloped, third world, developing,
etc., are yet pervasive when Africa is the story. Historically,

since at least the issuance of the Papal Bull of 1455, when the Pope of Rome authorized Spain and Portugal to go out into the world, the one east and the other west, to bring salvation to the heathens, -and, coincidentally, set up new territories for the crown-, word of mouth initially and now sophisticated, globally reaching electronic news organizations, maintain a negative reportage policy when the subject is Africa. Balance is rarely evidenced; why? Must a news organization demonstrate objectivity, responsibility, ethical standards, and fairness? Images of Africa in the Western Media, many times, are deeply troubling psychologically and emotionally.

Africa's image in the media of Europe and the rest of the west is not a self-portrait. Rather, it symbolises global ignorance on the part of the west about what is really happening anywhere else! So, whether Europe agrees or not, the first civilization started in Africa and the last civilization before this Earth is decimated will come from Africa. Europe and the rest of the west are spent forces that lack the morality to lead the rest of the world out of the present worsening global connectedness. Africa will surely rise to the challenge and help restore a new global order.

In 1980 during the heat generated by the UNESCO sponsored review of international communication to empirical back up the developing world's claims that there are so much imbalances in global information flow; the MacBride Commission submitted its Report and gave it an apt title – "Many Voices, One World" (MacBride, 1980). Thirty-two years after, is it "many voices, one world" or "one voice, one world"? Europe and the rest of the west pretend it is one world and so should have one voice. This may explain the derogatory portrayals of other worlds. In conclusion, even when a "many voice, one world" theory may seem attractive, we are practically in different worlds and so must allow alternative voices. The Creator himself knows this that is why pluralism was a hallmark of God's creative ingenuity. We cannot shy away from this truth otherwise we will continue to hear sounds of dissent from disgruntled and sometimes silent voices.

Based on some of the situation already highlighted in this chapter, the present author advocates for post-modern Afrocentricity in communication scholarship as a viable counter to negative and abusive portrayal by Western media agents and institutions. Post-modern Afrocentricity advocates for a pragmatic, resourceful and intellectual handling of African scholarship and problems from a pro-globalisation perspective. This is not necessarily supporting globalisation as an acceptable situation in the 21st century; it rather understands globalisation as a key variable in any attempt or push for Afrocentricity or even Africanism. For the believers in the post-modern Afrocentricity school of thought, a failure to appreciate globalisation trends in the current global order is to anchor African intellectual emancipation on a one-and-half-legged tripod – it cannot stand without falling!

In the immediate time, Africa should re-evaluate her news evaluation standards to reflect African realities of what news is. The need to deconstruct the Western news evaluation standards to reflect unique realities of individual societies and people can no longer be delayed. News can no longer be the man-bite-dog phenomenon. News should be a reflection of societal and cultural realities and happenings that affect or touch the lives of the people who live in such communities or society.

This will also mean that the current curricula used in teaching in our media training institutes and higher institutions of learning must also change. African institutions of higher learning must redesign the outdated curricula adopted from the colonialists and their apologists who continue to influence and meddle with policy issues related to curriculum reviews and development. The communication curricula that should be taught in our institutions of higher learning must emanate from the rich African cultural and communication heritage. African indigenous languages and communication systems were developed in their own rights before the unholy invasion by the colonialist. So, we cannot justify the continued adoption/application of alien communication policies, philosophies, curricula in our educational system.

Following from this preceding point, African institutions must evolve their own unique Journals and communication channels that must circulate widely and measure up to any so-called 'international' standards. This will help preserve our values and make sure our voices are no longer drowned or our stories killed by the murderous hands of Western editors and their African cronies. As a follow up to the publication of this book, we could establish the *"Journal of African Communication Sciences", Voice of Africa (for both Radio and Television) etc.*

Of course, African Governments, corporate organizations and individuals of African origin must begin to invest heavily in the media industry in terms of ownership of media production and distribution businesses so that Africa can have her own voice and tell her own narrative.

Let us begin to have more conferences and workshops that focus on deconstructing our Universities from the leprous grips of

Western imperialists. Then we must begin to research within our African traditional communication systems to develop our own New African Communication Technologies (NACTs) or African Information Communication Technologies (AICTs). These are achievable through focused research and innovations.

In conclusion, we should not merely aim to reject everything European or Western in our drive for Afrocentricity and Africanism. No! We should engage them, deconstruct the lies behind their notions, thoroughly interrogate their philosophies, question their standards and probably reinvent the wheels of progressive and the true African communication sciences and scholarship.

These are practical ways out if the current negative portrayals, stereotyping and dehumanizing tendencies must change. These are part of the ways to drive Afrocentricity in communication sciences in a hostile world.

REFERENCES

Agba, Paul C. (2002) 'International Communication: Issues, Concepts and Perspectives', in Okunna, C.S. (ed.) *Teaching Mass Communication: A multi-Dimensional Approach,* Enugu, New Generation Books

Ake, Claude, (1981) A Political Economy of Africa, London, Longman

Akintoye, S. A. (1976) *Emergent African States*, London, Longman

Asante, M. K. (2006) 'Afrocentricity and the Eurocentric hegemony of knowledge: Contradictions of place', in J. Young & J. E. Braziel (Eds.), *Race and foundations of knowledge: Cultural amnesia in the academy* (pp. 145-153), Urbana, IL, University of Illinois Press

Brown, M. B. (1976) *The Economics of Imperialism*, England, Penguin Books

Carragee, K. M. & Roefs, W. (2006) 'The neglect of power in recent framing research', *Journal of Communication*, 54 (2): 214-233

Chavis, Rod (1998) 'Africa in the Western Media', Paper presented at the Sixth Annual African Studies Consortium Workshop, October 02, 1998, http://www.africa.upenn.edu/Workshop/chavis98.html, Accessed October 24, 2011

De Beer, Arnold, S. (2010) 'News from and in the "Dark Continent": Afro-pessimism, news flows, global journalism and media regimes', Journalism Studies, Volume 11 (4): 596-609

Ekeanyanwu, Nnamdi T. (2008) *International Communication,* Ota, Covenant University Press

Entman, R. M. (1993) 'Framing: toward clarification of a fractured paradigm', *Journal of Communication* [online] Available from <http://www.questia.com/googleScholar.qst;jsessionid=MN3pZ2Wgc2y15c7yv412H35nH59y8B0yytthLGcfhRGp4CqT7cyr!-1788688887!-122474816?docId=96440060>, Accessed June 30, 2010

Garyantes, D. M. & Murphy, P. J. (2010) 'Success or Chaos?: Framing and Ideology in News Coverage of Iraqi National Elections', *The International Communication Gazette,* 72 (2): 151-170

Harcup, T. & O'Neill, D. (2001) 'What is News? Galtung and Ruge Revisited', *Journalism Studies*, 2 (2): 261-280

Karenga, M. (2002) *Introduction to Black Studies* (3rd ed.), Los Angeles, CA, University of Sankore Press.

Lenin, V. I. (1975) *Imperialism, the highest stage of capitalism*, Peking, Moscow Publishing Coy, Ltd

MacBride, Sean et al (1980) *Many Voices, One World*, NY, UNESCO

Makunike, Ezekiel (n.d.) 'Out of Africa: Western Media Stereotypes Shape Images', http://www.medialit.org/ Accessed October 10, 2011.

McNair, B. (2006) *Cultural Chaos: journalism and power in a globalised world*, London, Routledge

McQuail, D. (2000) *McQuail's Mass Communication Theory*, 4th ed., London, Sage Publications

Miike, Yoshitaka (2010) 'An Anatomy of Eurocentrism in Communication studies: the Role of Asiacentricity in De-Westernizing theory and Research', *China Media Research* 6(1): 1-11

Okigbo, C. (1996) 'International information flow and the challenge of the twenty first century to communication research', in Uche. L.U. (ed.) *North-South Information Culture: Trends in Global Communication and Research Paradigm*, Lagos, Longman

Okunna, C. S. *et al* (1993) *Theory and practice of Mass Communication*, Enugu, Abic Publishers

Oladepo, Tomi (2010) 'Framing the Abdulmutallab Event: A Comparative study of BBC, CNN and Aljazeera's Coverage', Unpublished M.Sc Thesis, Coventry University, United Kingdom

Rodney, W. (1972) *How Europe Underdeveloped Africa*, Dar es Salam, Tanzania Publishing House

Rogers, E. M. (1999) 'Anatomy of the two sub disciplines of communication study', *Human Communication Research*, 25(4): 618-631.

Rogers, E. M. (1982) 'The empirical and critical schools of communication research', in M. Burgoon (Ed.), *Communication yearbook*, Vol. (5):125-144, New Brunswick, NJ, Transaction Books.

Scheufele, D. A. (1999) 'Framing as a theory of Media Effects', *Journal of Communication*, 103-122

CHAPTER EIGHT

*The Myth of Poverty: African
Identities within an Ecosystem
Approach to the Gift Economy*

YVETTE ABRAHAMS

'So be like the sky and be like the sea
And be like the river running endlessly
And be like mountain, give shade to all
Be like the flowing waterfall
Be like the sun with arms spread out wide
Encircle all to your heart inside
And be like the moon that sees every face
And smiles on all
With equal grace
With equal grace
With equal grace'

—Schouw, T. (2010)

THE ROSE OIL

It is October in Cape Town and I am making rose oil in the old way. Not the old, old way (as in before the Flood old way) but following a newer tradition dating from the time after milking the wild Eland turned into herding the livestock, after the time when my mother's people, the Damara, began making iron pots and trading them. [1]

The rose is not an indigenous plant, although the only rose species native to Africa, *Rosa moschata var. abyssinica*, may well be an ancestor of the rose from which I now make oil (Phillips and Rix, 2004:18). Blush Damask has been growing here since the time of the birth of my spiritual ancestor, Sarah Bartmann, around the 1790's. Cape Town was a stopover for ships on the way from the East to Europe and the Americas, so this rose may well have come here before it reached Europe. I came across Blush Damask when researching which roses were likely to be growing here during Sarah Bartmann's lifetime, trying to answer the question: which flowers did she like? I think she liked this one, it is the loveliest of plants, pink and sweetly scented rosettes against grey-green leaves on graceful arching branches. Blush Damask grows happily on my heavy clay, too, in fact I initially planted it because it is said to be one of the most drought resistant of roses, often found on old graves where it receives no care whatsoever. Blush Damask has adapted well to the cool wet winters, the hot dry summers and the restless winds of every season in the south-western Cape, giving of its beauty in late spring just as the indigenous plants are going over.

Though the rose plant was not here much before 1670, the scent of rose has always been here ('always' in the oral history sense of 'since before anyone can remember'). The rose geranium, *Pelargonium crispum x radens 'Rosé'*, is a local plant, and the active substance which gives the rose its scent, geraniol, has been named after this plant. The geranium is a little bit more spicy than the rose and I love to mix some sprigs in with my rose flowers, it gives a sweet and spicy mixture which softens the skin and is wonderfully aroma-therapeutic. This is my art and culture. It is fascinating how the geranium family and the *buchu* family love to make scents, everything from mint, liquorice, lemon and rose, to those less easily described fragrances of the *veld* on a dewy morning. With such a tool box ready to hand I, like my ancestors, cannot resist playing with perfumes

This speaks deeply to our culture. Fragrance, like words and fire, is an archetypal symbol of the gift. You cannot keep a smell to yourself, it will give itself freely to everyone within sniffing distance. Words we can give to each other without ever impoverishing ourselves. On the contrary, our increasing inability to communicate with each other would be for me one of the markers of post-colonial traumatic stress and a warning of our hapless incorporation into the exchange economy. Fire, like words, is given over and over again without diminishing itself. These three great things which are the foundation of human life are the idiom of the gift. When we understand this principle we begin to understand what makes us human. Vaughan (1997:410) offers us this insight:

> '..everyone's giftgiving practice is being blocked by exchange and made difficult by scarcity, but also by patriarchal values, which interpret giftgiving as exchange, dismiss it as ineffective and weak, or overemphasize and sentimentalize it. Finding giftgiving in language makes it possible to consider

giftgiving as what makes us human. It is my hope that affirming giftgiving as the human way will promote its conscious practice.'

An ecosystems approach to the gift economy sees human beings as dependent on the plant world for our well-being, with plants in turn dependent on the welfare of the soil for their survival. It may depart from Vaughan's purist approach to the gift economy, which sees us as giving simply because we are creatures of language ('I give, therefore I am'), and indeed I was brought up to give with a good heart, not because I expected something in return. Yet I advocate ecosystems approach which muddies the clear waters of gift theory in political practice in equating altruism with self-interest. When we take care of the soil we safeguard our future. If we do not operate in a giving and loving way towards the earth and her creatures we simply won't be around for long enough to make a difference. Matthai (2010) has made a very strong connection between living sustainably and our use of language which seems to reconcile these approaches. Freedom becomes the gift which keeps on giving:

> '..I never differentiated between activities that might be called "spiritual" and those that might be termed "secular." After a few years I came to recognize that our efforts weren't only about planting trees, but were also about sowing seeds of a different sort—the ones necessary to give communities the self-confidence and self-knowledge to rediscover their authentic voice and speak out on behalf of their rights (human, environmental, civic, and political). Our task also became to expand what we call "democratic space," in which

ordinary citizens could make decisions on their own behalf to benefit themselves, their community, their country, and the environment that sustains them.'

Here, Maathai makes an important connection. Trees require a sustaining political environment in which to grow. It is a chilling fact, as Mbeki (2009:159) points out, that Africa spends something like US\$ 14 billion a year on security forces. The vast majority of that money is spent on civil wars and by repressive regimes fighting their own populations. The real enemy is seen to be within. Armies are wandering up and down this continent shooting people and despoiling forests, destroying where we should be building up. To demand some governance is necessary political work.

The reason why we need good governance is because the problem is not that Africa is poor. Our continent is easily one of the richest in the world, in terms of climate, resources and people. The problem is that we are squandering our inheritance. Mbeki (2009:146) points out that:

'One of the most disgraceful but underreported scandals in Africa is the extent to which African elites export capital from the continent. According to the Commission for Africa, nearly 40 per cent of Africa's wealth is kept outside Africa, compared to only 3 per cent of South Asia's private wealth and 6 per cent of East Asia's. The small surplus that remains, as we have seen, goes to finance elite consumption and to pay for the running of the largely unaccountable state.'

The African elite, it seems, does not trust its own armies to keep their money safe, and with good reason. I cannot remember when last a dictator died in peace in bed with his family around him. They do all come to a sticky end sooner or later. In the mean-time Africa is being bled of capital, like it used to be bled of pro-ductive labour during the centuries of the slave trade. It is not that we are short of money to feed, educate and heal all our people. At the same time as the African elite has money to invest in foreign banks, we continue to repay interest and instalments on foreign debt to the tune of US$ 15 billion a year (Mutazu, 2011:3). Most of this debt was incurred by undemocratic regimes to keep themselves in power. Now, we spend more money a year repaying foreign debt than we do on health and education. The poverty we experience is a social phenomenon, brought about by elites who put their faith in repression rather than justice. All empirical evi-dence to the contrary, they continue to believe this will work to keep them and their families safe.

I write this chapter in the first person because in my culture it is not done to tell other people what to do. When one wishes to advocate a course of action the correct form is 'I do this. I say that'. One leads by example. This tradition stems from the old days (I speak here of the colonial and immediate pre-colonial period) when leaders were chosen precisely because of their reluc-tance to lead. People who lobbied for power and position were automatically considered ineligible because they were deemed likely to be acting for self-aggrandizement. It was a good custom which should be revived. Yes, I know that generations of our true leaders were raped, beaten and assassinated into silence until only fools remained. Yet African hearths and homes continue to give rise to people of courage, character and honesty. To plant a tree so that the next generation of leaders can eat and survive spiritually is important work. It is the most precious gift we can give the next generation.

I try to commit one small act of resistance every day.

Since I first received the privilege of being the caretaker of the piece of land I now live on, questions of identity have become perfectly simple. I am the person who loves this land back to life. It has not been in Khoesan hands for over three hundred years. It has suffered multiple indignities. When I first came to it, it could have served as an exhibition of invasive, water guzzling, alien plants. There was not a particle of humus left in the deep, solid clay soil. In fact to this day, in order to plant, I first have to loosen the soil with a pick axe. I used to weigh the plant's roots down with stone so that it would not be blown away. Planting in a bare piece of ground like this is akin to planting in the desert. There is no shade, mulch or protection from winds to nurse young plants along. I had to think carefully about which plants could be summoned to my aid. I could not, as my ancestors did, work with only indigenous plants. Unlike my forebears, I am no longer nomadic. I cannot leave this land for two seasons to recover and prepare itself for my next visit. I ask it to yield throughout the year. So I have mixed our indigenes with those gentle immigrants who combine toughness with grace and utility. Loving this land back to health took all the skills, knowledge and experience I had inherited from my mother. Now, after six years and much ardent supplying of composted manure from the free range livestock farms surrounding me, some of the clay is looking almost like soil, and I find I am spending more and more time harvesting. In fact my role has increasingly become that of a peacemaker, keeping the plants from overgrowing each other. To me, this work of putting right what was done wrongly is decolonization. We cannot move backwards in time to what was. We can only use the wisdom of the past to move forward, meeting new needs, giving and receiving new gifts. It is a profoundly spiritual experience. Life has become too busy to wonder who I am. I am blessed.

I write of rose oil because it explains what identity means to me. It is about growth and change in culturally familiar ways. Cultures lend, cultures borrow. In fact, they even cross-pollinate. Still, inasmuch as the only thing constant is change, it is best to make sense of the universe by adapting to change in very old and familiar ways. The plant may be new, but the way I make the oil is old-fashioned and rather personal. In the same way identity is not just about what you do. It is about how you do it. That is why when some patriarch in a suit with a cell phone tells me that women cannot be traditional leaders because it is not 'culture', I just look at him. It is not the suit and cell *per se* that irritates me [2] (although I would like to see our glorious textile traditions worn more often and not just on festive days. It makes more sense in this climate). It is the use the patriarch is making of these things, transforming them into signifiers of western culture, and using them as instruments of power to enforce patrilinearity. This system, at least according to Diop (1959) and Amadiume (1997), is not indigenous to this continent. Are we adapting it to our ancient recipes or is it ruling us?

THE BIOGAS DIGESTER

I like to boil my rose oil on top of the biogas digester. It gives me comfort to know that I am making carbon neutral oils. My oil smells the sweeter because it is made in a way that makes the world better for the grandchildren.

I would like to propose the biogas digester as another metaphor highlighting what is wrong with a patriarchal social structure, or to give the thing its full name, hetero-patriarchal white supremacist capitalism. It is a system which creates poverty from abundance. Bosman (2011) points out that the problem with our social system is, fundamentally, that we do not return our manure to the soil. Our urban-based system, at best, treats humanure with nasty chemicals which eliminate their natural and very nutritional microbial balance. We then pump it into the sea, polluting rivers along the way. The upshot is that we have the sea full of nutrients which cause an excess of algae growth and while upsetting the fish, and a land which is increasingly deficient in soil humus. The rivers no longer provide clean water because we are using them as sewerage conduits. The part that hurts my brain and renders me in need of some rose oil, is the notion that this is called 'civilization'. There is nothing civilized at all about it. It is astoundingly silly, and creates poverty from abundance.

Think about it! Here we have this prolific and infinitely renewable natural resource, which we are expensively pumping into the sea under the impression that this is actually a better system then the ones our ancestors used for hundreds of thousands of years. Under the influence of European post-'Enlightenment' thinking, I know we like to see ourselves as somehow separate and 'above' nature (and if it were true, why would it be an improvement?). The truth is we are not. We are, like all animals, surprisingly efficient fertilizer producers. When left to themselves, mature plants take a long time to decompose, at a minimum one year. This means it will take long before their nutrients are available to feed the next plant. Add some animal nitrogen and stack them, and it will take three months. Or even better, crush plants finely with some liquid, place them in an anaerobic environment, and you will have the same result within a day or two. That is exactly what we do when we eat and excrete. It makes me want to praise our Great Creator. What an amazing idea! Tie is the secret element of good gardening. By adding animals to plants, we can play with time in growth and change, and create new possibilities for the infinite diversity of life. It provides more space in the biosphere. All we have to do is keep the plants and animals in a reasonable proportion to each other, and we have a wealth of species. This is not new. We have existed in peaceful symbiosis with the plant world, creating abundance from abundance for millennia until, that is, we lost confidence in our own ways of thinking. Then, we allowed the mad patriarchs to rule us. We have disrupted a perfectly sensible system in favour of 'civilized' technology. Now we have rivers full of disease, seas full of algae, depleted and eroded soils, and deforestation. Patriarchy has created poverty from plenty.

At worst, this system of treating sewerage is lethal. It is silly enough in the global north, where people have plenty of money to waste on idiocies. But here, trying to imitate it is like those Tintin cartoons of the Black man in a ragged shirt and too tight waistcoat. We do not have enough money to be silly in style. All over Africa, our sanitation systems are failing under pressure from corruption, population growth and urban sprawl. It is an open secret that municipal sanitation systems are not coping with the pressure. In South Africa, one of the richest countries on the continent, we had a typhoid and cholera outbreak in December,

2008. When we looked the cause, it was found that nine sewerage works were discharging under-treated sewerage into the river. Four rivers were found to contain illegally high levels of cholera bacteria (Makhubele, 2009). The shocking part was not just the personal human tragedy of crying human mothers on the evening news. Dying before your time is such a sad waste of human potential. Still, it is not just that our geniuses, the beautiful ones who perhaps held the key to new technologies, were lost. That argument is often made. But what price our poets, our artists, our dreamers of dreams? Lost to the need to crap like the colonizers? The poverty of the spirit thus caused is too sad for words.

Biogas digesters are an elegant solution to this problem. In essence, a biogas digester is an artificial stomach. It provides an anaerobic environment which ferments animal and plant waste at stable temperatures. The result of the decomposition is, on the one hand, biogas (technically known as methane). Yes, it is exactly what you think it is, it is the same gas your stomach produces when you eat too much beans. Produce enough of it and it can be used as cooking gas or to drive a turbine to produce electricity.

On the other, a biogas digester produces some of the finest liquid fertilizer this farmer has been privileged to see. In fact I think of mine as primarily a giant liquid fertilizer maker and fill it with good things for my plants: gentle migrants like comfrey, borage and yarrow, and also the leaves of unscented geraniums and succulents which grow without any help at all. You should see my roses. Fed on this rich diet they grow, bloom in profusion, and keep me sane, without any need to buy fertilizer, pesticides and the other abominations of agribusiness. It allows me to recycle every drop of water which enters this place, and my garden is rich in abundance while using as little of our shared resources as can be.[3]

Biogas is classified as a carbon negative technology. Organic waste will give off either carbon dioxide or methane, depending on how it is allowed to decompose. The amount of carbon it contains cannot be increased or decreased, whether it is in the sea or in a biogas digester. To decompose it anaerobically and create energy from it instead of coal, oil or natural gas is used reduces carbon emissions. But its greatest virtue is in restoring soil carbon. The significance of re-vegetation of former forests and grasslands lies not just in the above-ground biomass provided but also in the fact that forests and grasslands provide wonderful environments for the retention of soil carbon, or humus. Bell and Lawrence (2009:1) estimated that:

"Carbon stored in soils worldwide represents the 3rd largest sink in existence, after oceans and geologic sinks. There is 2-4 times as much carbon stored in soils as there is in the atmosphere and approximately 4 times the carbon stored in vegetative material (i.e. plants). It is therefore understandable that the soil carbon sink is being viewed as one that could potentially have a significant impact on sequestering CO_2 emissions".

The technology to do so is perfectly straightforward, and has been practiced by indigenous, organic and agro-ecological farmers or foresters for centuries. Lasalle and Hepperley (2008:5) summarized almost three decades of research as follows:

"In the FST organic plots, carbon was sequestered into the soil at the rate of 875 lbs/acre/year in a crop rotation utilizing raw manure, and at a rate of about 500 lbs/acre/year in a rotation using legume cover crops."

During the 1990s, results from the Compost Utilization Trial (CUT) at Rodale Institute—a 10-year study comparing the use of composts, manures and synthetic chemical fertilizer—show that the use of composted manure with crop rotations in organic systems can result in carbon sequestration of up to 2,000 lbs./ac/year. By contrast, fields under standard tillage relying on chemical fertilizers lost almost 300 pounds of carbon per acre per year. Storing—or sequestering—up to 2,000 lbs./ac/year of carbon means that more than 7,000 pounds of carbon dioxide are taken from the air and trapped in that field soil."

The same paper cites longitudinal studies to show that a depleted soil farmed organically will show rising levels of soil carbon until a steady state is reached after about three to five decades. It sounds like just what we need to reach 250 ppm.

Human beings, no matter how intellectual, all need to eat. We cannot do that without the plants which are nourished on the thin layer of soil enveloping the planet. To state the obvious, there can be no change in our social circumstances if we cannot generate the material conditions enabling us to organize and sustain a revolution. Ergo, food is one of the most ideologically radical concepts which allow us to think about social systems and human ecologies.

We need to care about the soil which nourishes us and the world we live on. Biogas serves as a useful metaphor for thinking about such deeply political matters as what we eat, how it is produced, and what its real costs are. While not ancient (as in before the Flood ancient), the history of biogas technology is respectable, dating back three millennia. (Climate Lab, 2011) There are designs old enough not to be patentable. The first documented usage is in the Middle East, but it is a technology which fits in comfortably with my culture and tradition. Instead of the economy of scarcity created by neoclassical economics it creates an economy of abundance – a gift economy. The more you give, the better it gets. Once we can make that mental revolution, the technology is ready to end man-made poverty. Are our minds?

CONCLUSION: THE WAY FORWARD

I work with sanitation because it allows me to deal with Africa's ills – corruption, cronyism, maladministration, inefficiency and cowardice – at a local level. A lack of adequate sanitation affects the potential for women's liberation in that, where there is no or inadequate sanitation, women bear the brunt of dealing with the consequences. Their burden of unpaid labour increases, as they are the ones who clean the mess up, and take care of the people who fall ill from infectious diseases. What I have tried to show in this essay is that the problem is not a problem of poverty, it is a problem of ideas (Nyeck, S.N., personal communication). I have argued that even very rich people with the cleanest of anti-septic sanitation are contributing to the madness of the exchange economy and assisting in the creation of poverty.

It does not take a lot of money to remedy the situation. Biogas has a proven track record in rural environments with low levels of literacy. Thus in India one organization has distributed over 43 000 biogas from cattle manure digesters to rural villagers since 1993. Each of these plants saves about four tonnes a year of carbon dioxide and about three and a half tonnes of fuel wood (Ashden Awards, 2007). The human ecology outcomes, however, are even more profound. As one woman villager says: 'With wood, our hands used to itch when we cleaned off the soot from the pots, our eyes had tears, our chests were painful and we coughed a lot. We had headaches and we had sight problems. With biogas, all these problems are gone.' (Ashden Awards, 2007)

Biogas from sanitation projects accomplish four things at once. Sanitation has to break down anyway, whether we pump it into the sea or use it to generate energy. It follows that a life cycle analysis of biogas from sanitation projects would show lower net carbon emissions as compared to processing sanitation separately and generating energy from fossil fuels. Therefore they assist in mitigating climate change. Further, by providing an economic use for sanitation, local governments save money and are vastly encouraged to extend waterborne sanitation services. The communities, and in particular women, benefit because they can access cheap energy for heating, lighting and cooking. The improvement in sanitation collection provides health spin-offs which again benefit women in their social role as family caretakers. Kiyaga-Nsubuga, J. (2003:85) demonstrates that, in a biogas from sanitation project in Uganda: 'Medical reports for the project site indicate a sharp reduction in incidences of water-borne diseases.'

I strive live consciously, to be mindful of what I eat, of how it has been produced and of the social implications the way my waste is managed. I seek to solve problems where I live. It is well known that too much free time leads to idleness and other subversive actions (like thinking critically). When a technology makes so much sense one can only wonder why we do not do it. Is it because when African women are no longer coughing, overworked and unpaid, they might find time to attend a feminist workshop or (even more dangerous) perhaps just catch up on their rest? Is it because biogas is a technology which does not lend itself to corruption? After all anyone can build one. Or is it because if we were eating well, and no longer had to fight merely to keep this planet alive for the next generation, we might actually find the energy to ferment some more social revolution?

ENDNOTES

1. It is generally agreed that domesticated sheep, goats and cattle made their appearance in southern Africa about 2000 years ago (Clarke, 2003:221).

2. This is not to say that technologies are value-free, or innocent of relations of oppression, on the contrary. It is simply that I believe we can achieve the power to choose which ones we need. It is not the scissors which are dangerous but the maniac wielding them.

3. Some people advocate irrigating your vegetables with digester effluent, but I do not approve of this. It makes the ecological cycle too short. I like to see my bodily substances go through a few more species before returning to me. The liquid is wonderful on the roots of trees, though.

BIBLIOGRAPHY

Amadiume, I. (1997) *Re-inventing Africa: Matriarchy, Religion and Culture*, London, Zed Books

Ashden Awards for Sustainable Energy (2007) 'International Finalist: SKG Sangha, India' , Page 2 of 3. Available at http://www.ashdenawards. org/media_summary07_skg . Last accessed October, 2011.

Bell, M and Lawrence, D (2009) 'Soil Carbon Sequestration–Myths and Mysteries' The State of Queensland, Department of Primary Industries and Fisheries

Bosman, C. (2011) 'Farmers To Measure Water Use' *Farmer's Weekly*, 27 May

Clarke, J.D. (2003) 'The prehistory of southern Africa', in J. Ki-Zerbo (ed.) *General History Of Africa, Volume 1: Methodology and African Prehistory*, Glossderry, New Africa Books.

Climate Lab (2011) http://www.climate.org/climatelab/Domestic_Biogas_ Plant Last accessed October, 2011

Diop, C.A. (1978) *The Cultural Unity Of Black Africa: The Domains of Patriarchy and Matriarchy in Classical Antiquity*, Chicago, Third World Press.

Kiyaga-Nsubuga, J (2003) 'Turning Human Waste Into Domestic Gas' *Service Delivery Review* 2:2:2003, pp. 85. Available at http://www.dpsa. gov.za/documents/service_delivery_review/vol2no2 Last Accessed October, 2011.

LaSalle, T.J and Hepperly, P. (2008) *'Regenerative Organic Farming: A Solution to Global Warming'* Rodale Institute, Pennsylvania

Maathai, W. (2010) *Replenishing the Earth: Spiritual Values For Healing Ourselves and the World*, Doubleday Religion.

Makhubele, H. (2009) 'Water Quality Cholera Report in Mpumalanga', Department of Water Affairs and Forestry, Mpumalanga, South Africa.

Mbeki, M. (2009) *Architects of Poverty: Why African Capitalism Needs Changing*, Johannesburg, Picador Africa.

Mutazu, T. (2011) 'African Debt crisis—a human rights perspective', African Forum On Debt and Development, Harare, Zimbabwe. Available at http://afrodad.org/downloads/Africa%20Debt%20crisis%20-%20 Human%20rights%20perspective.pdf Last accessed October 2011.

Phillips, R. and Rix, M (2004) *Best Rose Guide: A Comprehensive Selection*, Buffalo, Firefly Books.

Schouw, T. (2010) 'Equal Grace' on *Winds Call*, Cape Town, Tick Tock Productions, Cape Town.

Vaughan, G. (1997) *For-Giving: A Feminist Critique of Exchange*, Austin, Texas, Plain View Press.

CHAPTER NINE

Exploring Indigenous Healing Methods: A Personal Account

PETER ONYEKWERE EBIGBO

INDIGENIZATION OF UNIVERSAL PRINCIPLES

Indeed there is a psychic unity of mankind[1] but the various languages and cultures make it imperative that an indigenization of universal knowledge be undertaken[2]. It can only be so that people's mentality, belief systems, culture and indeed habit should be considered before a psychological test is developed, a psychotherapeutic method is formulated and even research undertaken[3]. That was why earlier a journal which Karl Peltzer and I founded and in our enthusiasm to pay respect to Africa titled "Journal of African Psychology" was so much criticized. The criticism was that there is no such thing as African psychology and that the body of psychological knowledge should have universal application. We had to change the title of the journal to Journal of Psychology in Africa as from the 3rd volume[4].

MY STORY

It is easier to undertake this assignment by using the prism of my own activities. I trained at the Julius Maximilian Bavarian University of Wuerzburg, Federal Republic of Germany a university with an institute of psychology which has a proud history of phenomenology and introspective studies of Narcis Ach, Kulpe, Malbe, Charlotte Buehler etc. the fathers of the so called "Wuerzburger Schule" that is Wuerzburg school/connection/ working group. In Germany as of that time (1974) you cannot complete your studies as a clinical psychologist without specializing in at least one psychotherapy method. As of then, psychoanalysis was very strong in Germany alongside mainly Behaviour Therapy and its devivates and Client Centered Talk Therapy.

GETTING SET

As a student although I was attracted to undertake Teaching Analysis, a self-analysis necessary for qualification and admission into the membership of the German psychoanalytic society, I had no money. Teaching analysis is mercilessly costly. My teacher and mentor, Prof Ludwig Pongratz himself a psychoanalyst and former monk called me and told me that I would not have much benefit from a Teaching Analysis, may his soul rest in peace. I should not waste my money, he said to me. The reason is that psychoanalysis was structured to analyze the European, with Christian background from a nuclear family from mostly Western civilization. He advised that I should study psychology to go home to help my people and therefore I should gather knowledge from as many therapeutic models as possible but remain open to what, teaching, research and practice will bring when I go back to Africa.

I pondered over his advice, accepted it and then specialized as a group therapist in which I learned in a group therapy training course called "interaction in small group" using various therapy models and their group therapy variations. I ended up with my master thesis as "model of group therapy for homosexuals". Supervised in 1974 by Dr Hendrick Roth. This paved the way for my PH.D with thesis on "Developmental conditions of Homosexuality, a theoretical and empirical study" under again Prof Luduig Pongratz in 1977.

RETURNING TO LEARN

With this preparedness to learn about how to apply psychology to help my people I returned to Nigeria September 1977 and was employed at the University of Nigeria Teaching Hospital Enugu. I made a number of observations which will form the background to our intervention strategies[3].

The test I brought back with me such as Mimmesota Multiphasic Personality Inventory, Freiburger Personality Inventory, Pauli Test of Concentration were not useful to me. I had to free myself of all tests and listened, observed and investigated with a view to learn the root of the basic problem of our people.

I observed that our people have their way of thinking, belief systems and cultural rights. The idea that our fauna and flora in our environment spoke and had to be understood to even understand those who live in this environment was widespread. For example if you find somebody talking to himself it must not be a sign of schizophrenia but can be a sign of heightened self awareness and being one with the environment and even the ancestors. There is an adage that if the penis starts itching you too much, you have no choice but to display it outside.

I observed three groups who were over represented among our patients and who bore heavy burden in various ways imposed by society. The first were married women, followed by single males and then people from polygamous families[5].

I observed that due to our hierarchical but close body tactile contact in child rearing leading to late discharge to adulthood there was external locus of control and undue concentration on the skin as a very sensitive modus of communication, therefore the widespread paranoic tendencies and somatization as idioms of distress [6][7].

I observed that there is widespread belief in pre-life plan and sworn condition of life, deviation from which in real life one is visited with death or mental illness such as Abiku, Ogba Nje, Agwu etc.

Evil eye, curse, breach of oath to shrines and gods, jealousy of fellow citizens and relations are all causes of mental illness[9].

Life together with fellow humans is key and one is healthy, who has peaceful relationship with relations, friends and those with whom one entertains relationship and one is ill, who is in disharmony with his world.[10]

I observed that there was widespread belief in spirits or collective power. God is the absolute spirit the collective power who handed down spirits to the various gods, thunder, harvest, sun etc., then there is spirit handed down to the ancestors, then to the eldest and o r the traditional ruler and spirits in the fauna and flora. Spirits, these collective powers can be peaceful and useful, if their terms are kept and destructive if negatively applied[11].

The thinking here is holistic and no line is drawn between living and non living, natural and supernatural, material and mental, conscious and unconscious (Lambo) both fuse into one holistic entity. The phenomena which are conceived in the West as opposites, one understands as a unit. Everything exists in a dynamic inter relationship, the seen and the unseen, past and present and future go into one another in harmony. The world is the same as in dream at night as in the awake conscious state during day light for people. In this manner there is a steady relationship between the dead and the living. If something unpleasant happens, there are a holocaust of natural and supernatural reasons for it [12].

We observed that the patients, who came to our clinic were divided into three types namely: The traditional type, the westernized type and the mixed type by far the larger group. The traditional type is born and bred in the village. He/she normally goes to the traditional healer but comes to us because he/she has left the village. The western trained clinical psychologist usually is perplexed by this group of patients.

The westernized type is born in the town and grew up there. He/she has little contact with the cultural life in the village. Parents are city dwellers, educated and Christians or Muslims. The western trained understands and treats this group easily and successfully. The mixed type born and bred in the village had maintained contact with the city, is a Christian or Muslims and is educated. He/she believes he has seen through the practice of the traditional healer but has at the same type internalized the traditional concepts and belief system. This group will try out all sorts of treatment methods pari-parsu[13].

The first observation I published from my observation in the clinic after return from Germany in 1977 was on 20 women, who had all kinds of somatic complaints who were given into marriage at an underage period (9-13). Each had traumatic first sexual relationship with their husbands. I was able to observe two types. If a positive reaction follows the first traumatic first experience, a kind of imprinting fixation of the girl on the man occurs, she attains satisfaction and recognition with the man. If however the man should later die or send her away there is a disorientation and inability to have sex with another man. This is when we see them in the clinic. If the reaction is negative the girl will react with frequent pregnancies, which she uses to limit the frequency of sexual intercourse. If she should stop the pregnancy or want to stop it, she develops symptoms such as crawling sensation, constant headache etc. to prevent future sexual intercourse between them. Once this was understood, treatment became easy[14]

Going through hundreds of case notes of psychiatric patients at the Enugu Psychiatric hospital. I found somatic complaints such as heat in the head and head, weight sensation in the head and body, dizziness, palpitation, blurred vision, weakness in memory etc.

When this body of knowledge was combined for example with hearing of voices the diagnosis was schizophrenia, if combined with feeling of in-sufficiency, it was labelled depression etc. in addition only 1/3 of the cases treated had a sure diagnostic label. This made me feel that there was uncertainty in the case of western diagnostic Illness categories for labelling mental illness in Nigeria. This made me to abandon the diagnostic categorizing and resort to listening and observing carefully what our mentally ill people were telling me with their bodies. I found support in local and international literature and became reinforced in my quest for better understanding of the problem.

As soon as we made this recognition we were able to find that heat in the head leading other somatic complaints indicated goal frustration conflict. We observed a constellation of sexual conflict in connection with recent traumatic event. The feeling of heaviness in the head and shoulder indicates ambivalent sense of responsibility (especially financial in nature), which a person symbolically carries. If the entire symptom group appear together they could attract a fourth symptom such as internal heat. Internal heat or biting sensation all over the body both symptoms show alarm states of the patient. We gathered a holocaust of such meaning enabling quick translation of idioms of distress into social and psychological problem which the patient is helped to solve if possible or also helped to accept if not possible to solve. Both scenarios mean healing[15].

I observed that there were others, who were doing the same work as a clinical psychologist within the society, namely the traditional healers and the prayer house priests "To know their methods and to possibly draw from their healing methods is especially important for us. As already mentioned, the traditional healers in this connection are seen as the mediator between gods, spirits and human beings. They recognize the message of the supernatural and through them find possibilities for the treatment of human beings. Traditional healers possess above average knowledge of the human and have an especially deep insight into the native cultures, beliefs, rituals and customs. T. A. Baasher described the factors which help them to achieve success as follows:[16]

1. Strong belief of the patient in the healing power of the traditional healer.
2. Unison in the belief of the healer and the healed as regards causes and manifestation of mental illness.
3. Exact explanation of the therapeutic intervention practices and the strict adherence to the therapeutic regimen by the patient.
4. Support of the patients by the family and community. The traditional healers involve relations in the various stages of therapy.
5. Strong belief of the traditional healer in personal ability and exactitude in the treatment.

In the prayer houses I could observe that especially the senses are aimed at in order to increase the power of expression. Colours and symbols play a lot of role as well as the scent of incense. Patients sing and dance until they see visions (a sort of cathartic projection in a sort of trance state) and begin in a sing-song to confess, how to improve their life style. Monotonous prayers have a relaxing effect on the participants. Artificial enemies or evil spirits are construed and made responsible for the illness. At the same time they are fought against with God's help and power. The participants quickly become a group in which members help one another[17].

In Nigeria here, there are alongside traditional healers also a group of wandering healers. They go to town and literally capture mentally ill people, whom we call here vagrant psychotic". They transport them into an empty house, give them a lot to eat and pray with them.

Already at 6 o'clock in the morning they wander in a row

through the town and drum rhythmically on plates and other improved musical instruments.

In this manner they wander the whole day and collect money. In the evening they return to the empty house totally exhausted. Again they get a large portion of food and a sort of drink concoction got from the back of some trees and which has a sedating effect. The aspect of eating a lot and well has not yet been researched into in this connection. The social relationship which is created by the action of this group appears to have a favourable effect on these patients. Similarly the daily wandering and the consequent bodily exhaustion appear to have a useful effect as a therapeutic method. These "healers" who capture their patients by force appear to be very strong personalities[18].

But how does the treatment method of the clinical psychologist trained in Europe look like? We are confronted- as already mentioned- with patients who described their complaints through bodily symptoms. They come from far and expect ready-made help through injections and tablets from the traditional healers. They are accustomed, to get a clear diagnosis, medicine and special instructions.

Psychoanalysis or behavior therapy is foreign to Nigerians. Because however, most people can easily be influenced and they already know about dream interpretation from traditional healers, the experienced clinical psychologist will try hypnosis at the first meeting. If he succeeds in hypnotizing the patient, the patient will be ready to believe in him and give up tablets and injections.

I made the experience that one has to speak with the patient before and after hypnosis to clear doubts and questions. Some patients will otherwise call the hypnotist a magician. Patients want something concrete, want it, if possible, to be directed into the healing process, want to be able to classify a therapist into herbalist (healers, who use drugs) or traditional healer (healer without drugs, who uses incantations or the like to heal). The hypnotist is seen to be more the traditional healer. Hypnosis and suggestion are so effective in Nigeria that some people have made it their stock-in-trade to hypnotize people on the streets, in taxis, in churches and then exhort money, trinkets, or electronic equipment from them. These people first claim to be great prophets, healers, religious leaders, people from beyond etc. they get into contact with their prey, make a few tests of suggestion and put their clients in trance before commanding them to go home to bring money supposedly necessary to carry out rituals for their benefits, to pray for them, to double money for them, to heal their sick and avert evil from them and their relations. This suggestibility of Africans should be utilized therapeutically [19]. This had led me to use hypnosis in a dyadic therapeutic situation and then I went ahead to start a relaxation clinic for staff and patients of the University of Nigeria Teaching Hospital Enugu, a programme captioned Stress Inoculation Programme. I made the experience that this was successfull. I used the autogenic relaxation method modelled after Schulz, 1932[20] and the programme of Muscle relaxation according to Jackobson 1948[21]

I started them with an intensive exploration and carried out several tests, which impressed the patients and made them inquisitive of the "European medicine" as western medicine was called then.

Goal of therapy is to make it clear to the patient that he/she is not bodily medically ill. Otherwise, they would not accept psychotherapy. Also I send the patient to other medical doctors or to laboratory tests, where it is confirmed that the patient has no organic illness.

It can then happen that the patient, who realizes that he/she is bodily alright, loses his symptoms or he produces others. I let my patients also to write essays. The topics are the persons' auto-biography, "the story of my life" or "my present situation", or "the story of my mental illness." I use them to try to awaken conscious-ness for their own problems. Later the essays are read back to the patients in a kata-thymic state for the purpose of re-experience. We exploit therapeutically the ability for fantasy and imagination of Nigerians, as well as their readiness to subjugate themselves to inexplicable things, to accept interpretations of symbols and images. After reading the written topics we animate the patients to bring forward remembrances, experiences, fears and hopes, real and unreal possibilities of solving the problems. The therapist understands and interprets the produced materials.

Other topics are "how I can overcome my emotional problems", "why I believe that my situation is not so bad", "how I used to heal myself",. I also, give them topics in which they should describe very concrete states after recovery. We also let them write down their dreams and I read it back to them later. Remembrances and interpretations are digested. The traditional method of guided affective imagery according to Karl Heinz Leuner can also be suc-cessfully applied among our people, only that we have to replace the European standard motives such as meadow or edge of the wood, with other motives which correspond to the symbols of the natives like house, forest, farm etc. Relaxation trainings, desensi-tization, psychodrama and family therapy have proved to be very useful. The family is often times willing to co-operate since they have been accustomed to be involved in treatment by the traditional healers.

In our attempts at group therapy we have built in traditional group methods in an analytic model which simplified can be reduced to two parts.

1. The phase of interaction, getting acquainted, inter-personal attraction, group formation. Traditional interaction methods such as singing, dancing and other rituals are made use of.
2. Phase of analysis, digesting of problems and possibilities for the solution of the conflict. For the African psychologist it is especially important to be flexible and full of ideas, to command as many therapy methods as possible and to apply them, even in case of necessity, to each corresponding case.

My father was a traditional ruler and as a young psychologist I observed how he settled disputes in his palace and adopted it to what I labelled the Native Judgment Model for Polygamous families. This method I applied to the Traditional Type and some mixed type of Nigerians. Mental illness is seen as the manifestation of ill feeling of a family member who feels he or she has been wronged in the family. Usually when a person from a polygamous family feels he or she has been wronged, he/she proceeds first to the eldest man in the family, for example a woman who has been wronged brings cola and a fowl to the eldest, reporting the wrongdoing of the husband. He calls a family meeting. Both parties will be heard by the family "court" and a judgement passed. We attempted to incorporate parts of this judgement system in our family therapy model. The therapist is the key member. The extended audience replacing the extended family, comprises workers in the hospital, psychologists, doctors, nurses, social workers, etc. All sit down in a circle or semi-circle just like in the native method. The therapist tries to verbalize the problem. If possible, key members of the disturbed polygamous family are invited, for example parents, a brother or a sister. Each get a chance to mention his present needs and motives (Schmidt, 1975, Toman,1973). The audience listens. The members of the audience help the individual family members to present their problems and act them out. Members of the audience base their help freely on sympathy, empathy, identification, transference etc. After the first stage of acting out comes the phase of self reflection, in which one searches for older motives and needs (Beese, 1992, Overbeck 1979 Schmidt, 1975, Sperling, 1972, etc), that could be responsible for the sick-making role delegation (Richter, 1968) or narcissistic transference relationship (Overbeck, 1979).

In these sessions, which at one time have the character of a group therapy and at another time, the character of a family therapy, there are no winners and no losers. The therapist seen at the beginning as a judge or head of family loses this role in the process of therapy and becomes one who understands and helps.

Contrary to the native judgement model, the family members do not need to get partners to support their case. They can speak for themselves and act out their feelings. The hospital audience are not only passive on-lookers but spontaneously participate in the therapy process and help the individual family members to solve the problems. The family soon learns not to defend their positions doggedly and with bitterness. It is no family disgrace if they give in. They really act it out. The distress of the family with regard to its ill members and above all, the high financial expenditure in the course of treatment, help to break the family defence mechanism.

We have often succeeded in solving family problems which not even the chief could solve. It is very necessary that the therapist speaks with the family members individually. Some men react by withdrawal from family therapy if they feel that we in the clinics are departing too much from the cultural methods. They need some explanation in such situations. The westernized type and some mixed Nigerians would find the native judgement model too autocratic. We then adopted the family therapy model of Schmidt (1975), who describes four ideal process stages of a family therapy although he warns that these are not sharply distinct from one another.

In the first phase, the family speaks about its conflicts, each one highlighting which motives have been deprived. The theme is: "what is wrong at the moment?" in the second phase, the family talks about the history of the conflicts and discovering earlier connection between the main earlier motives. The theme is: "How did the conflicts arise?" the therapist tries to appreciate connection between the main (earlier) and constant (present) motives. In the third phase, the members of the family, especially the parents, learn more about the connections between their individual (earlier in their parental homes) basic, earlier or main and their present (within the marriage) constant motives as well as the motives of the children. The theme is: "what are my/our real problem." The therapist can be of help here. In the fourth phase, the family members learn more about their individual wishes and expectations and the background to these. The theme is: "what can we do in the future?" A new "modus Vivendi" is sought that will make family members more satisfied.

Very important in this process is the breaking of the vicious circle of obsessively repeating the parent's childhood in their children (Missildine, 1979; Miller 1980; Dinslage 1982). Without knowing it or wanting to, parents repeat the tragedy of their own childhood in rearing their children. They exercise their powers on their children who are also dysfunctional because the parents were also. Parents have to experience the pains of their childhood. In the family therapeutic transference situation they can verbalize their childhood misery and consciously experience anger and sorrow that they were forced to suppress. In this manner they reconcile with their own parents so that present parent child relationship can be characterized by acceptance and partnership.

Paediatricians often referred cases of childhood psychopathology to us and we found that the symptoms of children could not be understood or treated without recourse to the family. We therefore adopted family therapy for treatment of children's emotional problems[30] Here we adopted the family collusion model according to Willi (1975, 1978) as exposed by Budderberg (1982). According to Willi, collusion means a common way of behavior unaccepted and hidden from one another by two or more partners because they have similar and undigested basic conflicts. The interaction between the family members is influenced by internal and external family factors. The principle of functioning will determine whether disturbances in the relationship or symptom formation will appear in disturbed families. Three principles of functioning determine a family's common way of behavior.

1. The ability of the family to withstand environmental influences and contacts. How far is the family unit together? Are the family members as loosely tied as a club or as rigidly organized as a monastery? This determines the ability of the family to resist external influences.

2. The second principle of functioning relates to the ability of the family to resolve problems of maturity in the family e.g. pregnancy, birth, separation, illness, death etc. (Bibering, 1961) as well as problems emanating from situations of transition of family members from one developmental stage to anther (e.g school entrance of a child, professional life, change of accommodation and place of work, entering pension age etc)

3. The third principle relates to social contingency which refers to the way and manner a family entertains contact with other social groups (neighbours, clubs, interest groups, political and religious groups) and especially how it reacts to the demands and expectations of these groups. It can react with adaptation or rejection of the norms of these groups.

The central rules which govern the way a family functions, can be demonstrated according to Budderberg in four main dimensions:

- The identity formation of the individual and the family as a group. Here the following questions must be answered: "who is who? And "who are we?"
- The material care and emotional attention. The question is "who caters for whom?"
- The distribution of power, the question being "who dominates whom"

- The exchange of affection with the question "who loves whom?" being in the forefront.

Each family is governed by the above rules. The rules can be openly declared, be hidden or be missing. Family rules result from a mixture of conscious and unconscious motives which have been inherited in their contents from the family rules of the parents and the goals of the individual family members.

The goal of family therapy is therefore to discover the way a family functions and the rules that govern that way of functioning especially in disturbed families, who always present the paradox on the one hand wanting to understand and explain their problems and on the other hand frustrating efforts leading to that explanation and understanding. In the case of very disturbed families the relevance and existence of these problems may be denied completely

In treating cases of drug addiction we have encountered people with weak ego or very weak will power, who need a well grounded method to help them keep away from drugs. The method is based on using cultural methods to rehearse the moral order.

As the client comes in, either alone or in company of family and relations, cola nut is harmony by rehearsing the moral order and inviting every body to keep to it and praying to God to bless those who keep it and to punish those, who deliberately do not keep it. For example let the kite perch, let the eagle perch whoever denies the other the right to perch should lose its wings.

"As I say let everybody live in peace and prosper. Whoever says I shall not live should be buried deep inside the earth. Let the rich be, let the poor be, let the man be let the woman be, let the adult be let the child be. The way we prepare our bed so shall we lie on it.

If we work under the heat of the sun, we reap and enjoy under the shade. I did not kill the first to be the first, I did not kill the second to be the second, I did not kill the last to be the last, wherever I am was brought about by circumstances. He who eats alone will die alone. He who does not make enquiries about whether a food is edible before eating will also die without sickness" etc. Proverbs get to the heart, to the mind and to the head. In Igboland there are behavioural patterns that are loathed and every Igbo man will utter rejecting loathedsome words distancing him/herself from the behavioural pattern.

Different sections of Igbo land utter different kinds of words but cultural is "Tufia kwa!, Azi gba kwa'! If you ask the Enugu Igbo to break the moral order for example to go against his brother, he will say "wa"! Meaning no! if you repeat the same thing again to him, he will say wa!wa! meaning not only decisiveness in reject-ing the temptation but warns you that you will face his anger, if you continue with the temptation. Wa!wa! means that you even wish me the evil consequences of breaking the moral order and therefore wa!wa! declares you an enemy if you do not stop the evil temptation.

When therefore you are facing a tempting situation and you say "tufia" meaning I spit on it you are also just saving yourself from destruction. "Azigbakwa"! It means evil will follow the person who said something abominable "Arusokwa gi" means let the evil follow you in your evil deed!

On another occasion one shouts moving both hands over the hand using the thumb and the pointing finger to chick a sound shouting "Uhiem ei", which means calling on the ancestors and denying ever to be part of the deviation from the moral order.

Wawa technique positions one as a normal citizen, rehearses the moral order to the person and invites him to reject the offensive behaviour .eg. Taking drug to ruin my family! Tufiakwa, wa-wa neglecting my family uhiem! Taking drug to impoverish me Wa! Wa!. The whole problem is discussed analyzed and shown to have several evil consequences that impede the moral order. The person is invited to break the negative consequences into short sentences and to shout Tufiakwa! Wa!wa! and to deny being part of it by shouting uhiem ei!

We have had very positive experience. The rehearsing is continued at home and anytime the temptation is at hand. Wa!wa! technique creates a dissonance within one's cognitive structure and invites the person to change his attitude or behaviour to establish consonance[34].

A similar method was developed by Awaritefe namely the Meseron Therapy. Meseron meaning "I reject it" His method and explanation goes in the direction of cognitive behaviour therapy of Ellis[35]. Here is the establishment of the moral order though breaking of cola nut and idioms. Declaration of the behaviour in question e.g Drug abuse and inviting the person to reject it, to spit on it, to loathe it and deny to the ancestors that one is not part of it. To continue doing it until it clicks.

I observed that dreams mean a lot for the Nigerian and that there are people who claim to interpret dreams. Various theories are put forward by various individuals as to what dreams means. Some believe that what they dream of will happen. If they dream somebody died, that person will also die, if they dream of eating food they will become rich etc. We studied dream contents of 30 psychiatric patients from the Enugu Psychiatric Hospital, now federal Neuropsychiatric Hospital. Classified into broad types, we find two main types of dream namely, fearful dreams and dream of sexual nature. In order to determine whether or not people with similar complaints have similar dreams, we classified our patients into two main categories according to their complaints, namely, crawling sensation and headache patients. Patients who complained of crawling sensation tended more to have sexual dreams while patients with headache had more fearful dreams. Those who complained of crawling sensations tended to be unsure, shy, withdrawn and weak ego personalities. No particular trend was found among headache patients. Means of assessment was systematic psychological exploration.

Furthermore, patients who complained of crawling sensation and who had sexual dream contents tended to be over 28 years old and had unsatisfactory sexual life. We also collected dreams of 74 students of the University of Nigeria Enugu Campus.

Again, we have tried to group the dreams contents extracted into clusters together with their interpretative symbols.

The 74 dreams reveal that the Nigerians in this study are very much preoccupied with family and natural phenomenon. Many of them believe that dreams can forecast events. The more educated they become, the more the tendency to believe that dreams are a reflection of the waking state and a sort of a stage to act out the unconscious drives, fulfill repressed wishes,, compensate insufficiencies both directly and symbolically, help the brain to get rid of excessive and unused stimuli coded during the day, etc. The university students in our sample more often than the other groups explained their dreams in terms of incidents in their lives emanating from the unconscious. The extended family system, material needs, fear of robbery, sexuality, religion and interpersonal relationship form the main dream contents of the interviewed subjects. The Nigerian as seen in this study seems to use death, blood, pursuit by dangerous animals, (snakes and reptiles), mermaid, evil spirits, masquerades, etc. to symbolize his fear of something. Sometimes his wishes are satisfied in the negative. Instead of dreaming that a brother lives long, as he would wish, the Nigerian may sometimes dream that his brother is dead.

Natural phenomena like darkness, unknown destination, a lonely road or a desert house covered by a thick wood is used as a prelude to fearful incidents. Most of the dreams have always one fear element or another and when the dreamers fear something, that thing pursues them in the dream. In Nigeria no one dies without people saying he was poisoned or that someone was responsible. This has important implications for the treatment of manic, phobic and schizophrenic (especially delusion) cases in our psychiatric hospitals.

It is tempting to hypothesize, though without experimental evidence, that the Nigerian generally tends to a manic exposition and paranoid translation of events. This is contrast to the more depressive and obsessive translation of event by the European[36]

Having studied several cultures and belief systems in Nigeria we note that the Nigerian has an internal yearning to reach out and be at peace with his world. His world being the web of relations (cosmos) he entertains in himself- mind and body (endocosmos), between him and his fellow humans with whom he maintain important relationship (mesocosmos) and between him and his ancestors, spirits, gods, God (exocosmos). He is at peace and healthy if there is harmony in his world (cosmos comprising of endocosmos, mesocosmos and exocosmos) the yearning to reach out and be at peace with his world is the cosmos expansion drive and the drive that would want him to do things on his own, based on his needs alone, is the cosmos reduction drive. There is harmony, peace and good health if the cosmos expansion drive gains the upper hand, the height of which is cosmic atrophy, leading eventually to chaos and death. **Ebigbo (2008)** Harmony restoration Therapy is just a therapeutic framework to determine the level of harmony distortion in the cosmos, where it is located and to restore the harmony selecting any form of therapy that is best suited for it such as Communication Therapy, Family Therapy, Behaviour Therapy, Psycho dynamic methods, wa-wa technique etc. Crucial to this is the development of the harmony restoration measurement scale[38]

Finally we are at the moment working on applying harmony restoration to heal the nation with the Nigerian psyche comprising of the development of the Nigerian psyche measurement scale and the igerian Psyche Hand book is to collect the attributes of Nigerians.

THE FIRST STEP

Some of such attributes have been listed by Ebigbo (2001)[39] as follows:

i.   Lateness (African time)
ii.   Over estimation of one's ability
iii. Respect for authority
iv.   Group mindedness
v.   Clan loyalty
vi.   External locus of control
vii. Over confidence

viii. Very friendly stance to strangers ans suspiciousness against relations and friends

ix. Paranoiac tendency. The feeling of being harmed by others.

x. Get rich quick and immediately (no delayed gratification)

xi. Easy to reconcile and easy to quarrel

xii. Interest in the whole than in parts

xiii. Use of the body to communicate psychic difficulties (Somatization)

xiv. Bird ostrich phenomenon

xv. Impatience

xvi. Strong will

xvii. Fearful and superstitious

xviii. Eye service

So also Achebe 1983 [18]

The idea here is to use these attributes to develop the Nigerian Psyche Scale Each of these characteristics will have a scale to measure them. [19] [20] Take for example characteristics (xiii) the Somatization scale was developed to measure this.

How can items for the Nigerian Psyche scale be generated?

1. Organize workshops and symposia for relevant stakeholders in various ministries with a view to raising items for the scale

2. Organize sensitization programmes for young people in schools: primary, secondary and tertiary with the view of generating items for the scale

3. Raise items to measure the attitudes and determine which attitude that should be emphasized and give score accordingly

4. Planning meetings for the development of the Nigerian Psyche Scale

FOLLOW UP ACTIVITIES

Thereafter

1. Develop modules for inculcating the Nigerian Psyche into nursery, primary and secondary schools as well as universities and tertiary institutions, the military and civil service and finally foreign missions.
2. Conduct a pilot study for the scale for item analysis
3. Organize seminars for pedagogical, military, civil service, foreign mission experts on the description of what the Nigerian Psyche is all about
4. Making use of the item generated for the measurement of the identified characteristics of Nigerians, establish norms for the scale
5. Organize workshops for relevant stakeholders in the mainstreaming of the scale into their various organizations.
6. The Nigerian Psyche Dissemination: A community mobilization and empowerment for the building up of the Nigerian Psyche will be undertaken. The sole aim of this phase is to set up a community support mechanism for the inculcation of the Nigerian Psyche into the society.
7. To this end a **Handbook of the Nigerian Psyche** will be produced dealing in detail with the attributes anybody, who is a Nigerian should have in order to have a Nigerian identity; qualities like honesty, punctuality, decorum, industry, self confidence, peacefulness, being one's brothers keeper,

fearlessness in expressing the truth, acceptance of responsibility, appreciation of the importance of education, pride in being a Nigerian, patriotism, national loyalty etc.

Thereafter community members comprising of local leaders, law enforcement officials, representatives of community based organizations, NGO representatives and religious institutions will be trained. The trained community task force members will reach out to the wider community through awareness creation on the Nigerian Psyche.

If this process accompanies the industrial and technological effort, there will be sustainable growth, where all hands are on deck

End Goal/Vision: The **Nigerian Psyche measurement Scale** and the **Nigerian Psyche Handbook** will be produced, one for screening of who has sufficient psyche to serve the nation in various capacities and the other for dissemination and training of the populace on the Nigerian Psyche. The transformation of Nigeria would have then started.

There have been other efforts to indigenize psychotherapy in Nigeria. I have chosen to use my self as a case study. I know of Awaritefe's Meseron Therapy, efforts of Oladimeji to apply behvaiour therapy to Nigerians, the efforts of Ohaeri to apply Cognitive Behavioour Therapy, also Yakassai had applied some Muslim prayer method for psychotherapy, Ayo Bimitie had devised his Psychotherapy through environmental manipulation, Dr Ossai applied spiritual behavioural methods to treat spirit possession.etc

The challenge here is to join the trend and devise further ways of diagnosing emotional and mental disturbance in Nigerian and ofcourse also developing psychotherapy methods of reaching our people. This done we would gladly beat our chest that we are relevant as a professional group having indigenized universal psychological principles in the diagnosis therapy and prophylaxis of mental illness among Nigerians.

REFERENCES

1. Kroeber, A. I. (1981) Anthropology Harcourt Brace New York

2. Ebigbo, P. O. (1989) Somatization in Cross Cultural perspective. In Peltzers, K & Ebigbo P.O (1989) Clinical Psychology in Africa (South of the Sahara- Afro Latin America Chuka Printing Company. Working group for African Psychology Enugu p. 225-233

3. Ebigbo, P. O. (1982) Psychotherapie in Afrika Schwarze Kultur und weisse Psychologie. Psychologie Heute No. 4, April 1982 p. 64-71

4. Nsamenang, A. B. (1990) What's in a Name? Journal of African Psychology vol 1, No. 3 p. 1-5

5. Ebigbo, P. O., Onyema, W.P.J.C., Ihezue, U.H, Ahanotu, A.C., (1981) Familien therapie bei polygamen familien. Zeitschrift psychosom med. 27, 180-191

6. Ebigbo, P. O. (1986) The Mind, the Body and the Society, an African Perspective Advances (Institute for the Advancement of Health) 3 (4) 45-57

7. Ebigbo P. O. & Onuora, A. N (1987) Paranoia und Somatisierungser scheinungen bei Nigerianer Zeitschr. Psychosom. Med 33, 78-90

8. Ebigbo, P. O., Anyaegbunam, B (1989) The problem of student Involvement in the Mermaid Cult- a variety of Belief in reincarnation (Ogba-Nje) in a Nigerian Secondary School.Journal of Afri PSychol. Vol . No 1 pp 1-14

9. Ebigbo, P. O., Oluka, J. I., Ezenwa, M. I., Obidigbo, G. C & Okwaraji, F.E (1996) Clinical Psychology in sub-saharan Africa. World Psychology 1, 2, 87-102

10. Ebigbo, P. O. Oluka, J. Ezenwa, M. Obidigbo, G & Okwaraji F (1995) Harmony Restoration Therapy. Paper presented at the annual scientific meeting of the Royal College of Psychiatrists Riviera centre, Torquacy July 4-7, 1995

11. Ebigbo, P. O. (1981) The belief in Reincarnation (Ogba-Nje) and its meaning for Psychotherapy in Nigeria Zeitschr. F. Psychosom. Med u. Psychoanal. 27(1)84-91

12. Ebigbo, P. O(1984) Psychotherapy in Africa, Quo Vadis? In Scientific Programme Committee of the Korean Academy of Psychotherapists Seoul International Congress on Psychotherapy East & West Proceeding p. 275-285

13. Ebigbo, P. O & Ihezue, U.H 91981) Uncertainly in the use of Western Diagnostic Illness Cathegories for labeling mental illness in Nigeria. Psychopathologie Afriacine 3, xvii (1) 59-74

14. Ebigob, P. O. (1979) Arranged Marriages of Underage girls and their psychic consequences. Zeitschr. Psychosom. Med u. psychoanal, 254, 367-381

15. Ebigbo, P. O. (1996) Somatic Complaints of Nigerians. J. Psychol in Afric. 1, 6, 28-49

16. Baasher, T.A (1975) Traditional Treatment of psychiatric disorder in Africa Afr. J. Psychat. 1 7-85

17. Ebigbo, P. O. (1989) Vagrant Psychotic Healers in Nigeria. In Peltzer & Ebigbo (1989) Clinical psychology in Africa. Chuka Press Enugu. 482-484

18. Ebigbo, P. O. (1989) Participatory observation of the healing methods of a Nigerian prayer house in Peltzer & Ebigbo (1989) Clinical Psychology in Africa. Chuka Press Enugu 485-489

19. Ebigbo, P. O. (1989) The Role of Hypnosis and relaxation therapies in the Management of the Mentally ill in Peltzer and Ebigbo (1989) Clinical Psychology in Africa. Chukka press, Enugu p. 634

20. Schulz, J. H. (1932) Das Antogene Training Konzeatrative Sebstenrspannung Versuch einer klinish-praktischen Darstellung Thieme Stuttgart see also 5th Edition 1978

21. Jackobsen, E (1929) Progressive Relaxation International Edition University Press Chicago

22. Beese, F. C. (1972) Neurosenstruketur und familien dynamik (Theoretische Grundlagea) Praxis der kinderpsycholegie u. kinderpsychiatrie 4, 126-130

23. Overbeck, G. (1977) Das PSychosomatische Symptom. Psyche. 31, 333-354

24. Schimidt, R. (1975) Psychoanalytic Oriented family Therapy according to the Duplication Theorem Praxis de kinderpsychol. U. kinderpsychiat 7, 254-258

25. Sperling, E (1972) Besonderheiten in der Behandlung von Magersucht Familien Psyche 26

26. Ebigbo, P. O. (1989) The Practice of family Therapy in the University of Nigeria Teaching Hospital, Enugu. In Peltzer & Ebigbo (1989) Clinical Psychology in Africa. Chukka, Enugu 551-574

27. Missildine, W. H. (1979) In Der lebt was warst. Fraukfurt, Suhrkamp

28. Miller, A. (1980) An Anfang war die Erzeihung Frankfurt Suhrkamp

29. Dinslage, A. (1982) Familie in der Krise (11) was soll aus dem kind werden? Psychologie Heute 9, 31-36

30. Ebigbo, P. O. & G. I Izuora (1983) Family Therapy in Paediatric Practice in Nigeria Nig. J. clin. Psychol 3, 1&2, 57-67

31. Willi, J. (1975) Die Zweierbeziehung Reinbeck Rowohlt

32. Willi, J. (1978) Therapie der Zweierbeziehung Reinback Rowhlt

33. Budderberg, C & Budderberg, B (1982) Family Conflicts in Collusion- A Psychodynamic view for family Therapy Praxis d. kinderpsychul u. kinderpsychiat 4, 143-150

34. Ebigbo, P. O. Oluka, J, EZenwa, M. Obidigbo, G., Udeoke, B & Okwaraji, F (1997) wa-wa technique in Harmony Restoration Therapy Meddika 5-11, July 1977 also in Ethnomedizin Verlag fuer Bildung und Medizin

35. Ofovwe, C.E & Awaritefe, A (2008) Rational Emotive Therapy and Meseron Therapy: a comperative analysis Nig. J. Clinic. Psycho. 6, 1&2 p. 29-36

36. Ebigbo, P. O. (1982) A Psychoanalytic approach to the Dream contents of some Nigerians Nig. J. Clinical Psychol. 1, 1, Jan. 1982, p. 64-75

37. Ebigbo, P. O. (2008) Positioning Culture and Psyche of Nigerians Towards Attaining Rapid Technological And Industrial Development Goals for vision 2020 through the Development of the Nigerian Measurement Scale and Nigerian Psyche Handbook. In: Adegoke, O. S, Ademolekun, L & Mu'azu, A. B (2008) (Eds) Developing a Roadmap for the Rapid Technological and Industrial Development of Nigeria Part 1 Proceedings of the Second Forum of Laureates of the Nigerian National Order of Merit (NNOM) P. 16-51

38. Ebigbo, P. O, Elekwachi, C.L, Ukoh U.C, Eze, J.E, Nweze, F.C & ABoh, U (2011_Development of the Harmony Restoration Measurement Scale. The cosmogram for Harmony Restoration. A paper presented at the Annual & Scientific conference and workshop of the Nigerian Association of Clinical Psychologists Covenant University Ota. 20th-24th September 2011

39. Ebigbo, P. O (2001) In search of the Nigerian Psyche. A contribution to NationBuilding NNOM Merit Award Response Lecture organized by the Nigerian National Merit Award Board. Chumez Enterprises, Enugu.

CHAPTER TEN

Beyond Revolution: Who Shall Lead Afrika's 21ˢᵗ Century Transformation?

PAULO WANGOOLA

ANTI-COLONIAL RESURGENCE, INDEPENDENCE AND THE CHALLENGE OF OPEN-DOOR IMPERIALISM

I present a story; the story of my long journey in search of and struggle for a self-determined Afrikan Black Nation. As struggle is a social activity, mine is, in fact, the search and journey of a generation of thousands, may be millions, of people across Afrika and in the diaspora who, during the 1960s and 1970s, attended high school and university, or other spaces of learning in which, with the support of role models and mentors, they cut their teeth of Pan Afrikan awareness.

'"Mpambo" is an ancient <u>Afrikan</u> word. In the ancient dialects of the ancient Afrikan language spoken by the twin peoples astride the Nile at her Source, on the shores of Nalubaale (Lake Victoria), the Baganda and Basoga, it means the undying precious seed of life. The best and most potent seed, forbidden to be eaten, but put away for safe custody, for propagation at the next and subsequent planting seasons and opportunities.

++**In Afrikan indigenous governance at the Source of the Nile, "Nabyama" means a person entrusted with the community's strategic secrets, because they have reached a stage in their physical and spiritual development when they cannot use the secrets entrusted with them, or the ones they are privy to, for any o purpose other than the protection, defense and advancement of the community. This is critical as no community can possibly hang together and competitively prosper without a core of privy secrets of its own. In the governance of Mpambo Afrikan Multiversity, Nabyama is the title given to the Multiversity's spiritual, academic and administrative head.**

The 1960s and 1970s were times of Afrikan resurgence and awakening; a historical moment of explosion of hopes and aspirations, confidence and belief among Afrikans that they can be the authors of their own future of national unity in pan Afrikan solidarity, democratic and participatory governance, national independence and social progress. In varying degrees this generation was energized and urged on by the inspiring Pan Afrikan ideas and thought of several Afrikan leaders at the time with a global outreach and appeal; for example, on the continent: Kwame Nkrumah **of Ghana,** Patrice Lumumba **of Congo,** Jomo Kenyatta **of Kenya,** Julius Nyerere **of Tanzania,** Sekou Toure **of Guinea,** Miriam Makeba **of South Afrika and Idd Amin of Uganda;** and in the diaspora: Martin Luther King, Malcolm X, Mohamed Ali,

Andrew Young, Stockely Carmichael and Walter Rodney. The energizing influence of this crop of Afrikan leaders was reinforced further by third world anti-imperialist leaders, particularly Abdel Gamal Nasser of the United Arab Republic of Egypt, Ben Bella of Algeria, Yasser Arafat of Palestine, Mahtima Ghandi and Jawalal Nerhu of India, Fidel Castrol of Cuba, Che Guevara of Bolivia and Cuba, Ho Chi Minh of Viet Nam, and Ayatolla Khomeni of Iran. Mao Tse Tung of the Peoples Republic of China stood out in a category of his own as the deepest, all round, principled, imaginative and nuanced revolutionary free spirit: anti-imperialist and anti-social-imperialist, anti-revisionist and anti-hegemonist, third world mass-line Marxist-Leninist theoretician and proponent of the "Theory of Three Worlds". By negative example Afrikan activists learned from Afrikan leaders in their midst who stood out as unashamed, eager and willing agents and stooges of imperialism; for example Moise Tshombe and Joseph Desiré Mobutu of the Democratic Republic of Congo, Hastings Kamuzu Banda of Malawi, Bokassa of Central Afrikan Republic, Kofi Busia of Ghana, Abel Muzorewa of Zimbabwe and Tubman of Liberia. By even worse negative example Afrikans with a Pan Afrikan outlook learned from the excesses of ethnic white supremacist apartheid settler tyrants on the Afrikan continent; particularly Voeword and Botha in South Afrika, and Ian Smith in Zimbabwe. Beyond the Afrikan continent there were substantive negative examples of leaders who oppressed their people in league with foreign powers or as agents of those powers; for example tyrant Salazar of Portugal and agent-dictator Batista of Cuba. Then there was the ultimate negative example of the elected, double-tongued Presidents of the USA who throughout the 1960s and the 1970s committed numerous ruthless wars of aggression and sabotage, including the bombing of Viet Nam into the stone age, and by way of chemical warfare, ecocide which rendered much of the land into a wasteland.

Between 1960 and 1970 scores of Afrikan countries attained independence and joined the United Nations Organization, the mixed bag international club of independent and sovereign states, both de jury and defacto. For several years into the first decade of independence it appeared as if all would be well for Afrika, for example: primary and secondary school enrolment was vastly expanded, correspondingly with tertiary institutions of professional and technical training; existing university colleges were upgraded and expanded, as entirely new national universities were established. Side-by-side with these developments in the education sector on the Afrikan continent, thousands of Afrikan students were airlifted in a crash programme to study in the belly of the **NATO** countries (Europe, North America, Australia, New Zealand, Japan) of the "political West" on the one hand, and on the other, countries of the **WARSAW PACT** (Soviet bloc), who constituted the "political East". The "East" and "West" represented two aggregated centres of essentially confederate ethnic white power (of people who, in the commonwealth of peoples of the world, and in international relations, defined themselves as "white"), although they were opposed to one another on the basis of homegrown Eurocentric ideology: that is, socialism/communism; and capitalism, in competition and rivalry for global hegemony. In any case, both the East and West each sought an imperial and parasitic relationship with Afrika. Of the two, whomsoever won the hegemonic contest, or in the event that they cooperated, the world remained saddled with white hegemony.

It took the elite analytical mind, ideological clarity, foresight and steadfastness of the Communist Party of China, on account of being deeply embedded in Chinese history and culture, to way back in the early 1960s, lay bare the global terrain of social forces and fault lines which defined struggle and engagement. In the Chinese Communist Party Chairman's (Mao Tse Tung) "theory of three worlds", which held until the collapse and disintegration of the Soviet bloc and Soviet Union, starting in 1989: the **first world** consisted of the two super powers, the US and the USSR, as lead imperialist powers of the same feather which vied and jostled for global hegemony; while the **second world** consisted of the medium imperialist powers of Europe and Japan, none of which then, as today, could by themselves uphold their imperialist interest, designs and ambition, save under the umbrella of US super power imperialism. It is a world of powers which are subordinate and look up to the USA; like hyenas they hunted behind the trail of lions and lionesses. The third world consisted of colonies and territories, countries and nations under occupation or invasion, as well as recently independent countries, the vast majority of which are located in Afrika, Asia, Caribbean, Pacific, Latin America and the Middle East. It is a world locked in multi-pronged and multi-level struggle for independence in the case of countries; for liberation, in the case of nations; and for revolution, in the case of peoples – all ultimately under-girded, shaped and driven by the global working class in all countries of the world.

Under colonialism Afrikans were kept so far away from the treachery of inner workings of colonial government and the juggling of competing foreign covetous interest at play that on assuming power at independence the bulk of Afrika's top echelons of leadership must have been shocked by what they saw and were ill-equipped to handle. Moreover, the post independence period presented an even more complex and more treacherous environment. For example, whereas the colonial governor mainly mediated competing political and business interest of one colonial power, as a result of the policy of open-door imperialism agreed upon particularly between the United States of America and the colonial powers of Europe, an Afrikan President found himself or herself at the centre of the power play of competing political and business interest of the former colonial power, as well as the competing and even hostile political and business interest of the two super powers, as well as all the intermediate imperialist powers of Europe, Canada, Australia, New Zealand and Japan, combined. The magnetic field was charged, manipulative, dirty, divisive and corrosive. In fact, while formerly accepting the independence and sovereignty of Afrikan countries, behind and not-so-behind the scenes the two super powers and the intermediate European imperialist powers and Japan looked at their new status (as newly independent countries) in international law, merely as an occasion which provided a better environment and wider opportunities for the intensified exploitation of Afrika. The ground work for this to happen had been long laid.

COLONIAL SOFTWARE AND HARDWARE TO NEGATE AFRIKAN INDEPENDENCE

The colonial software and hardware infrastructure carefully laid down, tested and certified by the colonial powers over decades to be effective and efficient instruments to lock the Afrikan continent in an imperial and parasitic relationship with the big powers was preserved and entrenched at independence, to be subsequently improved further. Key elements and subsystems of the infrastructure were: the general cross-cutting ideology and propaganda that Afrikans are innately backward and inferior to Europeans, the church and mosque to disorient people's spiritual, religious, value system, cultural coherence and cognitive autonomy, and in the process and thereafter engage and challenge them in the Western knowledge system they can never effectively be masters of; colonial education system to degrade and stunt Afrikan knowledge base and ways of knowing, so as to deny Afrikans community cognitive autonomy; colonial and foreign languages, particularly English, French and Arabic, as the official and exclusive medium of instruction in the school system, research, intellectual and academic discourse, literature, official government communication and documentation, trade and commerce, etc. Language is so critical to colonial and imperial order that in an Afrikan country nobody can rise to a position of top national leadership in the public or private sector, civil society, church or mosque without knowing and being fluent in a foreign language: English, French or Arabic. Indeed today it is common for the modern Afrikan elite at regional and international gatherings, to proudly and zealously present themselves as representatives and spokespersons of "Francophone", "Anglophone", "Lusophone" or "Arabophone" Afrika!. The software and hardware infrastructure for colonial bondage also included the following: agriculture for Afrikans to grow what they did not eat, for the colonial/imperial market, and to import what to eat; medical services and hospitals; the system of administration, the army and police, laws and the judicial system, agreements and commitments entered into by the colonial power – all these and more were inherited intact by the newly independent state. Indeed in all cases Afrikan states inherited as well citizens of the colonial power earlier recruited as civil servants to help subjugate the natives. What is more, following independence Afrika was increasingly swamped by all manner of publicly-funded and privately-funded paid-to-care "volunteers", missionaries, "experts", "advisors" and interns, covert and overt, whose objective purpose, notwithstanding the good intentions of some individual functionaries, was to spiritually, philosophically, culturally, politically, ideologically, technically and scientistically (pseudo-science) disorient the awareness of the governments and people of Afrika to the point when they become the ones who are the ideologues, implementers, supporters and defenders of white supremacism on the continent and globally. Such is the logic within which by 1990 an auxiliary software force of occupation of over 100,000 people from the **NATO** and **WARSAW PACT** military blocs roamed the breadth and length of the continent, as self-declared and self-appointed experts, advisors, volunteers, interns and friends of sorts. The consolidation and intensification of the exploitation of Afrika under open-door imperialism required an occupation force larger than was necessary under colonialism. It also required this occupation force to explore and occupy or have a presence in places, spaces and nooks not occupied under colonialism. This trend has not ebbed.

With each passing year following independence Afrika was besieged and overwhelmed by the numerous competing, corruptive and corrosive external interest, which conditioned and fueled corresponding internal interest, dissent and strife among the people. Indeed, the two super powers, together with the intermediate imperialist countries did not recognize the right of Afrikan countries, severally or together, to have a mind of their own, or to have legitimate and overriding interest on the basis of which to conduct domestic policy and external relations. As was the case for all countries of the Third World, Afrika was a theatre over which the two military blocs, NATO and WARSAW PACT, competed and rivaled for hegemony. Afrika was presumed to exist only as an estate of one of the military blocs or as contested territory. As for Afrikans, they could only be pro-East or pro-West; meaning subjects of NATO or the WARSAW PACT.

The imperialist powers were far ahead of the people, leaders and government in the preparations they made to subvert Afrikan independence. Ameripean Eurocentric confederate ethnic (Nato-Warsaw Pact) interest cloaked and couched in universalist ideologies and principles, (as if all the peoples of the world had one and the same history), particularly around issues such as science, race, society, development, progress and civilization; capitalism-socialism-communism, private-state ownership of the means of production and distribution, foreign aid, democracy, human rights, equality, modernization, etc. – was employed to wage all manner of software and hardware wars against the people, leaders, communities and government, until Afrikan states were fine-tuned into instruments compliant with the requirements of covetous and gluttonous open-door imperialism. As had been the case under colonialism the Afrikan state continued to be an instrument to pursue and secure an undemocratic agenda. Such state could not stand by or with the people to defend the highest common social good. In what strategically mattered, it instead stood with foreign powers, and by diktat, deceit, duplicity and cunning, preyed on the people. It was impossible for Afrikan countries and peoples to realize their dreams: participatory and democratic governance was out of the question; national unity was tenuous under dictatorship and repression; without participatory democratic governance and national unity, the people, directly and through their leaders and government, could not assert their national independence; while broad-based social progress was smothered by the imperial and parasitic relationship between Afrika and the big powers. The ensuing struggles and uncertainties generated across the continent instability, repression, wars and proxy wars. Military coup d'etats and assassinations became the standard method of changing leaders and regimes; for example in Nigeria, Congo, Burundi, Ghana, Uganda and Ethiopia.

DEBATE, DISSENSION AND RADICALIZATION OF POLITICS

The nipping in the budd of Afrikan independence in the 1960s and 1970s under open-door imperialism generated considerable debate on the continent in which the author participated while at high school and at university. In the author's circles and magnetic field, initially three fault lines were manifest:

- Those who believed that the colonial state was essentially good, but run badly by colonialists because they discriminated against black people on the basis of race; this was the change of guard maintenance school.
- The second school held that the colonial state had serious impediments which required some major reforms to bring it into line with Afrikan values and principles; this was the reformative school.

- The third school of thought contended that independence should pave the way for Afrikans to revert to their values, philosophy of life and indigenous governance, which had been usurped and degraded by colonialism; this was the restorative school.

As the situation deteriorated the debate was radicalized and globalized around the ideology of the West that is Nato-capitalism; and that of the East, Soviet socialism-communism. The radicalized school of thought argued that Afrikan independence was compromised by continuing to work closely with the West, who had built their power base on slave trade and slavery, colonialism, outright genocide and massive theft of land globally: particularly the entire continent of North, Central and South America, Afrika, Australia, New Zealand, the Caribbean, etc. It is a power whose future well-being and prosperity could only be assured on the same foundation. This school of thought contended therefore, that it was naïve to imagine the West could easily surrender its advantage and leverage in Afrika. In the circumstances the way forward lay in embracing the East that is the Soviet ideology of socialism/communism, which was the twin anti-dote to capitalism and imperialism. It was a powerful argument for those with a free mind insistent on an Afrikan self-determined Black Nation. Within countries socialism promised an end to one class (tiny minority) exploiting the rest (vast majority), and between countries socialism promised an end of one country or set of countries (a handful of them) exploiting the rest. Globally socialism promised the proceeds of socialized labour would be equitably available to all: from each according to their ability, and to each according to their need.

The radicalization of politics was global, as it embraced all the newly independent countries in Afrika, Asia, the Caribbean, the Pacific, as well as Latin America's nominally long-standing independent countries. The NATO countries exerted all the carrot-stick pressure they could to dissuade third world countries from aligning themselves with the Soviet Union or the ideology of socialism-communism. What third world countries really wanted was self-determination. In time there emerged the Non-Aligned Movement of countries which sought space, elbow room and leverage between the two super powers and their respective power blocs, to advance their interest and agenda. Afrikan countries joined the Non-Aligned Movement. Their participation in the articulation, establishment and running of the affairs of the Non-Aligned Movement seems to have strengthened many Afrikan leaders' resolve to be independent of the hegemonic power blocs. In pursuance of this the socialist school of thought coalesced in Ghana and Tanzania in what came to be called "Afrikan Socialism". In Tanzania the ideologues of Afrikan Socialism submitted that it was under-girded and under-pinned by **"Ujamaa"**, the community and communal-based Afrikan cooperative spirit of brotherhood-sisterhood, empathy, caring, sharing, justice, mutual support and reciprocity.

Around mid-1960s from the author's vantage point, two broad ideological schools contended on the Afrikan continent:

The Afrikan socialist school of thought lead by Kwame Nkrumah of Ghana and Nyerere of Tanzania, with two tendencies: towards Afrikan values and culture; and towards Marxism-Leninism. There was all manner of talk about "socialism", "scientific socialism", Marxism-Leninism, Maoism, etc.

The second school of thought did not want to rock the boat too much. For example, Tom Mboya of Kenya used to argue that Afrika was too poor to be socialist. For that reason therefore, it was prudent to keep close to the imperialist powers, learn from them the science and art of accumulation, accumulate wealth, and after there is enough for all, become Afrikan socialists when there will be enough to distribute.

By the turn of the 1960s two ideologies dominated the continent, Afrikan Socialism which found different expressions and forms in Ghana under Kwame Nkrumah, Tanzania under Nyerere, Zambia under Kaunda and Uganda under Obote on the one hand, and on the other capitalist enterprise with a warm and positive attitude to the USA and the former colonial powers of Europe, for example Kenya, Congo, Nigeria. The two ideologies drew from the same Eurocentric text, and together they shunted into oblivion the Afrikan school of thought which advocated a return to Afrikan values, ideas and institutions of governance, culture and language. These were presumed by the two schools to be "backward" and "primitive". The socialist school of thought helped in the popularization of the categorization of people into "progressive" and "reactionary" or "feudalist"; with the ultimate prize reserved for the Maoist, particularly defined by embracing Mao Tse Tung's theory of three words.

The author participated in some of Afrika's ideological struggles and some of the corresponding action during the 1960s while at high school and the early 1970s while at university; always as part of the "radical", "leftist", "progressive" or "revolutionary" school. At high school and at university many students believed they were destined to change the world for the better. After we started to work the struggle certainly continued, although it required of a former student to virtually reinvent himself/herself to maintain some viable revolutionary content. The situation continued to deteriorate as the IMF/World Bank-led attack on the people intensified to grab even more of their land, labour, natural resources, values, language and culture. In the ensuing further reflection on the Afrikan problematique, many Afrikan leaders were puzzled as to why Afrikan countries were not holding against the imperialist powers. There emerged particularly among the progressive forces the idea that the Afrikan revolution was stunted by the early granting of independence on a sliver platter, before the purification and hardening of independence movement and leadership, such that at independence there was no adequate ideological clarity, camaraderie between and among the leadership, or hardened, robust revolutionary institutional framework to fire the task of transforming formal independence into a self-determined Afrikan Black Nation in fact. According to this view, what Afrika needed, and was missing, was the baptism of fire by way of a people's protracted warfare. This view became so strong in radical, socialist and Marxist-Leninist inspired circles that it became folklore within and among these circles that without holding a gun and waging war, one could not be a revolutionary! One ready example where a people's protracted war had internally delivered and sustained revolutionary change, and externally acquired the capacity and ability to stand up to imperialism, was the People's Republic of China; moreover, who subsequently supported the anti-imperialist struggle worldwide.

The idea of the centrality of force of arms to liberation and revolution at one time was so widespread that it was vulgarized; to the point that every armed soldier who took up a gun over people's heads to entrench open-door imperialism announced they had carried out a revolution. Indeed it was this logic which informed Jerry Rawlings of Ghana following a military coup d'etat he led in 1979 when he lined up all former heads of state and had them executed by firing squad, including Afrifa, Ankrah, Acheopong and Akufor.

PRO-WEST, PRO-EAST OR NON-ALIGNED AFRIKA REMAINED DOOMED!

During the 1960s and 1970s Afrika worked very hard on the euro-centric development project. Yet by mid 1980s it did not matter what path an Afrikan country had taken; "pro-West", "pro-East" or "non-aligned", "capitalist" or "socialist", whether independence was attained on a "silver platter" or by way of armed struggle (e.g. Kenya, Mozambiuque, Angola, Algeria), all found themselves in a dramatic economic melt-down – a melt-down so dire even the United Nations Organization convened its Special General Assembly in 1986 to address what was officially themed to be "The Critical Economic and Social Situation in Afrika". This was the time, for example, a senior professor at Uganda's prestigious Makerere University earned a monthly "wage of death" of $10, and the Vice-Chancellor $25.

Events moved really fast a few years later when in 1989 the Berlin Wall suddenly fell, and the Soviet bloc subsequently and quickly collapsed and the Soviet Union disintegrated. At a time when Afrika writhed in the pain of an accentuated economic, social and cultural melt-down, the West, led by the USA, euphor-ically announced that capitalism (imperialism) had triumphed over socialism (socio-imperialism), and that in the process capitalism had proved itself to be the qualitatively superior and natural system ordained by God, with the US Presidents as the High Priest, to which there was no alternative, remedy or relief. A new world order started to emerge, whose defining moment was the inheritance of the mantle of the Soviet Union by white Russia, that is the Russian republic, which was ethnically close to Western Europe, consummated by Russia's willingness to cooperate with NATO. The cooperation between white Russia and NATO, and the subsequent search by imperialism and socio-imperialism of a "common European home" exposed the underlying yearning for ethnic unity between the two, over which they projected and put to the fore supposedly opposing universalist theories, ideas, principles and ideals; the latest formulations coalescing into,, for example, "war on terror", "pre-emptive" strike, "humanitarian" intervention, "protection of civilian populations". These developments triggered the world's major peoples and their polities, except the Afrikans, to go back to the drawing board, to read and size up the emerging new world order, and to strategize how to position themselves with advantage and leverage.

THE TURNING POINT

As a native of the land astride the Nile, at its source on the shores of Nalubaale (Lake Victoria), throughout the 1970s the author wrestled with the menace visited on this beautiful land by dictator General Idi Amin. In the ensuing community-based people's struggle against military rule, two schools of thought emerged: one contended that the struggle was essentially military, to be led by armed fighters, supported by civilians as the mouthpiece

of the fighters to announce the exploits of the fighters, do diplomatic work, and mobilize financial and non-financial resources
to support the war effort, as well as a "strong" leader. The second
school of thought, to whom the author belonged, submitted
that the struggle against Idd Amin's military junta was essentially political and civilian. It required political unity among the
people, with an institutional framework through which they
would pursue the goal of national unity, democratic governance
where the military was subordinate to civilian political authority
and leadership, national independence, and generally create an
environment in which social progress for all would be pursued.
This school of thought argued further that Idd Amin was not a
problem on account of being a "weak" leader but, on the contrally,
for being "too strong". The point therefore was not a governance
system which concentrated power in the hands of one leader or a
handful of them, but rather a system which diffused power among
the people.

As the two schools took root, each came to derogatively refer
to the other: those who advocated the primacy of fighters were
referred to as "militarists"; while the "militarists" referred to those
who advocated for the subordination of the military to civilian
leadership and authority, "brief-case" or "armchair"-politicians/ or
"revolutionaries". In the meantime, Idd Amin's military machine
was such that none of the several militarist factions which prolif-
erated, each by itself, could dislodge it; yet the ideology of "power
to the fighters" was not strong enough to either unite the fighters under one command or to have persuaded them into a coordinated command. When the two leading fighting forces under
Milton Obote and Yoweri Museveni attempted to unite they failed

because Museveni's much numerically smaller force wanted unity on a 50-50 basis of equality of "strength", which was rejected by Obote, who preferred weighted unity, determined by the number of men under arms one had. In the end it took the arm-chair revolutionaries to provide the framework for all political organizations opposed to the dictatorship of Idd Amin to unite on the basis of equality. Some seven fighters in their respective political organizations were constituted into a Military Commission as a sub-committee to carry out its mandate under the authority and direction of the civilian National Executive Committee. The historical moment was such that the fighters had no alternative but to accept this arrangement, although they did so under protest. And so the Uganda National Liberation Front was born in 1978 and thereafter quickly threw Idd Amin out of power, and established a government of national unity.

The militarists never accepted to work under civilian authority, and looked for every opportunity to subvert it. They found in the Military Commission a convenient base and instrument. In a coordinated move the militarists degraded the Military Commission into a Military junta, and, like Amin before them, by force of arms overthrew the UNLF government, and claimed to be exercising the powers and authority of the UNLF and its government! Upon which the school of thought which advocated for "power to the people", established the Uganda National Liberation Front-Anti-Dictatorship, UNLF-AD, to dislodge the new military dictators. The UNLF-AD established several bases around the country, out of which it conducted political work among the population, recruited, trained cadres and, eventually, following the raising and manifestation of a good threshold of general political awareness, together with the emergence of a critical mass of political leadership, raised an army under civilian authority and leadership. In the meantime, the Museveni-Obote militarists who had acted together to overthrow the UNLF civilian authority could not hold together. Theirs was a fighters' marriage of convenience against the common enemy of being held accountable to civilian authority, to create a new environment in which each faction expected to overthrow the other. In the event, the bigger Obote faction outsmarted the Museveni faction in an election the two rigged the people of Uganda out of power. Museveni, and a variety of aggrieved militarist factions, took up arms to fight Obote, and before long UNLF-AD, representing those who believed in the dictum of "power to the people", found herself in the population contending for state power. In the event, Museveni's National Resistance Army, NRA, to which a "Movement" of subordinate civilians was appended, for purposes of public relations and legitimacy, badly wanted power for himself. In 1980 he teamed up with Obote to carry out a military coup d'etat, to enhance his leverage to later capture power from Obote. As personal ambition for material security, power and pomp can co-exist with imperialism, in fact, are best achieved under imperialism, it was common talk in the NRA leadership that what stood between them and victory over the Obote regime were guns, for which they would readily and happily do a deal with anybody, including the devil. In the end the devil presented himself in the form of Col. Muama Gaddafi of Libya and Tiny Roland, member of the British ruling class who has made a fortune out of his wide business interest in Afrika. Between them these two provided the guns and other logistics, including financial and non-financial

resources, diplomatic support, etc. which was critical in catapult-
ing Museveni and his army into power in 1986, following a five-
year stint of bush war.

AFRIKAN ELITE, GO HOME: YOU CANNOT LEAD PEOPLE OUTSIDE THEIR KNOWLEDGE!

The victory of the militarists ahead of the "arm-chair revolutionaries", sometimes referred to as "purists", occasioned deep reflection and analysis within the UNLF-AD. The militarists emphasized the primacy of the gun, the disciplined armed fighter with
the courage to fight "the enemy". With "enough guns" in place,
all that was required of the civilian population was logistics and
supplies, support and protection, for the fighters to deliver revolution or to liberate the people. In war the fighters are not subject to
civilian authority, and after victory they rule because they fought,
and the civilians continue to be subordinate to them, because they
did not fight, and have no guns. On the other hand, the "purists"
emphasize the centrality of people to build a civilian force of free
spirit, love for land, country and people-in-self-management, who
may raise an army under their authority and leadership, to be an
instrument at people's command and direction to achieve their
agenda. Thus in struggle for state power and in the exercise of state
power the people are in charge; they are not liberated but liberate
themselves. In this case revolution is not done on the people or
for them, but is the result of the fire they light inside themselves,
which then from the inside glows on the outside.

The question of why the people of Uganda, like the bibli-
cal Jews before them during the days of Pontius Pilate, chose
Barnabas, in this case, Museveni, over Jesus, was exhaustively

discussed at the time. Of interest here is the fact that the militarists were doomed to fail because their victory was predicated on a deal with the devil. Yet even if the arm-chair revolutionaries had succeeded entirely on the people's steam, sooner or later they too would have failed. The bottom line was that both Museveni's NRA and Nabudere's UNLF-AD received their inspiration from the same pool of Eurocentric social-democratic, radical tradition and Marxist-Leninist textbook. Leaders of both organizations were western-educated, and consequently variously distanced from the people on key issues, which mattered in their depth and complexity; including Afrikan spirituality, language, culture, narrative on ontology, history, the origin of God, spirit, matter, the universe; the origin and purpose of living things, including Man/Woman and his/her future, the nature of Afrikan thought and scholarship. At the UNLF-AD we came to the conclusion that as part of the Afrikan elite, the leadership was materially distanced from and misaligned `with the vast majority of Afrikan peoples who had not been touched and disoriented by the Arabo-Western knowledge, ways of knowing, philosophy, science and religiosity. We speak of men and women who do not speak, understand or think in the hard currency languages and Arabic. For that reason therefore, since Eurocentric social democratic liberal ideas, radical tradition, Marxism-Leninism, neo-liberalism, scientific method, philosophy and science, which inevitably inspire and provide considerable content and form of the Afrikan elite's social revolutionary thinking and practice, it follows that to such degree, he or she does not have what it takes for their words to translate into a phenomenon of mass engagement, and therefore mass action, the only basis for social transformation. For that reason therefore, it was decided to dissolve the UNLF-AD, to allow the members to go back to the people, learn from them, root amongst them, and as members learn anew, they will converge again sometime in the future, such that in the event there will emerge a critical quantum of people's knowledge, energy and inspiration, a new organization based on people's ideas, spirituality, philosophy, science and technology, education, governance, etc. will emerge from the people's bosom, complete with leaders who will have organically issued from the people's brain, brow and struggles.

THE CITIZEN THINK TANK ON THE AFRIKAN PROBLEMATIQUE: FRESH INSIGHTS

To locate ways back to the people, the author used an Afrikan Citizens Think Tank on the Afrikan problematique, to act as a compass to help indicate the ways back and forward to the people. The timing turned out to be perfect as it overlapped with the collapse of the Soviet bloc and disintegration of the Soviet Union, which ushered in a uni-polar hegemonic geo-political world order, dominated by a lone super-power, the USA, with unprecedented opportunities and temptations to degenerate into a super rogue power. The author was lucky to have been at a vantage position, with the connections and capacity to constitute and convene an Afrika-wide think tank. It brought together men and women from West, East, Central and Southern Afrika. They belonged to a multiplicity of political and ideological backgrounds and persuasions, but were united in their belief in the Afrikan's capacity to determine their destiny in the post-cold war era. In a series of think tanks between 1990 and 1993 the Afrikan Citizens' think tank interrogated the Afrikan predicament. In the process three interlocking strategic questions emerged, around which the strategic reflection and planning revolved.

- Why is it that Afrikans are probably the only people in the world who, in whatever land they find themselves, are the most oppressed lot; even in their Motherland Ancestral Continent, Afrika?

- Moreover, why is it that whatever they try to do to liberate them, never sustainably adds up?

- Is there a missing link to Afrikan development, one that, if found, would be the master key to open doors to a New Afrika of peace, harmony, unity, self-reliance, social progress and international solidarity? The sort of key which when systematically employed would earn Afrika a place of honour and note among the commonwealth of peoples of the world.

STRATEGIC FINDINGS ON WHY AFRIKA LAGS BEHIND

The core finding as to why the realization of Afrika as a self-determined Black Nation has been elusive was centred on what the Think Tank considered a stark truth; that intellectual self-determination and autonomy is the Mother of the entirety of a people's viabilities and sovereignty. For that reason therefore, a people can only be a self-determined, self-reliant and internally self-propelled nation on the basis of their own home-grown knowledge base, rooted in their spirituality, ontology, land, history, culture, language, philosophy, scientific thought, epistemology and ways of knowing. It is equally critical to have the means (education system) to maintain, deepen, renew and extend the frontiers of that knowledge, as the active, operational, practical living guide to that people in reading the word and world and, with advantage, locating themselves therein. On the basis of what they already know, internally people learn from, with and among them, as well as externally make sense of other people's knowledge, digest aspects of it until those aspects are transformed and absorbed, so as to peculiarly become part and parcel of the recipient people's knowledge, to enrich that particular knowledge. The act of knowledge creation is nurtured and driven by community cognitive autonomy. It is charged, enhanced, developed and transformed in the course of creating knowledge over millennial time and space.

Afrika's strategic undoing therefore, has been to have been stampeded into or somehow believing that by abandoning the Afrikan knowledge base and jumping onto the bandwagon of the white man's knowledge, this particular knowledge can as well do wonders for black people, even to the point of helping them to "catch up" with and to "be like" them, the Ameripeans. This is why it cannot work out for Afrikans:

- The white man's knowledge is tailor-made, for their own benefit and prosperity, in fact, as a rule, at the expense of black and non-white peoples. It is the personal to holder tool white people have historically developed, massaged, cloaked and couched such that it is in the overall interest of its authors. White people use the instrumentality of their knowledge to locate themselves in the universe, and to position themselves so as to effectively cooperate, compete and rival with the other peoples of the world, and whenever possible surpass and dominate them.

- The whiteman's knowledge is fully available to native whites who have grown up from the inside of white culture.

As a category, outsiders get only bits and pieces of necessarily culturally coded knowledge. On balance what outsiders are able to acquire is inadequate for them to excel or to be competitive so as to be equal with, let alone surpass the owners. Just as at the English language level a variety of outsiders manage with a variety of pidgin English, to become pidgin English speakers; even at the scholarly level in this language they perform at different levels and quality of pidgin scholarship, and therefore fall in the category of pidgin scholars, unable to be part of the cutting edge in the creation of new frontiers knowledge in the English language. Similarly the universities run by Afrikan scholars across Afrika are pidgin universities operating under Ameripean franchise, to produce graduates presumed to be inferior to the products of the mother university in Europe, North America, Australia and New Zealand.

- English, French and Arabic, the main languages culturally conquered and subdued Afrikan scholars work in, bring out full meaning in the context of the speech community owner's internally shared history, value system, worldview, epistemology, prejudices, mythology and myths, psychology and psyche – all of which will be beyond the reach and full grasp of the ordinary and not so ordinary Afrikan scholar who typically grew up on outside of the culture of the native language speakers. For that reason therefore, an Afrikan scholar in English works laboriously, to the detriment of the full bloom of his and her cognitive and creative faculties. Mercifully, in oblivion most scholars work with this impediment; and are therefore able each day to face the world with a sense of pride, accomplishment and honour.

The genius of Afrikan peoples, like that of any other people, is grounded and locked in their mother tongue. In the public, mass and community domain therefore, development or modernization is about a people accessing and unleashing their own and their community's inner energy, creativity and genius. Since Afrikans cannot access their own genius through the medium of English, French or Arabic, the missing link in Afrika's development endeavours is mother tongue education, from kindergarten to post-doctoral.

Indeed, it must be for this reason that history has no examples of a people who achieved internally self-propelling and sustainable levels of development in science, technology and literature, while using a foreign language as the medium of education, research and official Government communication. It is much worse if the said foreign language is also the language of a colonial-neocolonial power. Even today countries outside hegemonic Europe and North America which have something to show for their development effort are the ones which also officially take their culture seriously, and use their own language, a language not alien to the masses of the people, as the medium of education, research and official Government communication. Examples include China, Japan, The Two Koreas, Iran, Thailand and Malaysia.

THE EMERGENCE OF MPAMBO AFRIKAN MULTIVERSITY

On the basis of its core findings the Citizen Think Tank resolved to establish Mpambo Afrikan Multiversity as a centre for Afrikan mother tongue higher learning, based on the community and centred on men and women embedded therein, and are considered by their community and peers to be compelling experts in their areas of expertise and interest. At the Multiversity these men and women constitute the engine to energize the batteries of Afrikan community cognitive autonomy and security, as they power a new chain of knowledge creation and transfer: from the people, to mother tongue scholars, and back to the people again. The point about Mpambo is to raise a critical mass of world class mother tongue scientists, philosophers and scholars engaged in the generation of an own knowledge base, to fire and nourish the intellectual self-determination of Afrikan communities. It is a new knowledge chain in the sense that knowledge is not merely created close to its consumers and beneficiaries, the people, but in the very bosom of the community, spearheaded by exceptionally talented and skilled compelling experts who have emerged out of peoples struggles to be and to become their best, on the basis of their potential. The line between community and the Multiversity is blurred because knowledge belongs to people, is with people, comes from people to their own experts, and goes back to people for validation. In reality therefore, Mpambo Afrikan Multiversity are the people.

The Multiversity is based on the proposition that the peoples of the world and their knowledges, cultures, languages and epistemologies are horizontally ordered, such that each of the knowledge is valid in itself. Each of these knowledges deserves some ample space and resources to be advanced to its farthest frontiers, as well as to be enriched by, as it itself enriches, other knowledges, through cross-fertilization. Conceptualized that way, the Multiversity contrasts with the University. In Afrika's experience, the **UNIversity** is based on the claim of the vertical ordering of the peoples of the world, their knowledges, cultures and languages, such that Western knowledge, culture and languages are presumed to be superior to all other peoples. The University then, as a colonial-neo-colonial design, is an ideological outpost for "Bantu education", to advance the all-round supremacy of the white man, and the inferiorization and eclipse of the bearers of Afrikan thought, scientific knowledge, philosophy, spirituality, worldview, etc; that is particularly the knowledge Afrikans have developed over millennia, as a self-determined Black Nation. The disemboweling of the Afrikan scholar of their solid millennial knowledge assets, including thought, spirituality, philosophy, science, etc. cripples them, such that they cannot stand on the shoulders of their own greats. An Afrikan University therefore, typically raises scholars without a foundation or base, and therefore typically incapacitated to master much outside their own disempowered circles.

BACK TO THE PEOPLE: WHY IS CULTURAL UNITY HIGHER THAN POLITICAL?

Mpambo Afrikan Multiversity was conceived as a polycentric institution of higher learning, with multiple campuses, nodes and spaces on the Afrikan continent and globally which, in time would coalesce into an Association of The Afrikan Multiversity. The author had the responsibility to establish the Multiversity's first campus at the Source of the Nile in Uganda, to seed Mpambo the idea into Mpambo the praxis.

Until the Afrikan Citizen Think Tank of 1990 – 1993, the author shared the view that Afrika would redeem herself through the agency of the primacy of euro-centric politics; particularly the radical tradition of people's protracted war, as the extension of politics by other ways. Kwame Nkrumah had a dictum on this which admonished Afrikans in struggle to "seek ye first the political kingdom, and everything else shall be added unto it". It was politics within the Western modernization development paradigm. According to this paradigm the world was divided into two: the "advanced", "civilized" wealthy white world of Europe and annexed North America, Australia, New Zealand, which the author has called The Confederate Ameripean Republic, on the one hand, and the rest, "backward" and "poor". It is asserted that the backward countries are weighed down and back by their backward culture, languages, beliefs and ways; and somehow it is the responsibility of the white world to salvage the rest of the world, by walking its peoples the modernization path. This somehow entails the advanced teaching the rest, particularly the Afrikans, to abhor and abandon their backward knowledge, culture, languages and ways, considered to be mortal impediments to progress; and instead love and adopt the white man's "superior" knowledge, culture, languages, philosophy and ways, the "self-evident" engine to progress.

Until the break-up and disintegration of the Soviet bloc and Union, two options existed for backward peoples: either to be mentored by and therefore be like the Ameripean capitalist republic, or to be mentored by and therefore be like the Union of Soviet Socialist Republics.

More than anywhere else, the modernization development project failed in Afrika for several reasons:

- Far too many Afrikans expected far too much out of an

alien project designed to subvert, dismantle, subjugate and disposes them.

- Afrika was the last continent to be colonized, at the close of the 19th century. The European imperial powers approached the continent with the most lethal colonial weapons and tools, which for hundreds of years they had tested in far flung places, for example Scotland, Ireland, North, Central and South America, the Caribbean islands, India, Indonesia, China, Australia, New Zealand.

- The people were fragmented and weakened as minor and significant differences among them were exaggerated, and where none existed they were manufactured, and all raised to the level of antagonistic contradictions.

- Islam and Christianity were an essential part of the modernization project on Afrika. These two religions have been used to bring new divides among Afrikans; the followers of Jesus Christ and the followers of Mohammed. Yet even if all Afrikan peoples were to decide to follow Jesus Christ, they would not find unity under him, since, as a rule, he is introduced and presented in terms of vested interest groups locked in unending wars. Similarly, Afrikans cannot strike unity in all following Mohammed! [It should be remembered that fighting for God, that is religious wars, is strange in Afrika. According to Afrikan spirituality it is an entrenched belief that God simultaneously revealed Himself/Herself to all peoples of the world, and commanded them to worship Him/Her, each in their own languages and culture.]

- At the neo-colonial stage, political parties became an

essential element in the modernization package. More often than not they too fragment and exasperate sterile differences among the people, and therefore help to weaken them further.

- The bottom line of imperialism is to exponentially take people's land and sweat, as well as corrupt their awareness, and therefore repress them – all of which cannot be the basis for unity.

- At critical mass level, Afrikan leaders over generations have either not adequately understood, or in the alternative, they have feared to understand the system that enslaves their people, and therefore instead of leading them into liberation, they help hold them in servitude; a clear challenge to the people to raise their own leaders, from amongst themselves.

During the course of the Citizen Think Tank (1990 – 1993) the author came round to solidly be part of the school of thought which held that the primacy of politics as the vehicle to pursue national liberation and Pan Afrikan unity had failed mainly because Afrikan leaders lead compromised and in double jeopardy. They presided over an alien system systemically designed to enslave Afrikans, but one they did not understand. At the same time these leaders were culturally deficit in their own peoples' culture, and run a system which was the master's cultural expression and in the master's language he was as well shallow in. In such circumstances the typical Afrikan leader is a small alienated minority, fearful of the people whose overall interest he undermines, and leaning towards the Ameripean master, who looks down upon her and him as a tool to be used against their own people for a small rental fee. In the light of this we opted for Afrikan culture to be the basis of Afrikan peoples' unity-in-struggle to galvanize their quest for self-determination, pan Afrikan unity and solidarity.

By Afrikan culture we refer to the collective harmonious survival plan which Afrikans have developed over millennia; in fact, since the time of their creation at The Source of the Nile. This collective harmonious survival plan is recorded and captured in the Afrikan ontology and worldview, the Afrikan narrative on the origins of God, Spirit, matter, universe, living things, man and woman, purpose on earth and future; governance, voice, the word and language, peoples, nation and country; people-to-people relationships, relationships between the living, ancestors, and the yet to be born; the concept of people as the totality and unity of the living, the dead and the yet to be born, and the relationship of this totality and unity with their Creator, as well as with nature. The collective harmonious survival plan is as well recorded in the history of Afrikan peoples: the road they have walked since their creation in the sacred hills of Walusi, at the Source of the Nile, accomplishments, challenges and failure; finished, interrupted, on-going and work yet to be done; with whom have Afrikans walked, who have been their competitors and rivals, and who have not wished them any good?

When Afrikan culture becomes the basis of praxis for self-determination, leadership migrates. It migrates from an English-French-Arabic-spitting alienated elite, raised and nourished on the Bible and Qoran, Descartes, Plato, Hobbes, Locke, Rousseau, Hume, Kant, Marx, Hitler, Churchill, Roosevelt, Kennedy, De Gaulle, Thatcher, Blair, Putin, Bush, Obama, etc. to fight the white man's war on the Afrikan Black Nation; and settles on community-based organic mother tongue intellectuals, researchers and scholars who have acquired their knowledge and skills in the Afrikan indigenous learning system. These scholars are the direct descendants and heirs to Afrika's great scholars, authors of and contributors to Afrika's enduring theoretical and applied civilizational achievements in spirituality, science, philosophy, social organization and governance – including the ancient Egyptian high technical civilization.

On re-location to Uganda to found the first chapter of Mpambo Afrikan Multiversity at the Source of The Nile, the author was amazed by what he found on the ground. There was an elaborate nation-wide network of patriotic men and women who had participated in the struggle for independence, but were later disillusioned and "quit politics" after they were outsmarted by those leaders who chose to be agents of the colonial powers, instead of standing with the people for the highest common social good. Many of these leaders were sidelined because while in the struggle for independence they were formidable mobilizers without whom independence would have been impossible, thereafter there was no role for them in the running of independent Uganda because they were "uneducated". The best example of this category of leaders was Igaga Waiswa Kisambira. He attended a special high school set up by colonialists to raise junior native functionaries to service the colonial administration. In 1945 – 1946 he received specialized training in Dar es Salaam as a postal clerk. On return to Uganda he worked for only two years, upon which he resigned, to work as a full-time activist for independence, and secretary to the Chiefs and heads of Clans of the Kingdom of Busoga, at the Source of the Nile. He was as well a member of the Uganda National Congress, a political party. After his political party abandoned the people's line soon after independence, Igaga Kisambira channeled his political energies through the cooperative movement, a grassroots organization. After government policy weakened the cooperative movement in the 1970s, Kisambira migrated to the church, where he became head of the laity. While in church he spearheaded rebellion against the autocracy of his Diocesan Bishop, until reforms were effected to remove the incumbent and to make diocesan governance more participatory and accountable. By mid-1980s Igaga Kisambira migrated to the Council of Heads of Clans of Busoga Kingdom which had been shunted into oblivion by the military dictatorship of Milton Obote and General Idd Amin. By mid 1990s Kisambira had built the Council of Heads of Clans into a formidable social force which lobbied for and secured the restoration of the Kyabazinga (King) of Busoga in 1996. As Head of Heads of Clans of Busoga Kisambira developed an indigenous governance model which empowers the people of Busoga to run their affairs directly, through their families, through their clans, severally and collectively, as well as through their king.

By the end of the 1990s Igaga Kisambira had distinguished himself to be a compelling expert without equal on Lusoga (the language of Busoga Kingdom), the history, spirituality, governance, culture, literature and politics of Busoga Kingdom, in fact he was Busoga's greatest thinker, philosopher and prophet of the 20th century. The accelerated gestation decades of the 1970s and 1980s which birthed Igaga Kisambira the Great of Busoga, were generalized across Uganda and Afrika-wide. These conditions birthed multiple community-based compelling experts in a multiplicity of disciplines and areas of human endeavour in Uganda's communities. Visible compelling community-based, organic mother tongue experts, intellectuals, thinkers and scholars emerged across Uganda, particularly in the areas of indigenous governance, medicine and healing, spirituality, philosophy, engineering, history, language, astronomy, food and nutrition, entrepreneurship, etc. It was as if to prepare the ground to receive Mpambo Afrikan Multiversity. Indeed the Clans Council of Busoga provided the first home and base of the Multiversity from where it spread to the other parts of the host country, Uganda.

Slowly by slowly and step by step Mpambo Afrikan Multiversity inched into the fraternity of indigenous scholars; men and women who acquired their knowledge outside the Western formal education system, are anchored in the Afrikan worldview, do not speak or think in the colonial hard currency languages. Men and women who know as matter of fact that as a people, Afrikans are second to none, hold the view that it is by fraud, deceit, duplicity, hypocrisy and force that Europeans and Arabs have a stranglehold on Afrika; but that truth has no end, while lies have an end, and therefore Afrika shall be free! In time the author discovered that beneath the nose of the Western education and knowledge system there exists an Afrikan peoples knowledge system, the one which informed the ancient classical Egyptian high technical civilization, which in turn fed into its origins and source, at The Source of The Nile. It is the Afrikan knowledge system which is amazingly well and kicking, at the Source of the Nile, and operates through decentralized centres of excellence and knowledge transfer. Scholars and researchers in these spaces of specialized learning may not have formal ranks, but within their fraternity they have an informal protocol by which they recognize seniority among themselves, as and when the need arises. Amidst all this, it is intriguing that many a Western-trained Afrikan will go through the education system, enter the world of work, and rise to the very top of their career in their respective areas of training, as teachers, including at university, as engineers, human doctors, etc., without knowing that there exists a parallel system of knowledge in their midst. When opportunities come up to engage with this age-old knowledge, the Western-trained elite is typically impeded by the Western-inspired prejudice against this knowledge, characterizing it as "witchcraft", "folklore", "unscientific", etc.

The Game Changer: Spirituality, the Highest Level of Awareness and Unity

On engagement with the fraternity of the direct descendants to Afrika's greatest pool of scholars of all time, the author observed two broad categories: scholars who distinguished themselves on the basis of using their human intellect, reason and logic to master a significant body of knowledge in an area of their specialization or interest, on the one hand, and on the other, compelling experts who, in addition to having mastered what human intellect, reason and logic could allow, were exposed to the spiritual dimension of knowledge and understanding, direct from the Creator, the Seven component Spirits who Constitute the Creator or ancestors with qualitatively greater access to knowledge and understanding. By under-girding and supplementing their intellect with the qualitative amplification of insight which comes with being plugged into the spiritual sources of God's knowledge, and the knowledge of ancestor greats, the latter category of scholars stand head and shoulder above the rest. In fact, at the Source of the Nile the spirituality-inspired scholars are a game changer in Afrikan indigenous scholarships.

During the course of listening to and engaging with Mpambo philosophy over the years, step by step, consistent with mutual confidence and trust, community-based organic mother tongue scholars, led by the spiritually-inspired, pronounced themselves on the Multiversity as an initiative of Western-trained Afrikans in search of their roots, upon having hit a dead end with the white man's adventure. To begin with the mother tongue scholars told us of a prophesy, well-known in their circles, according to which the white man's knowledge expired and came to an end on 24th of May 1966; which marks the first day of the first month of the first year of the Afrikan Calendar of **Mulembe Mutinzi (MM)**; i.e. the Bridging Epoch or the Epoch of reaching out to other Peoples and Nations of Goodwill. 2016 will mark the 50th year of the Afrikan Calendar. It is only by sheer inertia of an expired regime that the world is still under the sway of the Western paradigm. In 1972 there was another prophecy. This one said that the time when Afrikan children who had been lost to the white man through interlocking mechanisms of education, materialism and lifestyle, exile, etc. start coming back to their community and people in search of their roots, know ye that victory is in sight. It will be so because all along it is the Western-trained elite who have been the key stumbling block in the Afrikan peoples' efforts to liberate themselves.

Continuing their critique on Mpambo philosophy, while also broadening and deepening it, the mother tongue scholars submitted that while culture represented a deeper level of awareness than politics, it was not the deepest. The deepest level of awareness was spiritual; and they substantiated: the core and essence of reality is spirit; in the beginning there was spirit, free spirit and the body came later as a transient housing for the spirit; in reality real life is influenced more by what cannot be seen, felt, touched, smelt, heard, etc.; what humans can see, touch, etc. is only a tiny percentage of the word of living things.

Of all the critiques of the mother tongue scholars there is one which cannot be overlooked. To quote a senior mother tongue researcher and eminent scholar of Afrikan Spirituality at Mpambo Afrikan Multiversity, Kiwanuka Kijjo, "The enduring problem with the Western-trained elite is always to imagine and to be obsessed by the idea that Afrikans cannot have their own valid and viable knowledge without reference to or stamp of approval from the white man".

Upon Nourishment at The Source of The Nile: Towards a Manifesto of the Afrikan Black Nation

During the course of the Afrikan Citizen Thin Tank (1990 – 1993) and subsequently, increasingly many Western-trained elites came to the conclusion which Afrikan mother tongue intellectuals and scholars had known since the 1960s, that: neither the Western, nor any other people's paradigm could possibly be the basis for Afrikans to liberate themselves; what is more the Western knowledge paradigm had reached a dead end, such that it now constituted a strategic threat to all peoples of the world, including those in the Confederate Ameripean Republic. It was in this context that Mpambo took root at the Source of the Nile. In the process the Afrikan problematique has continued to be refined and appreciated. Out of continued cooperative intellectual labours and labours of praxis, a Manifesto of the Afrikan Black Nation is emerging with the following as some of the highlights:

- Preciously far too many Afrikans unquestioningly work and give their lives in the service of institutions which are toxic to the interest of Afrikan peoples as a self-determined Black Nation; particularly the state, (domestic and other), multi-national corporations, the church and mosque, Western-based and inspired educational institutions, para-statals, inter-government, multi-lateral and international governance mechanisms designed, inspired and controlled by a force which describes itself as "international community", which is short hand for white power.

- Afrikans must wake up to the fact that they live in this world as a people, and share it with other peoples, particularly Arabs, Asians and Europeans, and they share it amidst life-and-death fierce competition and rivalry. If history and contemporary history is anything to go by, strategically speaking, Arabs and Ameripeans have not wished Afrikans the best, particularly in terms of peaceful, reciprocal relations of mutual respect and mutual benefit.

- The Afrikan neo-colonial state is the designer's instrument for the disempowerment and dispossession of the people. It is misaligned to the people's interest as it is not rooted in people's struggles for self-determination, in their history, spirituality or culture. What is more, Afrikan functionaries who mind the neo-colonial state, but pass for leaders, as a category, either do not fully understand this state or fear to understand it. It cannot be worked around in some sort of by-pass, or reformed so as to align it with the interest of Afrikan peoples as a self-determined Black Nation.

- To buy into Afrikan neo-colonial states as "countries", whereby, for example, Lesotho, Sao Tome are as much country as Sudan, Algeria, Brazil, India, China, Germany, Canada or USA is to embrace absurdity made in Berlin in 1884. The time has come to go back to reaffirm the Afrikan concept of space and nationhood, rooted in her people's history and spirituality. According to Afrikan spirituality at the Source of The Nile, as humans peopled the world following creation, they organized themselves in nationalities (self- governing people) under bona fide senior children of the soil and heads of their families, **Bataka,** as well as under heads of clans in kingdoms, Obwakabaka, which brought together many nationalities; as well as in empires which embraced multiple kingdoms. The first kingdom was formed at the Source of the Nile, and it was called "Buganda" which means the anchored, open-ended, perpetually expanding, but fluid and coherent black nation of inter-connected and related autonomous families, villages, communities, peoples, nationalities, kingdoms and empires. On expanding beyond the Afrikan continent, Afrikans started to refer to this continent as their country, (Nsi), their home and base, their sacred ancestral place of origin. Even today, among spiritually-inspired scholars at the Source of the Nile, the authentic sense of space still regards Afrika the continent as the Afrikan country.

It has become urgent for Afrikans to go back to the basis of their concept of space, and therefore to liberate themselves, from the fragmented stifling tyranny of unventilated spaces, and as a starting point, conceptually and spiritually reclaim the whole continent as the country, Afrika, and then organize around that.

- Without cognitive autonomy a people have nothing and they themselves are nothing; in fact they are slaves of the people whose cognition has swept them off their feet. Cognitive assets, therefore autonomy, are triggered, precipitated, nurtured and accumulate; are updated and transformed by a speech community, in space over millennial time, in the course of acting and being acted on by nature to procure the needs of their material sustenance: food and drink, shelter and clothing. A speech community's needs for material sustenance requires that community to read and understand the world and their God, the origins of the two, their generic origins as humans, location, purpose and nature in the nexus of life, and therefore the best way to survive and prosper. This is what the creation of coherent, self-referencing knowledge is all about; it is created by speech communities. The understanding and creativity of a people reaches full bloom only in that people's mother tongue. It is for this reason that only those people who create and transfer knowledge in their mother tongue can be competitive or comparable with other peoples who work in their own mother tongues, in the sense of achieving internally self-propelling levels of science and technology, literature and art, or notable civilizational levels.

- Afrikans have their God, the one who created them at the Source of the Nile, in His/Her own image, and upon creation gave them their divine inheritance of: awareness, knowledge and understanding; land of the Afrikan continent; voice, that is language; culture and colour. By divine right and responsibility Afrikans have the inescapable duty to enjoy, advance, protect and defend their divine heritage, particularly against encroachment by people who have their own share in EurAsia.

- God created the peoples of the world, and simultaneously revealed Himself/Herself to them. He created them to know and worship Him/Her, each in their respective language and culture; and in the process know and understand the world. In their languages God communicates, knows, guides and judges them. He/She created them to live in awareness, knowledge and communion with and celebration of all living things and types and forms of being as the basis of their abundant life.

- There are no people who were not created by God; and none were created so dumb they do not know who their Creator is, or have no name for Him/Her. There are no chosen people, and if there were, it would be the ones created at the Source of the Nile; they are the only people God created, others having issued out of them. Consequently therefore, in Afrikan spirituality proselytization does not arise. In fact, a people who lose or abandon their own God become slaves of the people whose God they rent or adopt.

- When God created people at the Source of Nile in His/Her image, he created them good and to lead; certainly not to be slaves. Indeed they led, and in leading they blessed the world with a lot of undying good: the first bearers of

God's voice (**Ddoboozi**), and the first to break voice into syllables, words, phrases, sentences, language, ideas, theories, treatises and philosophy. The Afrikans were the first to be civilized, in the sense of elaborating rules, regulations and rituals to guide people to live in reciprocal peace with their neighbours (people with people as the living, ancestors and the yet to be born, with nature and their Creator), instead of living a life of commandist violent relations guided by the threat and use of force. Afrika's gift of civil living has been captured in the now popular dictum of "**ubuntu philosophy**": "I am because we are; and because we are, therefore I am". Having authored the first civilization at the Source of the Nile, Afrikans as well authored the pioneer high technical classic civilization in Phaoranic Egypt, or Kemet, as they called their country, which means Black Nation; it is a civilization subsequent civilizations have built on. Kemetic high technical civilization is classic in the sense that a critical mass of its commanding heights cannot be scientifically improved upon, because they are in tandem with the laws of nature, while many of its achievements have not been equaled since. In this sense then, the Source of the Nile is not merely the headwaters of a river; it is a source of much more and deeper in meaning: the source of God (where He/She first touched earth to create); the source of voice and language; the source of knowledge and civilization.

- During the course of reading the world and reading the word in the Nile valley and across the continent, long before Arabs and Europeans, Afrikans created coherent and internally self-referencing knowledge. Indeed, until Arabs and Europeans accessed this knowledge they remained barbarians. Afrikans can only sink into barbarism if they forgot their own knowledge. To be able to move forward the Afrikan has to start from his own beginning and foundation at the Source of the Nile, and at his base in the Nile valley, which culminated in the high technical classic civilization in Egypt, Kemet. When Afrikans start at the point at which they were created, they start from the unshakable base of their own God, **Katonda we Butonda;** and they start as the first twins, Musoke and Namusoke, children of God's emissary to earth, Ssewamala and his wife Namala who, on reaching the earth as pure spirit, contacted the first holy matrimony. The Afrikan started good and pure, without any inherited sin. Only on the basis of reclaiming his own knowledge will he have the foundation on which to build new and greater knowledge. Just as the knowledge he now seeks to reclaim he created in his own mother tongue through indigenous scholarship, thousands of years ago, even in reclaiming it for greater purpose he will need to do so in his own mother tongue, and by way of Afrikan scholarship. For this Afrikans need a new breed of scholars; one who writes to and for Afrikans, and therefore writes in their mother tongue. Afrikans who have written in English, French, Portuguese, Arabic, etc. have not written for their people; they have instead written for people to whom those languages are their mother tongue; communities to which Afrikans writers are peripheral, and cannot be part of the cutting edge in the creation of new frontiers knowledge in those languages. In fact, without the old, our own old, we cannot create the new, our own new; without standing on the shoulders of our ancestors we cannot be their equals, let alone surpass their achievements. Besides we cannot possibly compete with the peoples who stand on the shoulders of their own ancestors.

- Afrika is the ancestral home and base of Afrikans. It is as well home to Arabs, Europeans and Asians. In the building of Pan Afrikanism therefore, it is critical to differentiate it from continentalism. Afrikans need to capture Pan Afrikanism as the solid unity of all Afrikans, wherever they may be, on their ancestral continent and base, as well as in the diaspora; it is the unity of the children of **God of Butonda** (Katonda we Butonda), the children of Ssewamala and Namala, God's first twins at the Source of the Nile who peopled the whole world. Only upon anchoring themselves in their ultimate unity, spiritual, historical, cultural, psychic and emotional, as children who can locate their common ultimate origin at the Source of the Nile, will Afrikans be able to enter meaningful collaboration and alliances with other peoples at the lesser levels, for example, the economic and political (Afrikan Union, etc.); as common residents on the Afrikan continent and, indeed, with other peoples with whom they share space in the wider world.

- According to prophesy at the Source of the Nile in the early 1970s, the realization by Western-trained elites that as a people, Afrikans could not expect liberation, self-determination and social progress under the Western development paradigm, and the decision by a sizeable part of these elites to return to their roots in search for solutions, will be a sign that victory is at hand. It seems that victory will be realized on the basis of and by the extent to which by Afrikan scholars will write in Afrikan mother tongues, for an Afrikan audience, and therefore engage Afrikan peoples in the creation of knowledge, in debates to illuminate knowledge further, generate enlightenment, new awareness and consciousness which will birth a new Afrika, by far superior to anything that can be produced by force of arms. At such moment Afrikans will transcend revolution; they will have entered the realm of transformation.

CONCLUSION

The Afrikan problematique is fueled by the over-arching, elaborated and well resourced fiction, which seems to have gripped the Afrikan, that he is systemically deficient, and therefore not viable except under tutelage. This has hamstrung and disabled him at four strategic inter-connected and mutually reinforcing levels:

- At the **primary level** the Afrikan has been spiritually disoriented, such that he has forgotten or is hazy about his origins which otherwise directly connect him with God who created him in His image, pure and full of goodness, at the Source of the Nile, at the very beginning of time. Amnesia at this primary level has opened up the Afrikan to all manner of inferiorizing junk and speculation; in particular the notion that he was born in sin and helpless; has no God of his own, and that he therefore needs some exotic God to save him from total destruction. It should be noted that convincing the Afrikan that at the spiritual level he has no God and therefore in deep trouble, prepares the ground for him at the mundane level as well to have no viable means, plan and programme to procure the material requirements for his sustainance; that is development/modernization – so he needs the White man, Arab or Chinese to help him by taking over his country and economy.

- At **the first strategic secondary level,** the Afrikan has been disabled by taking away his history of sterling achievements at the Source of the Nile, in Kemet, in Ethiopia, in ancient Ghana, Mali and Songhai, in Buganda, Bunyoro-Kitara, Asia, etc. He is instead tricked to believe Afrikan history is about the history of the white man and Arab in Afrika; and therefore it is the history of the Afrikan at his weakest: the history of enslavement and entombment, colonial and neo-colonial plunder. Having lost the memory of his glorious history he has no clue he can be great again because he has been great before; in fact for a very long time he was the greatest!

- At **the second secondary strategic level** the Afrikan has been incapacitated by being tricked into believing that he has no knowledge, and none of his mother tongues can be the medium of knowledge creation for modernization. The point is this. If white men who were barbarians until by theft, robbery and genocide they accessed the knowledge and resources of Afrikans, Arabs, Chinese, Indians, the Caribs, the first nations peoples of North, Central and South America, Australia, New Zealand, etc. hardly 500years ago, what greater civilizational heights would

Afrikans scale if they were to reclaim and stand atop their great pyramids at Giza, Egypt? What greater dreams and possibilities?

- Finally, Afrikans have done themselves incalculable disservice by ignoring the centrality of community cognitive autonomy, which can only be triggered, nurtured and advanced through the medium of mother tongue education throughout the entire education cycle, from kindergarten to post-doctoral.

There is no space here to go into the work and programme of Mpambo Afrikan Multiversity. Suffice it to say that it emerges out of and feeds back into the Manifesto of the Afrikan Black Nation, outlined above. Even then, it is important to point out that the Multiversity's premier work is around the preparation of a sacred text on the sources, values, philosophy, beliefs, laws and practices of Afrikan Spirituality; as a guide to the Afrikan desirous of a modern lifestyle, in tandem with the light of their God and the revealed light of Afrikan greats. Of course it is in the mother tongue.

In the final analysis the search for a self-determined Afrikan Black Nation is the search by Afrikans of their own knowledge, understanding and wisdom – which is the search for their God, the ultimate source of all goodness. The author has told his story and journey. It is not a blue-print. Most likely only some aspects of it will make sense to the reader; even then only when consistent with where they will have come from to be where they are, and where they want to be. The point is, by negative example or positive, what does the reader learn from this author's journey? Walk on, you could meet!

SELECTED READING LIST

Diop, .C.A (1974) The African Origin of Civilization – Myth or Reality, Lawrence Hill and Company, Westport; and Civilization or Barbarism – An Authentic Anthropology, Lawrence Hill Books, 1991.

Bernal, M (1988) Black Athena – The Afroasiatic Roots of Classical Civilization, Vintage Books, London.

Prah Kwesi K.: **Afrikan Languages for the Mass Education of Afrikans; and Mother Tongue for Scientific and Technological Development in Afrika;** both published by the German Foundation for International Development, Bonn, 1995.

Kovel J. **Enemy of Nature: End of Capitalism or end of the World? Zed Books, 2007.**

Atleo, Richard E. Tsawalk, a Nuu-chah-nulth Worldview, UBC Press, 2004.

Akoto, Kwame Agyei, Pan Afrikan World Institute, Washington DC, 1992.

Asante, Molefi K. **Kemet, Afrocentricity and Knowledge**.

James, George G.M., Stolen Legacy. San Francisco: Julian Richardson Associates, 1988.

CHAPTER ELEVEN

Koru: Celebrating New Ecologies of Knowledges

IJEOMA CLEMENT-AKOMOLAFE

"We're told our old ways and our old knowledge aren't good any more. The local wisdom and the knowledge passed down from generation to generation are being destroyed...The education system actually helps destroy the old knowledge. Education has been designed to produce people for industry. Learning has become something that is bought and sold. Education is an investment and investors want to get a return on their money. So people who go through schools just end up like cogs in the industrial machine – sometimes without even realizing it. Our capability is actually going down because our self-confidence is ebbing away... We have to survive, but with dignity too".

COMING 'HOME'

Observing a busy street in Chennai, the Tamil Nadu capital city in southern India and a suburban street in Lagos, western Nigeria is a study in contrasts – especially when you are the hybrid birth-child of both worlds separated by almost 4000 miles of sea and land. Born to an Indian-Iranian-English mother and a Nigerian father, I grew up on both continents a friend to none in general, a strange spectacle to both. A 'moving mass of counter-arguments and contradictions', I never easily fit into the down-pat categories of identity I grew up to meet. In Nigeria, the 'unnatural' length of my 'Tamil hair', the milky colour of my skin, and my impenetrably 'Asian' appearance drew attention and cries of '*Oyinbo*' (which is the Yoruba word for 'white person') from street urchins whenever our protective father whisked my sister and I off to school in our very early years. Since my education was divided between Nigeria and India (though predominantly in the latter), I also had to endure unnerving stares from contemporaries in my hometown and birthplace in Chennai. The things that 'gave me away' were the extensive curliness of my hair and the strange sound of my name, *Ijeoma* (which is Igbo for 'good journey'), a name I struggled to come to terms with as a fitting description of my heritage, context and hopes.

Growing up an 'Indian' and fluent in the Tamil dialect, I began to learn the hard way how to negotiate my identities in two worlds that could not be any more different, two worlds that laid claim on my person and rich histories. Eventually I, in my early twenties, did take a 'good journey' to the African continent to briefly chase a doctorate degree in biotechnology in 2008. The 'predicament' of my multiple heritages at once granted me, through the storms and the din of my identity crises, a very peculiar appreciation of the similarities of the two worlds in question – a vision, I admit, that is not limited to 'in-between' persons like me, but is merely easily accessed by our unique circumstance. These similarities

assumed an almost sinister quality in my mind, through increasing doses of my growing proximity to stories about the imperialistic dominance of the so-called 'West' over the place I now called
home. In Chennai, it was (and still is) the large scale development
of glossy shopping malls, the invasion of the consumerist accou-
trements and trends of Christian Dior and the consequent relega-
tion of local cotton-spinners to the fringes of economic life. In my
new home, Lagos (which I have only just begun to have extensive
interactions with due to my recent marriage to a Nigerian), the
advent and hegemony of the 'West' is more or less evident in the
same emergent landscapes. Buried under newly tarred roads (or
the broken ones), hidden behind shopping malls, shadowed by
rising skyscrapers, and silenced by the rising ruckus of encroaching modernity are treasures, the wealth of which we once knew,
but have now forgotten. Our indigenous senses of community,
our notions of sacred belonging and reciprocity, our ideas of gift
and healing are all but lost in a globalizing regime of capital and
the universal creed of 'Western' supremacy. But the changing
landscapes I have observed in India, and now in Nigeria, hide a
much more menacing reality, a seemingly innocuous ritual that
has escaped scrutiny and remained invisible to our critical perceptions. Rarely do we talk about it except when we reinforce its
presence by berating the government for not creating more of it
– or celebrating private individuals for building more. It lies at the
frothy cusp of the imperialist tide washing in 'new' values from
afar, and doing away with 'old' ones. Indeed, one may trace insidious trajectories from the throbbing hearts of our fast-paced lives,
the growing isolation from community we all feel, our dependence on advertisements and the market for sustenance of our

identities, and the fragmentation of our ecological / sociocultural sensibilities to the engine room in the classrooms – the classrooms of modern schools.

The advent and proliferation of modern 'school' or the Western-inspired institutionalized public education system we have grown to accept as normal and even glorious conceals from public scrutiny the sub-text of knowledge imperialism perpetuated by a one-world view. Today, our children and young adults such as I am are trained to promote our cultural inadequacy and demonise our indigenous ways of knowing and being with each other. We are conditioned to believe that we are failed attempts at being Europeans. So we are fed stories about the glorious West and their habits, and we are trained to blush when our own histories are sometimes brought up. Our universities speak about excellence and reform, but when they do, they are almost always explicitly expressing a desire to look like Harvard or Oxford University – exemplars of 'global' excellence in tertiary education. The result is that we are left powerless to assert the compelling visions of life we were once possessed by; we are squandered by the one-way discourse that can only constrain even the so-called well-intentioned to feverishly build more schools and universities that are largely irrelevant to their contexts. In the backdrop of our noisy charade about how these schools should look like, and how we can clinch a higher rung on the ladder of 'world-class' pedagogical excellence determined in the boardrooms of Euro-American corporations, the purposes of Western imperialism find increasing accomplishment.

I write about Africa, my new home and in some ways my old home. I will speak about the disturbing influences of schooling on our ways of life in Africa. Though I am 'Indian' in more senses than I am 'Nigerian', I will aim the full force of my voice on issues surrounding the latter – that is, the African continent. Building on the conversations that must have been stimulated by George Dei in his remarkable chapter on schooling and the social sciences in Africa, my aim is to quickly get to thrilling imaginations of alternatives to institutionalized schooling (which includes universities) on the continent, articulations which reflect the power and possibility of our time. As always, I recognise the paradox of speaking for a 'continent' that was, until recent, a blurry memory of my childhood; there is therefore the problem of the representativeness of my voice. While it might be easy and convenient to tug at the paternalistic argument and insist upon my African-ness (given my father's), my perspectives and the deep ambivalence of identity construction compel me to query the taken-for-grantedness of the term 'African' – to contest what it means to be an African or half-African, while permitting me some confidence to speak about what I feel are the voices of the continent.

Summarily, I cannot but be aware that to speak is to be prejudiced, as Nietzsche nicely put it, and that there is always the problem of definitions, the danger of *essentializing* our objections, of uncritically submerging all manifestations of what we resist into one big stinking pile of rubbish, of first creating 'the enemy' and then attacking 'it'. There will be outliers to many of the key issues I and the authors of this book collectively resist – just as there are anonymous groups and persons working unnoticed (and probably vilified) within schools and universities in order to introduce paradigm shifts in orientation and relevance.

I believe that every position and perspective, no matter how noble, is a problem. The deep relativity and ambiguity of human be-ing ensures that there will never be a plateau without its own precipice, or a word spoken without another voice silenced. My offerings in this chapter have therefore been made with great enough pains to avoid demonizing the 'West', 'Europe', 'school' or any persons or communities associated with these constructs. This is an issue of systems, not persons; processes, not principles; 'us', not 'them'. Enunciating a pluralistic multiverse, the story that there are many worlds and not one, somewhat requires me to aver that the idea of schooling may have had salvific influences in a different context, time and place. However, the flipside of this acknowledgement is the recognition that there is no elixir, and that it might be in our best interests to be suspicious of long-lasting institutions that claim some kind of power over our lives.

This brings me to the point where I (with the contradictions of my Asian face and hair, African name, and Euro-Indian accent), a child of Asia-Africa-Europe, in spite of my reluctance to reify or romanticise our indigenous pasts and in lieu of the problems that must attend speaking in the first instance, refuse to be silent about the ways we are now educating our children and ourselves. I refuse to be silent about the knowledge claims to superiority and universality made by the historical 'West' – the shibboleth and the Trojan horse with which 'they' have gained entrance into our livelihoods, and by whose authority 'we' have continued to auto-colonise our peoples into believing that classrooms are the only place where 'real' knowledge-making happens; that we must nec-essarily give tests and exams and certificates to make sure 'learning' has occurred; that our lives cannot be significant without 'jobs' (a Euro-American industrial era invention); that 'development' and 'progress' must be meaningful constructs everywhere it is uttered; and, that there is no alternative.

MODERN SCHOOLING AND THE MYTH OF PROGRESS

When folk speak about modern schooling today, it usually is with so strong a sense of acceptability that the notion of *school* itself is hidden and only particular instances of *schooling* are brought to light. Popular culture teaches us to imbue schools with messianic qualities, thus we speak in ways that reveal a socio-cultural blind-spot. Thinking there are no possible alternatives, we do not see how schooling shapes us in ways that are problematic. We never popularly discuss why schools with 'white' teachers and a 'white' curriculum are generally preferable to schools with Nigerian teachers and locally relevant languages – we simply *know* that they are! Yet we paradoxically insist on the universality of schools and universities *by* striving to sound British, and celebrate the slightest upward movement of our educational institutions on ranking systems towards a zenith peculiarly crowded by only Euro-American colleges.

The new 'normal' evokes wise sayings that insist that 'education is the best legacy' and 'ignorance is more expensive than education'; by education, what is meant is a Western-type school, endless tests, regimented hours of passive listening, the marginalization of play, grades and policies for more and more standardization in instruction, foreign benchmarks for determining local excellence, the washing and dumbing down of indigenous knowledges and livelihoods, and the psychologization and subjugation of whole communities into 'human resources' fit for the operations of a global market agenda. Ignorance, on the other hand, is the political designation for everything suitably indigenous.

Our cultural maintenance of schools also means that Western schooling will almost always be preferable to their local counterparts. In the main, it is much more respectable to claim a degree from a European university or credentials from an American college. As for academics caught up in the quandaries of 'publish or perish' policies, the golden rule for bagging a promotion is a number of articles in international journals – never mind that indigenous people will probably never have access to these submissions. Recognising this, many academics, it seems, attempt to escape complicity in contributing to this crisis of relevance by claiming that they are adding to some 'body of knowledge', a popular phrasing of the academic imperative to research and publish that conveniently sidesteps the question – *whose knowledge?*

It seems deeply set into the logic of a globalizing centre to make increasingly irrelevant the emanations of the periphery, to feed the 'top' from the resources coming out of the 'bottom'. The structural violence inherent in the progressive 'centralization' of a *Western* centre and marginalization of its *non-Western* circumference continues to reinforce our dependence on modern schools today. As Nyamnjoh points out, 'Africans are still very much dependent on ill-adapted curricula, sources and types of knowledge that alienate and enslave, all in the name of modernity. Sometimes it does not matter whether or not school libraries are empty, since a full library may well be of little real relevance to the pressing problems and specificities of the continent, in terms of perspectives and contents'. But the problem, let us be reminded, is not our empty libraries in local schools and the richer ones in Western schools – for filling our libraries still does not address the problem of content, and addressing content does not solve the problems of pedagogical approach – and addressing this in turn does not solve larger contextual issues that situate schooling and answers the question: 'what is education for?'

The 'modern' African's unmoving faith in schools sprouts from the soils of an even more abiding trust in the *higher* accomplishments of the Western world and the popular predisposition to think that there is nothing amiss with talk about a 'global community' or a 'global village'. Call it 'globalization', 'development' or 'progress', this seemingly irrevocable drive towards global homogeneity, this distortion of boundaries and the non-contestation of our transforming socio-political landscapes hides the undercurrents of hegemonic interests made legitimate and, thus, invisible by the discourse of a one-world view. What we often do not see is *the way we have been taught to see* in our schools. Our evolving cultural visions selectively supports our continued colonization and, as a result, we are hopelessly subjugated by this 'irresistible imperative of power' called progress.

The point is that progress (like its counterpart – 'development'), which has captured our imaginations so effectively that it is barely even noticed in our conversations, and which grants popular Western-style schools its royal seal of approval, is not some disembodied law or the inevitable result of protracted social existence, but the hegemonic thrust of dominant power seeking to transform its assumed peripheries into colonies of itself. Progress

has to present history as following a vector, replacing the cyclical conception of time and discarding faith in destiny or providence. It portrays other religions as contemptible schemes for obedience, practised by oligarchical priests who invoke ghosts to humiliate man and who induce him

to waste his life on searches far removed from the perfectly feasible construction of a paradise on earth. It offers
the world as a resource to a unified humanity – headed, of
course, by those who have already progressed, but open to
all races and nations provided they jettison their tribal and
traditional bonds, which are but the capricious obstacles to
universal redemption.

On the tidal wave of motivations inspired by the Eurocentric
discourse of progress, Europeans 'championed the fight against
the moral power of those traditions representing an obstacle to
the expansion of the market, industry and the modern state', sub-
jugating all to their 'growing hegemony over the global horizon'.

The idea of progress, the grand aim and eternal burden of development, carved out of the historical anxieties and experiences
of the West, is the ground on which claims about the universal
validity and one-size-fits-all-ness of public schooling rests. What
seemed so innocent, so admirably disinterested, so removed from
conspiracy, turns out to be the holding vessel and the lifeblood of
the continued social engineering of our horizons. Our

faith in progress is entrusted with stripping the common
man – who as yet has not progressed, but has already been
cut off from his common land and deprived of his traditional means for autonomous subsistence – of all the cultural footholds that could give him spiritual autonomy and
personal confidence as he faces the market, industry and the
nation-state. Disembedded from his community and caring
only for himself, free from his elders' beliefs and fears,
having learned to look down on his parents and knowing he

will find no respect in what they could teach him, he and his fellows can only become *workers* for industry, *consumers* for the market, *citizens* for the nation and *humans* for mankind.

What results is the undoing of all the webbings with which Africans connected a glittering star in the sky to the mysterious workings of a community. Such stories are banished by the new regime of 'fact' and our lives are set in stone, robbed of all their creative vitalities and spontaneities, even before we are born.

Think about this. Right from school, the toddler will learn to discountenance the stories of her own people, will grow in the identity-shaping arenas of competition and isolation, and will learn to see her greatest accomplishment as *consumer* of the 'gifts' of corporate domination. 'Having been cut down (to the dimensions of individual), robbed of collective, solidaristic, shared features', stripped of her local embeddedness from which she can draw nourishing stories that enrich her sense of placement, confidence and identity, the African stands 'naked, shivering, wretched, before the array of commodities, services, adornments, experiences, sensations of the global marketplace; freedom indeed.'

Make no mistake about it. Our continued silence about the ideological entrapments of Western schooling and the hollowness of our vision has, and is, costing us dearly. What has been accomplished by the monologue of progress and its incarnations in form of schooling (a manifestation of the epistemological imperialism of the West) and the institutions that benefit from its existence is nothing short of the denial of our difference and the silencing of our lives.

Alien values are implanted into the lives of the people, precisely through the children; alien, not merely in the sense of foreign or exotic, but alien to humanity: a commerciogenic identity is formed...it has now become a major determinant on the lives of the young, displacing all earlier forms of acculturation, other ways of answering need, other ways of being in the world.

This is what our education accomplishes – the ossification of the rich possibilities for living and the progressive neutering of our identities, tainted by the filth of incompleteness and primitiveness. In so many words, by the time an African child passes through the series of factory-like processes we gracefully call 'school', he most likely would have learned that the world is a dangerous place where he must compete and strive to outwit his neighbour; he would have learned that his parents in his village are relics of an irrelevant time gone by, and he is an improvement of their lives; he will learn to see himself only in the matrix of images projected by our anxious landscapes, and he, empty of all sense of placement, will find his sense of worth as derived from his ability to participate in the global market. 'In the towns and cities of the Western world, the people haunt the shopping centres, because these are the bringers of answers, both surrogate and real, to need'. As such his sense of identity will never find internal integrity, but will be mediated through those shopping malls – unravelled almost as often as he passes by a billboard advertising a new car or the ideal attitude of the Marlboro man. His very life will be a distraction to his grand aim to accumulate more and more money in an endless quest for an inscrutably distant ideal of 'happiness' and content. He will learn to distrust others as competitors in a world with not enough value to go round – just as he competed with his colleagues for grades. His education will predispose him to think he is superior to his local counterparts, and will further isolate him from their community – banishing him to a life that can only be validated by his dependence and allegiance to the creed of the Market. This dependence will in turn reinforce the colonialism that 'substitutes the distant, the remote, the centralised for all that is local, domestic and familiar'.

SCHOOLING THE WORLD

Before modern schooling our education focused on the spiritual teachings. But now the emphasis is on material success. People go to school so they can make a lot of money, have a big house, drive a nice car...The whole idea of learning has been turned around to mean "how can I make a lot of money?"

The ideology of progress, which provided a strong impetus to the 17th and 18th century search for conquest and colony, bequeathed to the social sciences the impression that 'all societies are advancing naturally and consistently 'up', on a route from poverty, barbarism, despotism and ignorance to riches, civilisation, democracy and rationality, the highest expression of which is science'. This, of course, meant that the peculiarities associated with different cultures and radically divergent ways of life the Euro-American civilization encountered had to be envisioned and interpreted as features of retrogression, as instances needing intervention and, hence, the 'white man's burden'. The solemn *dama* gift economies of Mali that valorised the myths of interconnectivity and shared identity, the stories by moonlight in Senegal that weaved moral fabrics situating generations in relation to their own paradoxes and givens, and the yam festivals of Igbo communities in Eastern Nigeria that celebrated the bountifulness of earth and the ethics of work were all, by implication of the tyranny of progress, retro-grade practices needing improvement, order, and thought (for alas, we hadn't any!). The march of development, energized by the mis-sionary anthems of progress, has meant disaster and annihilation for competing articulations of the human question. Efficaciously disguised as a 'good', a self-evident necessity, the 'real' (as against the cosmetics of culture), the notion of progress and its accommo-dated strategies of development, has helped escort out of relevance, rather unthankfully, our own voices, histories and stories.

In the wake of the trumpeting armies of Western hegemony, the sounds of which are ever present, lay gleamingly new schools to console us and convince us that the horrors perpetuated on our worlds had to be so, had to be done. *Moreover*, it might be said, *today we have streets, we have cars, we have cash; we have religion, universities, their social sciences and banks.* Today, we have *knowl-edge and truth.* Surely these are true, but the verity of these state-ments hardly answer for the troubling Western colonial legacies on the continent of Africa or the present imbalances of power sus-tained by the insidious idea that, given a problematic definition of culture as merely decorative, the West is somehow cultureless (and therefore 'real' and unencumbered by frivolous distractions) and the Rest are 'feathers, bells and dances'. Somehow the social sciences taught in 'our' universities dispense the idea that African ways of life are fabrications of reality, and knowledge from the West is *that* reality we have, in times past, clawed at and tried, without success, to master. To our own disadvantage, we have con-veniently forgotten that

The world in which we are born doesn't exist in an abso-lutist sense, but is just one model of reality... [Africans and] the other peoples of the world aren't failed attempts at being [like the West], or...failed attempts at modernity. They are by definition unique facets of human imagination and when asked the meaning of being human, they respond with 6000 different voices.

Thus, the rhetoric of progress, or hierarchies of knowledge, of the dichotomy between the false and the real, the serious and the frivolous, continue to legitimise the existence of modern schooling. This is, of course, only part of the reasons why schools are growing up like mushrooms everywhere; there is also the externality of the ecosystem created by the triumph of modern schooling and the social sciences orthodoxies 'taught' in them: neoliberal economics and the imposition of central banks, the progressive disenchantment and stratification of human experience into jobs and job-seeking rituals (such as, well, going to school!), and the super stories of scarcity, survival, isolation and fear.

Depending on one's orientation to the phenomenon of modern schooling and its global reach, there is room for either cheer or despair; the Global Education Digest (2011) reports that 'the number of children attending primary school has exploded over the last ten years, thanks in large part to the tremendous resource mobilisation campaigns and political commitments arising from the World Education Forum in 2000'. In a sea of data supposedly representative of educational contexts from Sub-Saharan Africa to the Philippines, and using centrally determined indicators, the compilation reports a 9% global increase in enrolment of students in primary schools from 1999 to 2009 – a jump from 646 million to 702 million children. Of course, specific regions claimed the larger share of this number. While enrolment in South and West

Asia increased by 28% and by 17% in Arab states, sub-Saharan Africa enrolment rates jumped by 59%. What this suggests is an increase in the number of schools in Africa as well as the fact that the continent is still one of the most unschooled regions compared to other parts of the world – hence, the game of catch-up.

Additionally, Nigeria is currently experiencing a radical increase in its number of universities. With a total of 120, spurred by the dramatic entrance of more and more private universities into an arena traditionally occupied by state- and federal-run universities, and with more being planned for by the Federal Government, Nigeria now has more higher education institutions than most African nations. Yet, even with six proposed universities currently being developed, the British Council Country Director, David Higgs (2011), recently insisted that the number of universities are grossly insufficient to cater to the educational aspirations of Africa's largest country.

Most would immediately agree with Higgs' answer. I doubt if many understand the questions that we must find the courage to ask today: Why do we need more universities? Is the proliferation of modern schooling the only possibility for our education and that of our children? Are there no alternatives to the violence we have continued to perpetuate on ourselves in the name of knowledge, development and necessity?

I might as well allow that necessity might be the mother of invention – however, extravagance must be the mother of necessity, for modern schooling is only as much a necessity as we have decided it to be. This must be the case given that schooling, no matter how ingrained it has come to be in our political consciousness, is a colonial invention limited by the circumstances of a particular historical and ethical context – and not absolutely valid to all situations. Of course it is difficult to imagine life without modern schools, especially when we step back to see the larger portrait of the institution's economic and political utility to the realities of social ascendancy. Schools, founded on the ethics of uniformity and mechanistic efficiency, serve the globalizing need for a skilled force subservient to the interests of a corporate few – a line of thought that shall be developed in the next section.

A point can be made that there are different types of schools and that there is a growing mindfulness about the ways schools have perpetuated inequality, elitism, and the oppressive ecologies of capitalist hegemony. In response to this, it is important to note first that the collective critique of our social orthodoxies arises from a desire to do away with systems and paradigms of thought – due to their limitations – not individuals or groups. Therefore there are numerous individual cases of schools changing their curriculum to adapt to local needs; there are inspiringly noble pedagogical practices countering the hegemony-friendly method of lecturing. In my own work in a Nigerian university, I have courageously found different ways to question the notion that knowledge is a predetermined entity which we must simply find 'innovative' ways for transferring to a largely passive audience of certificate-seekers. I adopt an ethical space that mocks my authority as 'sage on the stage' and encourages creative and playful spaces of enquiry where long-accepted creeds are challenged. As a result, I constantly struggle with the inevitable at the end of every semester – when I shall be required to grade my students and assign scores, hence perpetuating the sorting mechanisms of a socially unjust world system. However, in spite of many occasions to celebrate, these practices are therefore more or less cosmetic – hardly ever addressing the hidden curriculum from which most traditional schools derive their sense of legitimacy, and almost never correcting the contextual problems that modern school inescapably contributes to.

The problems occasioned by the spread of modern schools, the agitated commissioning of newer universities, the escalating demands for successively 'impressive' certification and the critical failure of these many 'African' institutions to reflexively challenge the doctrines of living we have eagerly imbibed, clearly suggests in the least that we need to have serious discussions about where we are headed – and in the most, that the continuous spread of schools on the African continent (given the ethics of educational diversity) is most regrettable.

SCHOOLS AND THE 'ECONOMY':

> *One of the great tragedies of schooling is how it has ripped people out from nature and locked them up in rooms for 8 hours a day and I think that the profound kind of damage it's doing to us – only we'll recognise generations from now when we'll look back and say: "How could we have done this kind of thing to people...?"*

We can no longer afford to support the 'First World's cultural myopia that deceives us all into believing that there are no other ways we can live except mediated by the factory-like conditioning of school settings. I resist the claims of necessity in favour of the story of possibility. We do not have to perpetuate the broken narratives of schooling in our time – the failure of schooling. It is thus important to understand the ways formal education has been found severely wanting and unable to meet local needs.

I propose two ways to understand the failure of schooling – by the hidden curriculum of epistemological singularism it promotes (and, by consequence, the developmental pluralism it omits), and by its inflexible tethering to the colonial genius of 18th century social engineering. In other words, if we seek to understand the flaws of formal education, we must also understand the conditions that created it, and what 'schools' were actually intended for. A good way to start, therefore, might be to invoke the story of 'the Economy', the echoes of which we still hear today across forgotten times in Europe's history. It is the story that compels us to believe that the only way we can meaningfully frame our lives is in attachment to the demands of a set of 'natural' constraints we collectively call 'the Economy'. We are told with words and with silence that only the insane would think of resisting 'the Economy' – for to do so is to resist progress itself, which is utterly unthinkable.

One cannot make meaning of the astronomical rise of schooling as a modern institution with such pervasiveness and within a short time without understanding *this story* maintained–often at the price of blood-soaked fields and devastated traditional livelihoods – by the network of institutions (such as the nation-state), corporations, and knowledge production dynamisms that are responsible for the template of reality we inhabit. In fact, schools derive their sense of relevance from the same story about who we are and how we may best construct our lives. To this end, compulsory schooling has helped breed consumers based on a curriculum designed to best serve the interests of corporations and the nation-state – all at the expense of students' curiosity, critical thinking skills and creativity.

What is this story? What is the 'Economy'?

One may understand *it* as the narrative supported by the social science of economics and the set of assumptions the discipline promotes – which casts humans as self-interested profit-oriented rational players in a market space defined by unlimited wants but scarce resources to meet those wants. Additionally, the Economy captures the idea of a homogenous, 'highly-centralized, unified set of globalizing constraints, stringent conditions and corresponding institutions irrevocably bound to a set of policies and ethical considerations that are designed to ease the boundless dominance of 'free trade', monetary governance and supportive political configurations. The adoption of these constraints by individual nation-states, which also implies the loosening of locally compelling imperatives, traditional systems, myths, ceremonies and moral values, is always celebrated as a progressive step towards development. It is through this latter sense that the violence that attends the global spread of 'development' is clearly shown, as articulated by its proponents:

> Economic development of an underdeveloped people by themselves is not compatible with the maintenance of their traditional customs and mores. A break with the latter is a prerequisite to economic progress. What is needed is a revolution in the totality of social, cultural and religious institutions and habits, and thus in their psychological attitude, their philosophy and way of life. What is, therefore, required amounts in reality to social disorganization. Unhappiness and discontentment in the sense of wanting more than is obtainable at any moment is to be generated. The suffering and dislocation that may be caused in the

process may be objectionable, but it appears to be the price that has to be paid for economic development; the condition of economic progress.

A subtler appreciation of 'the Economy's' power over our lives can be gained from examining the ways it shapes identity, contains perspective – selectively allowing only what is agreeable to its logic to thrive – and determines meaning. By disrupting preexisting norms and social values the ethics of progress, as accommodated in the vehicle of the global market economy, re-engineers human relationships and forges a new kind of artificiality that presents itself as *natural* (and therefore, inescapable) especially to those who have been thoroughly schooled. Theorists publish knowledge and train students to view the *Economy* 'as if it were a fact of nature, the evolution of an inevitable pattern built into the very core of humanity and the world.' The entire enterprise of the social sciences in general, and economics in specifics, is founded upon the propagation of stories about the triumphant Western discovery of the laws 'at the heart of economic dynamics: supply and demand, maximization of gains, the necessity for growth, the harsh yet efficient reality of endless competition, the "productive" accumulation of wealth in the hands of powerful "job creators."'

Ethan Miller articulates the problematic by insisting that:

[The] economy was constructed by processes of enclosure, where people were forcibly separated from their means of subsistence (land, community, tools and skills) and pushed into dependence on wage-jobs and commodity purchases. It was constructed by the legal and military authority of centralized states who sanctioned the private property of elites and enforced their contracts. It was constructed by the specific, politically-enforced organization of wage jobs, in which workers were systematically excluded from democratic ownership and control over the products of their own labor. It was constructed through the outright theft of life, labor, land and resources from people in colonized places around the world.

Modern schooling is therefore part of an ecosystem of imperialism, and is a key component in the formulaic application of conditions imposed by a particular culture on the rest of the world. The prosperity of schooling in such a short time since its invention in the 18th century reinforces the idea – especially in the minds of the thoroughly 'schooled' – that indigenous traditions or non-western cultures did not have ways to educate their children, did not engage in work and productive activities, and thus needed the intervention of the West to bring some kind of order to an otherwise chaotic world. However, Euro-American cultural pretensions to universal validity and pretensions to superiority is found wanting with a little examination of the collective histories of African and other non-western communities. We have had non-monetary ways of exchanging value that do not introduce the peculiar disadvantages of fiat money or the deceptions maintained by centrally organised banking systems. We have had work which – while not organised into the industrial era invention called 'jobs' – enriched our local communities and nurtured our feelings of well-being.

Let's be clear, though, to avoid any confusion: humans have always engaged in diverse forms of production, distribution, exchange, and consumption. What the elite's self-fashioned concept of "the economy" did, in this specific historical form, was to create a kind of conceptual enclosure around a very particular set of human rationalities, motivations, social activities, and ways of life. Economic theory said: self-interest is the legitimate, and natural, economic motivation. Exclusive, individual private property is the legitimate, and efficient, way to organize access to resources and the means of livelihood. Accumulation of wealth (and the fear of poverty) is the legitimate incentive that will generate human well-being. Wage labor (a world divided into owners and workers) is the way to organize effective and innovative economies. Competition is the dynamic that generates efficiency in production and exchange. Bundle all of these things together, publish books about their necessity and build institutions on their certainty, lock the rest of life's complexity and possibility in a closet (or a jail) and call that ... *economics*.

It is worth mentioning here that I am not distinguishing between capitalism and socialism in critiquing the ideology of the globalist market agenda – for both forms of economic management are interrelated and separated only by degrees, socialism being a condensation of the incarnations and profit-generating activities of capitalist systems into a central authority, the State. However, given the failure of socialist structures, capitalism shines as the last beacon and thrives as the most competent carrier of the goals of development, and is indeed regarded as such.

Our schools and universities are therefore not innocent, disinterested, apolitical places where knowledge is dispensed. In light of the aforementioned, they are more readily conceived as outposts of a predominant power, perpetrators of an alien ideology,

priests of the doctrine of adherence to the 'Economy', and silencers
of thrilling possibilities in indigenous education. While I admit
that the tendency to over-generalise the limitations of schooling
and over-romanticise the possibilities of indigenous schooling is
always present, there are salient features of the world culture of
schooling that a less enthusiastic supporter of alternatives might
be ready to accept:

1. **The structure of modern schooling emphasises conformity and standardization**: It is not merely coincidental
   that schools seem like factories or industrial settings where
   'raw materials' are grouped in classes, 'categorised' and
   'graded' according to 'performance', and eventually produced to the market.

2. **Though sometimes employing the rhetoric of creativity,
   modern schooling does more to reinforce rote-learning:**
   This follows its internal logic of measurement and quan-
   tification. Regardless of persons in management, school
   systems need to establish uniform measures for assessing
   learning – a trend that often sacrifices individual learning
   styles for mass instruction and curriculum sturdiness.

3. **Modern schools disrupt indigenous realities and fragment identities – doing more harm than good by creating people lost in the crevices of society.**

4. **Modern schooling almost invariably acculturates
   persons into the dynamics of a market place**: This is the
   reason why schools remain big business, and why globalist corporations invest heavily in them. Schools are part of
   an organic whole, an incarnation of a consumerist system
   that must reify the market place as the most legitimate

dispenser of meaning and value; schools are portals to those systems. Thus, schools help create the externalities of these flawed paradigms.

5. **By branding millions as failures, Western education sees to it that the injustices associated with the stratification of society into elites and non-elites (along with the accompanying demonization of local knowledges) are perpetuated.**

6. **There will never be enough schools to go round:** Popular culture teaches us to labour under the impression that the multidimensional crises that threaten us, particularly in Africa, are traceable to our lack of education. As a result, we are driven to build more and more schools in the hopes that the educated persons will help create a just and equitable society with equal opportunities for all. What we so persistently fail to notice is that schools help perpetuate those inequalities in the first instance. Schools are part of a social sorting mechanism, embedded within a larger culture that relies on those inequalities to function.

7. **The tyranny of theory:** Our universities, often isolated from their host communities, promote theory in understanding the very communities they do not engage. This avant-gardism conceals the 'fact' that how people live their lives and understand their worlds could never be captured in little boxes. As the sole dispenser of credible knowledge, universities help build monocultures of knowledge that are linear, insensitive to pluralities, and most often insignificant to local experiences.

In today's half-lived world and on the continent of Africa, pregnant with possibilities, people continue to lead anti-lives determined and shaped by the advent and prosperity of modern schooling. We celebrate with much aplomb and colourful garbs the transfer of certificates from universities to their graduating students – satisfied in the promise for a better life a certificate supposedly gives its bearer. But 'none are more hopelessly enslaved than those who falsely believe they are free': the proliferation of graduates and certificates has not materialised into more meaningful ways of life, has not tempered the escalating rates of unemployment, and has done more to firmly entrench African communities into the discursive constrictions of capitalist ideologies.

In a paradoxical sense then, modern schools are succeeding – not at perpetuating liberation agendas and creating platforms of local relevance (for they are not designed for this) – but at continuing to destabilise the plurality of knowing and being, and by shaping people in ways that leave them fragmented, used and exploited.

Of course, assessing the impact of schooling on African culture for instance is not an 'objective' thing to do (for *objectivity* is very often the standardization of Euro-American *subjectivity*), but a value orientation. If the homogenisation of diversity, the perpetuation of the hegemony of the West, the banishment of traditional realities, and the dumbing down of rich alternatives to the Economy are perceived as positive developments, then modern schooling might as well be a *good thing*. However, it is difficult for many to come to terms with this perspective for, though some Western-styled schools have helped produce innovations and technologies deemed beneficial to our evolving cultural landscapes, it is important to realise that these are not direct effects of schooling. Indeed, a quick survey of the most compelling Western innovations shows that a significant proportion of their wealthy innovators are school drop-outs. Moreover, the world culture of schooling does not permit creativity and meaningful innovation, except these are tethered to the consumerism that motivates the paradigm.

> It is at this point that one can detect more clearly the failures of modern schooling. After a century and a half of development, there is not really much to show for this system... most people are utterly unable to see beyond the promises of unlimited economic growth, instead living blindly a consumerist lifestyle that has time and again been denounced as unsustainable over the long term. Ecological systems are in collapse, species are becoming extinct, and humans have become one of the few organisms (other than pigs) that consistently foul their own habitats...Perhaps it is too much to lay the blame for all this at the doorstep of school, to say that the mess the world is in today is due to schooling. But it is equally unrealistic to expect schools to fix these problems.

Yet most efforts at educational reform are still dancing to the same old tunes of economic growth and national pride, with the few exceptions to this uniform pattern, such as those feeble efforts at "environmental education" and "global awareness," merely serving to prove the rule.

THE NON-APPLICABILITY OF MODERN SCHOOLS TO ALL CONTEXTS

Today, Western schooling is responsible for introducing a human monoculture across the entire world. Essentially the same curriculum is being taught...and is training people for jobs, very scarce jobs, but for jobs in an urban consumer culture. The diversity of cultures as well as the diversity of unique human individuals is being destroyed in this way.

Over the past few years, spurred on by a renewed sense of pan-Africanism, there have been calls for the creation of educational institutions that reflect and focus on the plight of Africans. Remarkable activities have, for instance, served to intensify discussions about the Eurocentric bias of higher education praxis and how this is truly a disservice to our hopes for a better life. The search for the African university is still on, and this is attested to by various experiments in creating contexts that critique dependence on the West (at least rhetorically). Many of these universities are refurbishing their curricula, and embracing entrepreneurial training platforms to stop the rising tide of unemployment. The data on the entrance of record numbers of private investors and individuals into the development of new universities in Nigeria (some of which describe their ethos in salvific interventionist terms that are sympathetic to the 'African condition') is an example of the changing consciousness about education.

For reasons highlighted previously, these developments are reasons to be hopeful about reversing the monologue of schooling – however, a wealth of imagined alternatives to the phenomenon of formal education and the problems occasioned by its prolongation is yet to be accessed. It seems that we collectively *suffer* from what Arundhati Roy would have called 'the failure of radical imagination'.

Audrey Lorde placed it quite succinctly when she claimed that 'the master's tools will never dismantle the master's house'. In some ways, the proliferation of 'African' universities has been most detrimental to our collective hopes to fashion educational spaces that truly meet our needs and re-enchant our worldviews. This is because these so-called African universities tend to perpetuate the very same elitism that produced our initial disenchantment, so that they are really European universities located in Africa, not African learning spaces conducive to the resistance of the ideologies of the West.

> The education systems in postcolonial states in Africa appear not to have made much progress in shedding previously reified "modern" colonial knowledge to define and determine academic knowledge relevant for African societies and economies. Curricular in schools are deeply seated in the assumption that Eurocentric knowledge is superior to indigenous African knowledge, and this assumption is rife and regarded as "truth." The assumption has promoted the displacement and silencing of other belief and knowledge systems, which have largely been marginalized. In the

process schooling, in its current structure, tends to impose cultural essentialism and reproduce certain ways of viewing the world in the subordinate and marginalized groups. The reproduction of the culture of the dominant class in schools has a hegemonic effect that reinforces the fact that educational systems all over the world are not value-free and neutral. Schooling reproduces the cultural capital and worldview of the dominant social class in society.

In other words, the very same hidden curriculum of global social engineering which defines non-African schooling, the very same disciplinary strictures and departments built into our university frameworks, the unceasing hunt for global reckoning and world-class status, the maintenance of the same knowledge production dynamics, and the very same isolation from local relevance (the ivory tower syndrome) make it all the more certain that if there is such a thing like an African university, we probably have not created it yet.

It is not enough then to adopt entrepreneurship training platforms that churn out 'job creators', or champion the rhetoric of independence from Western academic imperialism, whilst the hidden curriculum is left unevaluated. What generally has become a blind-spot is our inability to recognise that schooling creates an *ecosystem* that invariably privileges the globalist agenda: the pyramid-building and social sorting that continually creates the artificial bifurcation between the 'haves' and the 'have-nots' (and, one might add, the 'have-mores') which are the very conditions that create poverty; training students who will be job creators, as against job-seekers, might seem a laudable goal at first blush, until one realises that it is a perpetuation of the whole oppressive paradigm of the elitist hierarchy of hegemonic knowledge by which the West maintains its assumed supremacy over the Global South.

Ironically, our so-called African universities are producing graduates ratified by content and textbooks derived from the West. These graduates, trained in economics, anthropology, history, psychology and sociology (among many other specialisations), rendered impotent by the non-applicability of their 'high' knowledge to the local concerns, problems and orientation of what is left of their communities, either return to the university system to teach the same things they were taught, or join the banks or some kind of business venture. Only a few radicalise their experiences and question the worth of their certificates enough to pursue life-scripts that are meaningful to their senses of beauty. As African governments continuously succumb to the siren songs of deregulation and the 'free market', opening up their economies to the control and manipulation of corporations in whose operations local peoples are an afterthought, the possibilities for truly meaningful employment are increasingly lost – replaced by highly selective job placement opportunities that deny untold millions, lost in the crevices of a system too big to unravel itself, a chance to thrive.

As alluded to in a different section, there will never be enough jobs to go round even if all the African universities decidedly adopt 'job-creation' educational objectives, since the global system which universities are designed to support is built on the myth of scarcity – the scarcity of knowledge, the scarcity of money, the scarcity of food, the scarcity of security, the scarcity of life itself. Just as the fractional reserve banking system is based on debt and the issuance of loans, modern schooling thrives based on the selective containment of a certain kind of knowledge as credible and trustworthy and the disavowal (and simultaneous creation) of *ignorance. As alluded to earlier,* universities, it turns out, actually need ignorance, unemployment and the continuous problematisation of statistical 'poverty' to remain relevant, which suggests rather painfully that university graduation ceremonies are not signalling the entrance of *bearers of light* into the larger society, but are maintaining its supposed paucity with every certificate handed out.

In response to what is rightly deemed the growing isolation and irrelevance of African universities to their local hosts, and the failure of researchers to embrace and promote indigenous knowledge systems, calls are being made for the integration of ethnic studies into pre-existing frameworks. Again, this move focuses on merely tinkering with aspects of a highly adaptable system or switching content – an approach that inspires Claude Alvares to remind us what we should be paying attention to is

> not just the content but even the assumptions and methodologies guiding the accumulation of knowledge in social science studies disciplines [which] have been uncritically imported from the European academic tradition. This framework is almost wholly Eurocentric – a charge made not just against European social science studies within Europe, but against practically every social science studies regime in the non-Western world. One eminent critic has rightly dubbed such disciplines as nothing but an extension of the 'white studies' regime. Though the critique of Eurocentrism in the social sciences is well accepted, there is

very little display of either courage or determination among academics in non-Western universities in raising their own distinct set of assumptions that would enable them to work and conduct meaningful research outside the framework of Western academic preoccupations and interests.

It is amazing how our best efforts at coming to terms with our indigenous realities often end up reinforcing the hegemony of the West. For instance, how we often label the newer disciplines we suppose will pay attention to our distinctive worldviews, such as when we say Ethnobotany, African Philosophy, and African History, betrays a predilection for conceptualising their European counterparts as 'real' or the default position. We do this by failing to label the work emanating from the West as European or American (as in 'European Psychology' or 'American Medicine') as if to say if it comes from the West it comes from everywhere and is meaningful anywhere.

How we approach the questions about the appropriateness of formal education to African contexts will depend on how much we are willing to critique the myth of knowledge as a homogenous entity primarily accessed and accurately dispensed using methods created in the West.

INDIGENOUS WAYS OF LEARNING

So what do we do with school in Africa? What do we do with our universities? Do we shut them down, and close them away from the public? If we were to advocate this, is there an alternative to modern schooling that could fill in the empty spaces?

When we frame the question of alternatives this way, we are most likely to fall into the trap of attempting to suggest the next big thing, another blueprint which we propose to implement in top-down fashion. But this would only amount to replacing one tyranny with another. I do not think that closing down our schools in authoritarian fashion is a wise way to resist the damaging effects schools have on our lives, our futures and our livelihoods. I do not also think there is an elixir, a silver bullet of some sort that could instantly maim the globalising reach and marginalising influences of the West and answer all our questions about how we can educate ourselves in meaningful ways. Progler considers the question about de-schooling society:

> Rid society of school? The mere proposition that Illich suggests in 'Deschooling Society' may seem preposterous, even treasonous, to many people. How can we live without school? Where will our children go? What will they do about jobs? When will they learn the heritage of their civilization? Civic values? Literacy and numeracy? But such questions only prove Illich's rule: we are addicted to schooling. And this addiction is to such an extent that it seems unthinkable to question the very existence of schooling. But is it really so hard to imagine society without school? After all, modern schooling is less than a century old in most parts of the world, and a little over a century old in its birthplaces in Europe and America. Prior to schooling, communities often found various ways to answer all the above questions, ways that were meaningful in their own cultural, historical and social contexts. Young people learned language, religion, cultural values, and social responsibility by living life. Apprentices learned trades by practicing them with those who had more experience. Education was often casual and

informal, and such an education was part of life, which was a life of learning.

I propose a wiser way to reframe the question at this time would be to ask, like Ethan Miller does: 'By what means, on whose terms, and with what guiding ethical principles will we collectively work towards new [educational spaces] and relationships?' In this way, at least, by emphasising processes that already exist and the need for conversations, we avoid having to respond to calls for a single solution and escape the urge to impose another monologue on our fragmented identity-shaping spaces. Seen from one perspective, the problem we attempt to engage is not the existence of schools, it is the silence of alternatives – it is the marginalisation of difference and the setting up of hegemony. Just as an illustration, we could probably say, for instance, that the lack of money is not equal to poverty; the adverse is more veritably the case: the *very existence* of money is poverty! Banks lend money into existence – as such our money-based economies are founded on debt that will never be repaid since loans always have interests attached to them. Thus money disrupts our livelihoods by first creating poverty, and then colonising the only means of escape from it. The hegemony of money over possible re-imaginations of economy resembles the domination of the school curriculum over diverse ways of knowing; we are dulled by our forced adherence to the rules of the classroom and, by extension, unsustainable lives of waste, isolation, and destruction.

It is not enough to merely resist schooling or to say 'no' to the ideology of progress (though saying 'no' does not necessarily compel us to say 'yes' to anything else). We can, if we will, begin to look at the many varied ways we have continued – under the radar of globalist concerns – to educate ourselves, shape our moral spaces and story our worlds. This might lead us to indigenous knowledge systems, about which Helena Norberg-Hodge said:

> There is no doubt that if we look honestly at traditional forms of education and compare them to today's modern education system...the traditional forms of knowledge fostered sustainability. All these cultures were not perfect, but they did know about their own specific climate, soil, water...

Though safely cordoned off and assumedly made of no consequence by the blinding legitimacy of the Western knowledge systems, our indigenous knowledge systems have for generations provided sustainable, spiritually nurturing, earth-affirming ways of configuring how we relate with ourselves, each other and our perceived worlds.

Indigenous learning contexts in Africa stress localisation of practice and emphasise community. They are not stratified and validated by the intrusion of examinations, centrally organised standardisation policies, or the award of certificates. These learning conditions generally depend on, and derive from, a cosmovision of interdependence and interconnectivity, as well as the valorisation of the invisible and the sacred.

The Yoruba, the Igbo – indeed almost all (if not all) indigenous African cultures – employed storytelling techniques and life creation systems that represent a critique of space and a return to place, the non-division between life and learning, the immediate application of learning experiences, and a critique of theory. Learning was a festival of sorts that never ended with graduation events and further classification, and the focus of these 'informal' ways of being educated was not distant and inscrutably abstract, but grounded in the lived experiences, the practical needs and the aspirations of the communities – leading to lives already relevant, not by virtue of a certificate, but for merely belonging.

Much can be said about African knowledge systems that may not be reproducible here; the most important that can be said, in my opinion, is that they represent many ways we can choose to re-enchant our world dulled by the crises of identity and meaning. Of course there are many questions to ask about the appropriateness of rejuvenating traditional indigenous traditions in an African context that is no longer 'traditional' but a hybridisation of modern and the 'pre-modern'. However to make such an enquiry is to reify the 'traditional' or create some kind of African essentialism, complete with media-induced images of huts, a group of barely clothed men hunting with spears drawn, or storytelling circles performed under a bright moon. The thing to come to terms with is that culture is not a 'thing', but a set of relationships, a conversation, and a dialogic moment by moment encounter with meaningful constructs of our world. Shifting spaces from the marginalising monologue of schooling and development is therefore not strictly an attempt to re-enact a fixed past, but an invitation to voice out living memories and to engage in conversations about what is meaningful to us today.

An attempt to embrace African indigenous learning systems is the reclamation of the local and the renunciation of the hegemonic relationships sustained by the allure of a universal centre. In place of the colonising spread of a single way of being, an irreducible plurality of knowledges and ways of being is found, which, radicalises knowledge as participation not as a reified given available only to a few.

When one casts a long vision down our trodden paths and how far we have come as a people, it is not difficult to appreciate the exciting moments and possibilities that are unfolding right before our very eyes. Across the world, even in the West, groups of people disenchanted with the globalist domination agenda and the ways schools and what is taught in them condition us to relate with each other are turning to the wisdom of old paths and re-enchanting their lives by out-thinking the limitations of our crisis-ridden societies. Bold visions are being articulated in concert with communities, and the regime of 'theory' and isolated academic knowledge production is faltering, leaving new spaces for radically empowering social constructions of meaningful wisdom. The 'lopsided and biased social sorting mechanism' we conveniently call modern schooling is losing its cherished space as the only possible occupant of our educational arenas. As this shift occurs, many other establishments that depend on the services that schools, certification, and jobs offer the monolithic global corporatist structure (that continues to side-line millions of people because they do not measure up to centrally determined, locally irrelevant and elite-imposed articulations of excellence or learning) are themselves giving way to locally vibrant practices.

It is most important for Africans to begin to see the futility of 'trying to catch up' with the West. The logic of development and the lifeblood of progress (which undergird modern schooling) necessitate the subjugation of peoples and the propagation of the myth of selective superiority, expertise and scarcity in order to console the restlessness of the subdued. What this means is that the 'game' has been rigged from the start. The interests of the global centres of power will always supersede and outrank the 'puny' concerns of the periphery. So long as we continue to insist on the precepts of universally valid knowledge, the primacy of formal education and the superiority of Western ethics and culture, we will always dwell in a state of dependence.

As Escobar insists, "There is always a tight connection between social reality, the theoretical framework we use to interpret it, and the sense of politics and hope that emerges from such an understanding." If we envision our world as existing beyond our discursive arenas and conversations, if we subscribe to the framework that privileges a few who 'get it' over those 'who don't', we will continue to create interventionist platforms that assume others different from us need our help and are disempowered without our policies, programs and projects. However, if we see our realities as politically created, mediated by interests and negotiated power, shaped and energised by cascading stories – in which there is no 'truth' except that which we have ourselves co-created – then the world becomes not a singular place filled with facts only experts can access, but a plural field enchanted with stories we can insist on telling. In such a place, we do not need to 'empower' others – for they are already empowered; we do not need 'development', because it shapes our subjectivities and frames our personhoods against relationships, and creates a monologue that blinds us to our untapped creative resources. We do not need 'schools', for in spite of the arguments that can be made about the benefits it produces for a sense of civic responsibility and civilisation, it is an arbitrary invention of industrial societies that is not designed to benefit more compelling and less destructive ways of living and learning.

Thus, it is important that we strive to understand the ways we have been taught to see, or else our visions will always be limited to the imposed familiar. In the stead of building more schools, submitting ourselves uncritically to new international policies that pretend to encapsulate the concerns and needs of our own people, we can choose to re-story our lives. We can choose not to participate in the ethics of factory schooling. We can make community, work, solidarity, cooperation, conversations (and all the challenges and paradoxes they will surely accommodate) part of our lives again. What I will propose subsequently is the fruit of our imagination (my husband's and mine), a vulnerable work of art, and a story-telling project we have begun to articulate, which we hope addresses the particular issues about the very political 'nature' of modern schooling as well as ways we can begin to turn to community for solutions to the existential problems plaguing the global systems we have hitherto maintained to our own detriment.

Resisting the Monologue of Western Schooling

A new consciousness shift is happening! A knowledge revolution is brewing!

Hidden away from the purview and interests of mainstream media are exciting puddles of resistance across the planet – including Africa. A radical reinterpretation of our world is afoot, giving birth to equally radical spaces for participation and new freedoms. By 'knowledge revolution' I do not mean that people are getting educated faster than ever or that there are many more scientific journals available for sale. I refer instead to a questioning of the discourses and orthodoxies of knowledge that have shaped our visions and constrained our possibilities for generations. Convinced that the only way to live meaningful lives was to allow the credible knowledge of the West to trounce our own learning, our fathers were schooled in the perceived superior cultures of the West. The formal end of national colonialism and the departure of the former masters was only just the beginning for a more sinister form of colonialism: academic/knowledge imperialism. So, thanks to our schools, we learned to discountenance the familiar – including our own languages – and looked forward to the foreign for meaning. Our identities shaped by the emanations of an increasingly global culture of consumerism, the fabric of our communities and stories by which we had once lived prosperous lives, began to atrophy. Today, we have replaced a life of learning and contextual relevance with the violence perpetrated by examinations and 'tests', certificate-seeking, theoretical abstractions of no import to our cultural aspirations, and the tongue-in-cheek promise of jobs that are not available or are only obtainable at great expense to our peers.

However, at the precipice, people change. A quick survey of emergent issues behind the hoodwinking intrusion of the mass media might reveal a rich plethora of initiatives, community platforms and resistances that collectively proclaim the death of knowledge.

In my home in India, a place that like Africa has long endured a regime of knowledge imperialism and continues to suffer from the myopia of her leaders (structural descendants of old colonialists) intent on carrying out the corporatist mandate of industrialism, a critical number of initiatives are charting new pathways for hope. These bold steps towards new frontiers are not merely indicative of curriculum adaptations, increased awareness of the Eurocentrism in modern schooling, or student-friendly pedagogies. They are holistic reappraisals of the very idea of education. What has resulted is not another monolithic monument to a masterpiece blueprint, but many voices speaking their differences to power.

For instance, the creation of Swaraj 'University' is an interesting resistance effort by young founders, Reva Dandage and Manish Jain of the Shikshantar movement. The name hides more than it reveals for Swaraj is nothing like your 'standard' university. The differences are more than cosmetic however as Swaraj University is a scathing rebuttal of the practices of assessment and examination. 'Students' are not conceptualised as passive recipients of abstractions, the regurgitation of which guarantees a certificate; instead, a 'khoji' (a rough equivalent of a 'student') determines the learning paths he or she would like to tread, and designs the learning environment where this happens – based on individual learning styles. Each *khoji* also liberally shapes a support structure (comprising of an *Ustaad* or a guide, peers and a feedback council) to help him/her on a chosen learning pathway. There are no 'disciplines' or 'departments' or 'certificates'; there is no 'campus' either! 'At Swaraj University, we believe the world is our campus'. Even more critical, in line with the courageous refusal to perpetuate the domineering epistemology of the West and the ethnocentrism woven into the fabric of the 'regular' courses of 'modern' universities, is the co-creation of praxis-based learning categories that are immediately relevant to the aspirations of their immediate community. There is no separation of theory and practice, or work and play. 'Jobs' are not the end result of this learning context, as being a khoji immediately links you up to a support network that helps you start community-sensitive enterprises. Unlike in most universities, which separate learning from immediate relevance, the hands-on approach of Swaraj makes learning deeply meaningful and rewarding.

The exciting paradigm shifts are not only occurring in Asia; as is evident in extant literature, Africans have always felt restless about the marginalising bias and disruptive effects of Western schooling models on their subjectivities. Dasen and Akkari credit Julius Nyerere, one time teacher as well as President of Tanzania, as one of the prominent few that voiced a critique of schooling:

> Nyerere realised that in his newly independent country, a school system keeping the colonial model, established to provide mainly local administrative personnel, continued to create a privileged 'elite' for the 'modern' sector, to the exclusion of the majority of the rural population. Most students would quit school with a feeling of failure, as the system was entirely oriented towards higher-level studies, being highly selective at the same time. The students, after only two or three years of primary school, felt themselves superior to their non-educated peers, and would refuse agricultural work, preferring to wait for an illusory job in the city. Thus the school system was the primary cause of rural exodus and widening generation gap.

Indeed, Nyerere's voice is but one out of a chorus of voices owned by prominent Africans still relevant to our concerns today. Ngugi wa Thiong'o, while characterising what he called 'the colonial system of education' as a 'pyramid', bemoaned the fact that schooling was taking us 'further and further from ourselves to other selves, from our world to other worlds'. He interpreted his call for the rejuvenation of our languages and the social realities they were able to conjure as a 'call for a regenerative reconnection with the millions of revolutionary tongues in Africa and the world over demanding liberation'.

Ngugi wa Thiong'o's concerns for a reappraisal of our educational systems finds even sharper clarity in Molefi Asante's (one of the contributors to this book) insistence on an overhaul, not a 'tune-up':

> Black children have been maligned by this system. Black teachers have been maligned. Black history has been maligned. Africa has been maligned... Afrocentric education... seeks to respond to the African person's psychological and cultural dislocation. By providing philosophical and theoretical guidelines and criteria that are centered in an African perception of reality and by placing the African-American child in his or her proper historical context and setting, Afrocentricity may be just the escape hatch African Americans so desperately need to facilitate academic success and "steal away" from the cycle of miseducation and dislocation.

Considering the aforementioned, Abdul Karim Bangura, a strong voice for the incompatibility of Western educational systems with African life, and an advocate for an African educational paradigm, asks: 'Why have Western educational systems not yielded much benefit for Africans? Did Western educational systems infiltrate African societies because Africans lacked their own?' He then proceeds to offer responses to these questions. Reading his astute responses, however, could never come close to the deep satisfaction of *seeing* the 'possibilities' – enter ABEK:

Alternative Basic Education for Karamoja.

In resistance to Western education brought by Western missionaries to the north-eastern arid region of Karamoja in Uganda, the Karamojong people buried a pen. It was a significant public renunciation of schooling and its effects on their world. Additionally, the Karamojong people, being semi-nomadic, could not find any relevance in Western systems for their ways of life. So the elders buried a pen in the ground as a symbolic rejection of formal education and Western faith – in spite of the Ugandan Ministry of Education's petitions, programs and development projects.

However, in another symbolic gesture in 1995, more than half a century after it was buried the pen was lifted out of the ground – not as a sign of capitulation to the demands of a 'modernising' world, but as a salutary gesture to support the work of ABEK. The initiative has since succeeded in bridging the troubling gap of irrelevance by adapting learning to the needs of the Karamojong, transferring ownership of content to the determination of the people, accommodating elders as facilitators of learning, and creatively adopting less intrusive places (under a tree, in a field, etc.) as training zones. ABEK still accepts some kind of literacy training and formal education as part of its approach in Karamoja; its actions however show a growing awareness and sensitivity to the need for localisation and cultural affirmation.

KORU: STARTING CONVERSATIONS FOR MANY KNOWLEDGES

Drawing from the wealth of discussions, controversies and paradoxes about profoundly emancipatory possibilities for affirming multiple knowledges, and as a gift to the current unsettling of mainstream education institutional foundations, I offer 'Koru' – a democratic process for engaging communities, revitalising conversations and pluralistic cosmovisions, and co-creating alternative, non-capitalist ecologies and learning societies. Employing the most radical strand of 'postmodern technology', internet social networking (for galvanising volunteers), Koru is an emerging non-interventionist way to confront the homogenising legacy of schooling and reclaim the cultural diversity threatened by the discourse of market globalisation.

The name, 'Koru', is inspired by an indigenous metaphor for an unfurling fern frond. The Maori of New Zealand consider the 'loop' or 'swirl' shape made by a growing fern to represent the sacred unravelling of new life, the birth of possibilities, renewal, paradox, growth and strength. The symbol is closely related with the Adinkra visual symbols, which originate from Ghana.

Koru starts by sparking generative conversations in different communities of interest. Anyone can start a conversation. Through this meshing of memory with memory, through these life-affirming conversations about our livelihoods, people are inspired to take action in fundamental ways. Whereas, practices that valorise the cosmovisions of the concerned communities are strengthened and celebrated.

Koru seeks to build coalitions or connected circles of polyvocal ecological arenas and educational prospects. It is not a vanguard thing – a blueprint for change or a new plan based on theory; it is an anticipatory process of approaching the other in a bid to learn new ways of being educated, of exchanging and gifting others with value, and for reinforcing these practices in resistance of the ethical constraints of our 'monoculturising' world. Koru helps with the sharing stories and brings people together to help build weave their own educational frameworks and ecological spaces.

In a sense, one can imagine different teams of people or plural communities of listeners helping to revitalize traditions in Africa, and in Global South; these conversations will re-enchant local knowledges about education, and hopefully help diverse peoples in Africa reclaim their own paradoxes, pleasures and wisdoms – a trend highly damaging to the monotony of schooling and the economic straitjacket modern schooling ushers our children into. Because mainstream schooling chiefly serves industrial purposes and feeds directly into the social sorting contrivances of an economy based on the myth of inadequacy and fear, which means that schooling is intimately linked with the economy (indeed certificates, degrees, and graduation ceremonies are artefacts and rituals of entrance into a globalising economy), Koru is also articulated as a process of co-creating local economies, which might mean adopting local currencies or totally doing away with centrally issued money (such as has been done in many awakening communities even in the West) – depending on the wisdom bases of the people concerned. These volunteers thus help revitalize ecological/educational livelihoods in small circles in communities of interest. One can with others initiate a Koru project of provoking generative conversations, identifying locally embedded practices that deny the consumerist-industrial complex their claims to universal applicability, celebrating indigenous practices of educating and relating with ourselves, and co-initiating new institutions that support the cosmovision of the community of interest. All these can be done with moral support from other circles via the internet

– thus building a coalition of difference, an brightening fresco of colours in the stead of the dour monotone there before.

Again, is this possible? Is it really possible to imagine alternatives to schooling? Is it possible to rethink the mechanisms of our consumerist system and the obsolescence built into them? If people stopped perpetuating these systems, we will find just how possible it is. What seems quite clear is the need for a consciousness shift – wherein the hidden possibilities of today's choking monoculture will give way to the smallness of a different world and new opportunities.

Small and slow initiatives such as Koru (which, at the time of writing this, is in its birth stages) represent the openings and opportunities afforded us by a consciousness shift now animating courageous people around the world. From the Kufunda village in Zimbabwe to the Walk Out Walk On adventures of the Berkana Institute to the local food initiatives articulated by Vandana Shiva in India, people are waking up to new dream worlds, and leaving the monologue of corporate monoliths and the educational systems they have inspired and popularised behind.

THE BEGINNING: ANOTHER EDUCATIONAL SPACE IS POSSIBLE

Perhaps no other words I know better captures the prospects buried in our slowly transitioning world as poetically as the oft repeated lines of Indian activist and writer Arundhati Roy, whose voice continually insists that 'another world is not only possible, she is already on her way'; and as my husband would insist, nothing disturbs the conveniences of our language, a monoculture of homogeneity, our identity markers and, by extension, what is excitingly possible in being human like the story of an Indian-Iranian-English-Nigerian! Through the kaleidoscope of vision seemingly offered me by my multiple heritages, I continually look upon the dangerous influences schooling perpetuates on the manifold visions of life's meaning with increasing apprehension.

However, just as describing my appearance and heritages often becomes to me a metaphor for the playfulness at the heart of language as well as the beauty of difference – what someone has called the 'irreducible dignity of difference' – it also affords me reason to hope. Through the upheavals of a restless age, it is indeed time to strengthen that hope and walk out of the constraints of a fading dream. Koru, among untold numbers of other small initiatives and social movements, represent ways to transgress the imperative of schooling and the Yellow Brick Road that begins from the gates of modern schools in Africa and around the world. Much more than an addition to the inventory of social technologies now extant, Koru represents a transition into new fields of consciousness, new ways of being with the world, new dimensions of sacredness and new celebrations of the awakening spirit of our disenchanted times – a spirit our continent will do well to latch on to, if future generations of Africans are to ever find some meaning behind their own names.

CHAPTER TWELVE

Dream States and Interrupted People

TSITSI DANGAREMBGA

A s I see it, the problem with Zimbabwe is its people. We have failed to fashion a national identity for ourselves that we all buy into. Without a national identity, we cannot act as a nation of people, nor as people of one nation. Without a common identity we cannot act in such a unified manner at any time. Certainly, without the prerequisite identity we cannot act in unity at times when unified action is most needed. This is to say that Zimbabwean responses will be desperately inadequate in times of uncertainty and challenge – for times of challenge and uncertainty unsettle even well-formed, integrated and stable identities. Where identity is poorly formed, the result of challenge is disorganisation and chaos.

The problem of disorganisation and chaos has been said to visit all African nations roughly two decades after the nation achieves independence. As I write, that group of people called Afro-pessimists are declaring doom on South Africa, where the post-independence grace period of twenty years will soon be over.

To be fair to these pessimists, though, the great majority of post-colonial African nations have succumbed to various degrees of chaos and disaster. The extent to which Zimbabwe has disintegrated has been the bitter disappointment of many people, both inside and outside the country. At its independence in 1980, Zimbabwe was proud of a number of educated political leaders, and of relatively good infrastructure and systems which latter had resulted from about one hundred years of British colonial rule. In addition, events on the continent had given the new leaders the chance to learn from history. Zimbabweans themselves and many others were convinced the country would get it right. Zimbabwe was seen as an island of progress and hope on a devastated land mass. The new nation was to embody a new prosperous beginning for a continent of wretched people.

Social reforms quickly carried out by the then almost universally popular ZANZ-PF government led to improvements in services such as health and education for the majority. Zimbabwe, like Nigeria, boasted to other Africans and to itself that its nationals were amongst the most literate at one end of the scale, and amongst the most intellectually accomplished at the other end, of the scale, on the entire continent. I remember personally benefitting from these reforms. Studying at the University of Zimbabwe at the time, I received a government grant which was fifty per cent scholarship and fifty per cent loan. Medical fees were computed according to income. Reforms in other sectors included labour and agriculture. The much maligned land acquisition programme in Zimbabwe did begin, immediately post-independence with documented successes. In short Zimbabweans were proud of their nation.

And then it all went wrong.

What most Zimbabweans failed to realise as we ran jubilant in the streets in 1980 and as we enjoyed the brief post-war period, is that independence does not make a nation. We know now that nations are built up painfully. Time, vision, forbearing, endurance, and (as my mother always says) statesmanship, are essential. Nation-building takes place over extended periods and different seasons. Progress is fitful. There are many setbacks which function as tests of capacity.

At some historical moment, nevertheless, there comes a moment of consensus. People acknowledge common history, common tribulations, toiling, successes, struggles and common vision. Individual people and groups of people freely recognize each other's commonality. This commonality is acknowledged and celebrated. The notion of a nation is conceived. In this context, Zimbabwe as a nation is not yet. Zimbabwe as a nation has been conceived, but it is still only becoming. When Zimbabwe will truly be born depends on the people, achieving consensus. And this consensus must be broad enough to engender a buy-in from all its people – including its leaders, its business and working class, its military and peasants,

With a large political elite still calling itself "Comrade", it is scandalous in Zimbabwe today to speak of 'peasants'. The phrase 'rural population' is often preferred to cover up the scandal. Yet, Zimbabwe has a huge population of peasantry, numbering roughly five and a half million individuals. This figure is based on general figures of a Zimbabwean population of 8 million following the exodus of the last decade. Of this eight million, seventy per cent are estimated to dwell in the rural areas. Some of those included in this number are small-scale farmers who acquired title deeds during the Rhodesian occupation, and subsequently. However the vast majority of this non-urban population consists of people who do not own land in their own right. Ownership of rural land is one of the banes of the Zimbabwean administration today. The debate over title deeds or no title deeds in the rural areas continues until the time of writing. The status of the rural population is seldom clarified publicly. From one point of view these people are granted permission to work the land they live on for subsistence. From another point of view post-modern Zimbabwean peasants have the right to work the land. In reality however, whether rural folk have permission or the right to subsistence from the land, these permissions and rights are ultimately granted by the state. Thus Zimbabwean peasants are state peasants. Many of the rural population understand the situation in this way. A friend of mine, who lives in the country-side, recently informed me that many rural people believe that all the land belongs to President Mugabe.

Since independence a new urban class of peasantry has developed. Today many urban Zimbabweans subsist on menial labour supplemented by urban agriculture. The picture is chillingly feudal and is prominent in Harare where many of the richest Zimbabweans live. Wealthy city dwellers who own title deeds to their land employ impoverished individuals for less than a living wage. These individuals supplement their income with urban agriculture in land owned by the City Council. In addition, farm workers who live on large estates and are granted the right to works small plots by the titled land-owner are peasants in the classical sense. Disturbingly, in more than thirty years of independence the Zimbabwean administration has not significantly emancipated its peasant population.

A large peasantry, analogous to today's rural peasantry, has characterised the Zimbabwean state since pre-colonial times. While the definition of state used by historians of pre-colonial Zimbabwe was developed as a historical tool, I find it instructive to return to this definition in my analysis today, because it allows certain comparisons to be made between the development of the old Zimbabwean state and the development of today's Zimbabwe.

Most historians agree that even before the Berlin Conference of 1884 set boundaries to the southern African nation, a distinct geographical structure in southern Africa had resulted in a certain group of people flourishing in the area. The geographical feature was a plateau ranging from roughly 2000 metres to 4000 metres above sea level. The northern edge sloped down into the Zambezi river valley. The southern edge descended into the Limpopo river valley. The eastern edge was the highest and descended abruptly into an area of lowveld that leads to the Indian ocean. To the west the plateau petered out into the Kalahari desert.

Historians are also generally agreed that the ancestors of present day Zimbabweans had settled on the plateau by the early Iron Age age or the Late Stone Age, in the last millennium Before Christ. These ancestral people followed the nomadic hunter gatherers of the late Stone Age onto the plateau.

Beach tells us that the lives of the inhabitants of the plateau were already fairly stable by the beginning of the Iron Age. While settlements were not permanent, the residents of the plateau were not entirely nomadic. There were two main reasons for this situation. Firstly, changes in altitude and rainfall patterns, as well as soil conditions from area to area resulted in changes of vegetation and therefore wildlife. These changes would render knowledge gathered over many years by a specific group of Late Stone Age people of the Plateau that was necessary their for survival useless in a new environment. Secondly, the new environment was unlikely to be uninhabited. While relative population density was low, relative population pressure had long been a feature of life in the geographical location of present day Zimbabwe. Although this was not pressure of actual numbers, it was pressure derived from the number of people the land could sustain given the lifestyle of the time and the technology that accompanied it. Therefore while portions of the southern African plateau might not have appeared to have been inhabited in terms of site territories, few areas for hunting or of edible vegetation would have been unclaimed by one group that inhabited the plateau or another.

According to Beach, there were two criteria for statehood on the southern African plateau. The first criterion was the ability to raise large armies. The second criterion, associated with the first, was the ability to exact tribute from less powerful political entities. Five great states that dominated the pre-colonial history of the plateau have been identified using these criteria.

The first great state was in fact called Zimbabwe. It flourished before the 16th century in the south of Zimbabwe around the area that is now called Masvingo. Masvingo means and refers to the stone enclosures that surrounded the households of the more noble families in old Zimbabwe. The second great plateau state followed the demise of Zimbabwe and did not coexist with it. It is known as the Torwa state, and its capital in the south west of the plateau was at Khami. It flourished from the late 15th until the late 17th century. The Torwa state was succeeded by the Changamire state with its capital at Danamombe to the west. The Changamire state lasted until the middle of the 19th century. This Changamire state gave way to the Ndebele state under Mzlikazi. Mzilikazi crossed the Limpopo to set up a mobile capital called Mktokotloke near Bulawayo in 1840. The Ndebele state was stable and safe for the next fity years, during which Lobengula succeeded Mzilikazi. Meanwhile, the Mutapa state dominated the north of the plateau from the fifteenth century until the late 19th century.

The Zimbabwe, Torwa, Changamire and Mutapa states are generally believed to have developed from plateau societies that had migrated to the southern African highground during the Stone Age. The , Nebele state, on the other hand, resulted from a migration north from what is now the Kwazulu-Natal province of south Africa in flight from the megalomania of the Zulu king Shaka. Having settled south of the Limpopo with their capital near Pretoria / Tswane, the Ndebele found themselves in conflict with the Afrikaaners. They departed from this conflict further north and crossed the Limpopo to settle in the south western part of the plateau. The newcomers consisted of original people from the south-east cost, as well as Sotho people conscripted en route. Plateau dwellers already in the south west where the Ndebele settled were incorporated into the Nebele state.

The social organisation of the newcomers and that of the plateau dwellers was very similar. The economic base of both groups was agriculture supplemented by cattle herding and trade, and exhibited more similarities than differences. This was the case even if there were somewhat different emphases placed on these practices. The Ndebele culture placed greater significance–justifiably, given its history–on militarization, and also on cattle herding. The main differences between the Ndebele and the earlier plateau dwellers appears to have been that of language, with the plateau Iron Age peoples speaking versions of what is called the Shona language. Due to its history, the Ndebele state always exhibited a greater linguistic diversity.

A private army belonging to megalomaniac Cecil Rhodes' British South Africa Company raised the Union Jack on 30 September 1890 at Fort Salisbury (now Harare). This effected a complete rupture in the flow of development on the plateau. By the time the British arrived on the plateau, Zimbabweans had had a long history of interaction with Arab and Portuguese traders. This trade had been carried out under agreements between the ruling dynasties and the foreign traders. Such had been the discipline of both sides that, not withstanding friction and conflict the traders and the Zimbabweans had observed practices that ensured co-existence.

Cecil John Rhodes' objective was complete domination of the plateau and not co-existence. A royal charter had been granted to Rhodes' British South Africa Company in 1889. The Encyclopaedia Britannica says the following about the company: "The BSAC's function was to take the risk of extending the infrastructure of modern capitalism (including railways) into south-central Africa for the benefit of the British but without the cost's falling on the British taxpayer. Unlike normal companies, the BSAC was permitted to establish political administration with a paramilitary police force in areas where it might be granted rights by local rulers. It was also allowed to profit commercially through its own operations or by renting out land, receiving royalties on the mining of minerals, levying customs duties, and collecting other fees. The British government guaranteed the BSAC a monopoly where it operated and, as a last resort, was prepared to support it militarily against rival European powers or local rebellions." Thus by granting the charter gave the company the British monarch consolidated subjugation of Zimbabwe.

From now on language ceased to be the major difference between groups on the plateau. There followed a new order of inclusion and exclusion, of being and non-being, of the right to the necessities of life and prohibition of this right. Whereas language had been the signifier of a distant homeland abandoned in favour of the plateau, with colonization language itself became a signifier that created boundaries between the human and perceived inhuman. The sad truth is that in time this perception came to work both ways. I remember being mystified as a young child when I asked the domestic help a question such as, "Who was that person?", and received the answer, "It was not a person. It was a European."

It is in this sense that the development of the people of the plateau can be said to have been interrupted. Earlier migrations had been gradual, allowing for assimilation, adaptation and integration. This was not the case with the British onslaught. The motive behind the British arrival on the plateau was not a new life, a beginning. The motive was quite simply conquest and the acquisition of new lands as resources for the British Empire and its people. The independent states of the plateau ceased to exist and in their place was created the colonial state of the British Empire. This colonial state was governed for six decades by the British Government through, its chartered companies and its colonial administration. This period was followed, beginning in 1965 by a brief decade and a half of unilateral independence declared by the white settler state of Rhodesia.

To a Zimbabwean, the events that followed the raising of the British flag on Zimbabwean soil was chaos and could not be termed development. By being denied the right to participate in the administrative processes of the first the colonial and subsequently the settler state, the people of Zimbabwe were effectively rendered stateless. Though the right to carry a Rhodesian passport was sometimes recognised if the individual was not seen as a threat to the abusive Rhodesian state, carrying the passport was not a guarantee of full human rights in the Rhodesian state. On the contrary, the function of the carrier as a useful resource for the Rhodesian state was recognised. The plateau dwellers saw themselves as being brutally socialised into a system of lawlessness and plunder. Colonial myth-making saw the plateau dwellers being socialised into civilization with its foundation of codified law and the rule of the same. It was a schizophrenic interim. The possibility of a true Zimbabwean state built on inclusion and consensus remained a dream. To one section of the new order it was a dream of hell; to the other it was a dream of heaven.

The definition of state used by historians of the 19th century Zimbabwean states applied to the new plateau state of Southern Rhodesia. It was able to raise large armies from amongst its people. It was able to exact tribute, in the form of livestock, land, taxes and labour from other political entities, who were the remains of the original five great plateau states. Soon, however, the dispossessed people of the plateau began to dream of a return to statehood. After a period of civil engagement that proved useless against the intransigence of hard line settlers, the Zimbabwean armed struggle was launched in 1966.

The foundation of the pre-colonial Zimbabwean state was the house, or the clan. Historians of the southern African plateau have made the distinction between the small society and big society. The small society refers to the small social unit bound by close kinship ties in which day to day activities were carried out, whereas the larger society refers to how these smaller units of society coalesced into states.

In reality there was a continuum from small society to the wider society. The basic unit of the small society was the household. The household consisted of a man and his wife and their children. The man might have had more than one wife, but this was the exception rather than the rule as marriage was expensive due to the practice of the male party to a union paying a bride-price. In addition to this nucleus, there were relatives who might or might not have been of the same blood-line as the male household head, and there were often also hangers on.

Physically the household was a cluster of huts used for various purposes—sleeping, storage, cooking and so forth. Several such clusters of huts usually existed within easy walking distance from each other. This group of clusters formed a village and was necessary to afford the villagers protection from beasts of prey or hostile groups of other humans.

The village also provided the inhabitants with access to necessary resources such as water, which were not available at simply any site. In addition, this organization into villages enabled the community to cooperate in the tasks necessary for the communities' survival, such as the backbreaking agricultural work that was the basis of the plateau inhabitants' existence.

A number of villages made up what has been called a territory, but the Shona word "nyika" is also used. In addition to geographical limitation, "nyika" implies the totality of all existence in a given area, encompassing human, animal, plant and spiritual. The number of villages that made up a nyika was again extremely variable, ranging from a mere handful to a large number. Where the territory was very large it was subdivided into wards. The nyika was governed by an hereditary ruler, who was chosen from one lineage, although not necessarily by direct descent.

The ruling house was the dominant lineage in a territory. However, as wives joined their husbands' villages on marriage, and relatives were welcome, not all the members of a nyika were of the same house or totem. Beach estimated that in a village or ward about a third of the households belonged to the dominant lineage. Three quarters of the remaining 66% were related to this dominant blood-line. Thus most individuals in a unit, be it village, ward or territory had kinship ties with the dominant lineage. This being the case, it was unusual for minor houses dynasties or totems to overthrow the dominant house. Power struggles and coups were usually carried out within the dominant house. Dynasties that were particularly powerful and which exercised dominion over a large territory or over more than one territory are those entities that constituted the historical states of the plateau.

Dominion was supported therefore by powerful ties of blood and kinship. This way of life had changed very little in rural

Zimbabwe until the last few decades. The imposition of colonial rule, however, rendered the blood and kinship ties of the once powerful houses impotent. In the camps that constituted the exiled guerrilla state, ties of common fate, common purpose and common oath filled the Zimbabwean power vacuum created by colonial rule.

The launching of the armed struggle provides an interesting case with respect to Beach's definition of statehood. Guerrilla leaders were able to muster large armies. They were also able to obtain tribute from some sectors of their native population, or the inhabitants of Rhodesia. Tribute was often freely given. However, it was also extorted using brutal reprisals and threats of brutality where individuals and communities were not inclined to cooperate.. Practically, therefore, the guerrilla movement based outside the physical boundaries of the plateau amounted to an exiled plateau state. The guerrilla state evolved into the political party during negotiations with the Rhodesian government and then into the ruling party.

At Zimbabwe's independence in 1980 the guerrilla state in exile finally took formal leadership of the nation it was created to administer. The beginning was promising. There was talk of reconciliation amongst former antagonists, who were divided conspicuously along racial and ethnic lines. Former internal and external armies were integrated. Social services and citizenship were extended to the majority. Soon, however, international capital decided to adjust Africa structurally, without specifying to what the continent was to be adjusted. Zimbabwe's own Economic Structural Adjustment programme began in the 1990s. Services, which were a sign of sovereignity, indeed humanity, to a people who had been disenfranchised of this humanity by the colonial project were the first casualty of the new policy. Discontent grew amongst a populace that had enjoyed a decade and a half of peace and relative prosperity compared to the previous decade and a half of guerrilla warfare. Pressure mounted on the ruling party, ZANU-PF's government to meet the first real challenge since independence and perform the function of a government, that of providing for its people. ZANU-PF proved in spectacular fashion that it did not have a clue what to do beyond shout abuse at the west. The identity of the guerrilla state as a civilian administration began to unravel. The identity of a guerrilla state that could muster a large army that could exact tribute had not changed. In the new Zimbabwe, ex-combatants became a reserve army. Tribute was and is exacted in the form of votes. Where this tribute was denied, the guerrilla state masquerading as political party remained true to its identity and reverted to guerrilla practices.

Rather than expound the array of atrocities committed by the new Zimbabwean state against its nationals, suffice it to say, post-independence events in Zimbabwe have made it clear that the exiled liberation movement did conceive of itself as the Zimbabwean state. ZANU-PF has repeatedly justified its cruelties against Zimbabwean nationals by asserting that these people, are enemies of the Zimbabwean state, when in reality the individuals concerned are enemies of ZANU-PF. Thus the guerrilla movement continues to this day erroneously to conceive of itself as the Zimbabwean state. Just as language and other constructs were used by the colonial state to justify inclusion versus exclusion, respect for human rights against disrespect, and appropriation of resources versus disappropriation, ZANU-PF devastatingly uses the dichotomy of membership of the former guerrilla state in exile versus non-membership of this entity to justify inclusion against exclusion, respect for human rights against lack of respect, access to resources against lack of access.

Zimbabweans reacted inappropriately to this evolution of the once idolized guerrilla administration in exile. Few apart from former guerrilla leader Edgar Tekere were willing to take the personal risk of founding a post-independence political party that could free itself of the brutal heritage of an indescribably atrocious liberation struggle where crimes against humanity were committed by every party involved. Others took up the post so-called World War 2 human rights discourse. These latter established civil society movements to monitor ZANU-PF abuses and create counter movements in the name of democracy. In the majority of cases this was done not because of personal conviction but because promoting human rights discourse was heavily funded by the west, thus these activities were an increasingly lucrative arm of the international aid industry. When I write my history book, I will rename those conflicts of the first half of the 20th century the European Wars and I will not call them the World Wars. However, as Zimbabwe approached the turn of the century, those Zimbabweans who were not bravely forming new political movements, nor cynically joining the post-independence inland manifestation of the guerrilla state in exile, nor jumping on the economically rewarding development aid gravy with its emphasis on the human rights movement, were hiding their heads in the political sand. By the time Zimbabweans woke up to the fact that they had been re-colonised by their own state, it was all but too late.

The most recent large scale manifestation of the murderous guerrilla state identity, when Zimbabweans slaughtered other Zimbabweans in order to retain power and to achieve political ends occurred in 2008. It remains to be seen whether the current tensions will explode into similar destruction during the next elections, expected to be held in 2012 or 2013. Important to note is that the criteria determining retention of life or the ending of life in present day national violence are the same as the criteria which guided the Zimbabwean on Zimbabwean carnage that characterised the liberation struggle: are you for the guerrilla state or are you against it? As was the case during the liberation struggle, Zimbabweans today are sufficiently complicit with the system to allow this brand of violence to persist as an influential Zimbabwean identity. My own awakening came during the disputed 2008 presidential elections when the psycho-technology of guerrilla warfare practices were imported into the city. No doubt if I had frequented the rural areas in the preceding decade, I would have understood that these indoctrination practices based on instilling fear and awe, and euphemistically called 'mobilization' continued in the rural areas at election time after independence. Many Zimbabweans, though, make peace with the staus quo and declare, in a clear way back to primitivism that people always die in African politics. Few Zimbabweans are thinking seriously of change. People are concerned with finding enough food, medicine, education in order to survive at one end of the spectrum, or with abusing the nation's wealth at the other end of the spectrum. In both cases the activity is consumptive. Rarely, if ever are Zimbabweans engaged in productive activity. Where activity is productive, as, for example, in the case of President Mugabe's line of youth fashion called "House of Gushungo", the aim is the continued political survival of the former guerrilla state. The aim is not to turn around Zimbabwe's creative industry through competitive product. The positive aspect of this development in the Zimbabwean fashion world, however, is that the guerrilla state seems finally to have understood that people will not vote for you if you cut off their limbs or kill them.

Clearly, we Zimbabweans have developed an array of dysfunctional identities. On one hand we have a Zimbabwean identity that stops at nothing, not even slaughter, one that socialises its youth into the culture of murder and butchery to achieve megalomaniac ends. If these practices are engaged in to obtain political ends, the picture is even more frightening. Politics is defined in my dictionary as pertaining to policy and government, or pertaining to parties with different ideas on government. Thus Zimbabweans have developed an identity that baulks at nothing in order to remain relevant in policy or government, or in contestation with parties that have different ideas on government. On the other hand, we have Zimbabwean identities that excuse, tolerate or condone the former in the interests of not rocking the boat. Protest is largely opportunistic, based on economic rewards. There are few protests voices in Zimbabwe that have defied hardships to endure without significant external funding. Finally, with respect to today's identities, there are those pseudo protest voices that purport to be sites of resistance. These attract large donations, but do not produce anything. In other words Zimbabwean identities almost always are instrumental to achieving a material end. Zimbabweans seem no longer to have an identity rooted in the essence of what it is to be human.

Fear is often cited as a reason for not engaging more fully and with righteous anger against the horrors of mutilation, rape, death and other crimes against humanity that are committed by the guerrilla state. Zimbabweans whisper that they know what the guerrilla state is capable of, and retreat into cowardice, hoping that the spirit of death will pass them over. Individuals are content to continue as though nothing is amiss as long as they can eke out another day in one way or another. Zimbabweans have retreated into moral cowardice. As Zimbabweans we have brutal war-mongering identities on the one hand, cowardly, self-serving identities on the other. We do not have an identity of national good, unity of purpose and respect for Zimbabwean life. We are a nation divided against itself, and thus we are falling.

Today's dysfunctional identities were conceived in the discontinuity caused by the interruption of the nation by the colonial era. A pre-feudal organisation of society characterised by communal property transformed at a stroke into a dual system of communalism and a wild west form of private property. The dual system was retained so that the colonial era, having caused it, could also exploit the disunity of Zimbabwean identity. The communal areas acted as a vast reservoir of labour, food and health care for the neo-British state. This colonial state was the first and only brush with modern statehood the Zimbabweans experienced before independence. As such this repressive state formed the model for the post-independence nation. The new Zimbabwean state had neither the will, the imagination nor the temperament to establish any improvement.

Identities are stable when they are accepted or preferred by the identity holder. In such a stable identity system, the identity holder acts in a way that maintains the preferred identity. Challenging an accepted or preferred identity leads to dissonance, or discomfort, in the identity holder. The identity holder initiates actions aimed at reducing the dissonance.

An identity that is not accepted by the identity holder, or that is undesired, is unstable. In this situation, the identity itself causes dissonance in the identity holder. The holder of an undesired identity is thus continuously impelled to act to reduce dissonance. It is reasonable to assume that undesired identities are imposed and not freely chosen. Thus dissonance reducing adaptations in situations of undesired identities will often be directed at challenging the source of the unacceptable identity. A variety of reactions aimed at reducing dissonance are available to the holder of an undesired identity. These reactions can manifest mentally, emotionally or in overt behavioural realms, or in any combination of these.

If a challenge to an unacceptable identity results in greater threat to well-being and continued existence, however, dissonance reducing reactions frequently involve changing cognitions concerning the acceptability or desirability of the dissonance-inducing identity. In other words, the holder comes to accept the initially unacceptable identity, or "becomes used to it", as we commonly say. Since unacceptable identities are imposed, dissonance reduction involves changing thinking about the imposer, and about oneself in relation to the imposer. This is how the identity of victim becomes a preferred identity. The new preferred identity then becomes resistant to change as other preferred identities are.

Amina Mama emphasises how vexed the question of identity is for the African. She informs us that there is not, in any of the African languages that she is familiar with a word for identity. Pointing out that "European psycho-technologies have been implicitly designed to serve the administrative, bureaucratic selection and social control needs of late capitalist welfare states," Mama emphasizes how African nation-states have failed to synthesize identities that serve their own nations. She notes that our African cultures did not produce 'a substantive apparatus for the production of the kind of singularity that the term [identity] seemed to require". In Zimbabwe, as seen above, in order to fill this negative identity space, the identities of guerrilla state and victim emerged.

Presumably, however, a 'substantive apparatus' did exist for production of the kind of identity in the pre-colonial Zimbabwean states that served the purposes of these pre-colonial states where identity of person was based on blood or clan membership in the first instance, and more broadly on kinship. The colonial interruption imposed the identity of colonial subject upon Zimbabweans. This identity was undesired and unacceptable. A range of civil and political actions were initiated to challenge the undesired identity. When these actions met resistance, two options remained. The first option was to change thinking about the nature of the undesired colonial identity. The second option was to intensify activities challenging that identity. The identities of victim and guerrilla fighter emerged.

The 'victim' identity was of a particular kind. For the first time in Zimbabwean history the colonial period represented a state whose purpose was to subjugate a whole and numerous group of its people. The Zimbabweans were thus victims of the state, leading to the development and the acting out of the identity 'state victim'.

Guerrilla fighters repaired to camps in neighbouring countries. Here again blood became a powerful bond. However, it was not the common nature of blood that flowed in veins that united, but the ritual of blood shed that by a common action. The guerrilla fighter became a member of a guerrilla movement held together by common cause which necessitated the shedding of blood. This movement coalesced, through military action and the exacting of tribute. Finally, the guerrilla state took on the identity of warrior nation where inclusion required identity with a guerrilla bond based on bloodshed.

Cognitions concerning the nature of the Zimbabwean guerrilla state warrior nation have taken on the character of myth. The average Zimbabwean is fearful of any activity that might raise the wrath of the guerrilla state and unleash the army of ex-combatant. The result is submission and a recycling of the 'state victim' identity where the villain is now no longer the colonial but the guerrilla state. The identity of victim of a guerrilla state has become acceptable to many Zimbabweans.

A common result of this identity is moral decay. Zimbabweans think "I may steal, defraud, terrorise, cheat etc because I am a victim". Ironically the guerrilla state justifies its excesses in the same way, by publicly, through its propaganda machine, identifying itself as victim of a malevolent world order. This seemingly cynical claim can, however, be better understood as a dysfunctional 'victim' reaction to the undesirable identity of failed state.

Zimbabweans have not seen many true efforts by the guerrilla state to change its identity into a true government of the people of Zimbabwe with the common good of the nation as its raison d'etre. Rather, the guerrilla Zimbabwean state appears to have chosen a victim nation identity over the identity of failed state. In doing so that arm of the Zimbabwean state justifies once more the need for a warrior nation.

More recently, however, as the discomfort associated with it grows beyond endurance,, the people of Zimbabwe are increasingly making attempts to prevail against guerrilla state domination. The negative consequences associated with the identity of 'state victim' seems finally to be outweighing the negative consequences associated with identity of 'fearful Zimbabwean', even in the absence of significant foreign subsidy. At a recent workshop held by the Zimbabwe Electoral Commission, twenty two parties were represented. The successes of the MDC have been well documented. These successes culminated in forcing the guerrilla state into a power-sharing arrangement.

However, these successes appear not to have resulted in identity change on the part of the old guerrilla apparatus turned state. The identity of exclusionist warrior movement persists, with army generals refusing to salute Prime Minister, Tsvangirayi of the MDC. It is unclear whether they have been ordered to do so.

The question of identity becomes particularly vexed in the African terrain when negotiating the spaces of group and individual identity and the grey stretches between these. However, as group identities require concordant individual identities, some generalisations may usefully be made. Clearly, to move into the future in a way that does provide a future for Zimbabweans, Zimbabweans must change identity and this refers to both group and individual identities. Failure to effect such change has cost Zimbabwe its nationhood before in history. Commenting on the decline of Lobengula's southern plateau state, Blake writes "The social structure of the Ndebele state militated against just those changes which were needed for political and military survival. Its economic bargaining power was on the decline with the exhaustion of its ivory. ...Worse still, the whole mentality of the Ndebele military leaders was resistant to reform. Like the Prussians before Jena or the French before Sedan, they were rigid conservatives who thought in terms of the tactics of a vanishing world" (p45).

Zimbabweans must develop psycho-technologies that are equal to the task of creating a new identity that serves a free, prospering nation, where inclusion is the paradigm rather than exclusion. Zimbabweans have to understand that the identity of victim in any context is the identity of failure. The identity of 'victim' whether as explanation of apathy, of petty individual moral degeneracy or of gross state decay, must be done away with. Notwithstanding any intrinsic worth it may have carried in the past, in today's post-colonial world the category 'victim" bears absolutely no value. What is needed is an apparatus that transforms 'victim' into 'victor'. When we see ourselves as generous, compassionate victors, we will map the steps that need to be taken to move from where we are and make the new identity a reality. Zimbabweans need a lot of imagination and courage. The apparatus at our disposal is that of culture. We must develop, with all the non-violent means possible, the courage, vision and will to change our culture. Zimbabweans must engage with culture in all its facets in order to transform the old malignant into a new beneficent identity.

REFERENCES

Beach, D N. The Shona & Zimbabwe 900-1850: an outline of Shona history, Heinemann, London 1980

War and politics in Zimbabwe, 1840-1900 Mambo Press, Harare, 1986

Methuen, R. A History of Rhodesia, Methuen, London, 1977

Mama, A. Challenging Subjects: Gender and Power in African Contexts. Plenary Address, Nordic Institute Conference: 'Beyond Identity: Rethinking Power in Africa', Upsala, October 4 - 7 2001;

CHAPTER THIRTEEN

Reflections on Black Politics

DARYL TAIWO HARRIS

Nearly two hundred years ago in 1827, the pioneering newspapermen Samuel Cornish and John Russwurm, launched *Freedom's Journal*, the first Black newspaper published in the United States. In the inaugural issue they exhorted Black people to seize the lead in defining and conceptualizing their own experience and direction, saying in self-determining assuredness, "We wish to plead our own cause. Too long have others spoken for us." No blurred lines in their self-conscious expression that might imply ambiguity, just the constant certainty of Blackness. That Cornish and Russwurm used "we" and "us" suggests they were very much conscious of being Black in 1820s America, as was their contemporary David Walker, whose 1829 *Appeal to the Coloured Citizens of the World* stands as a seminal expression of agency and Blackness.

At present, however, it appears that heuristic conceptions of Black experience—such as Blackness, Black interests, and unity, for instance—are being misconstrued, contested, and appropriated mostly by opponents of Black people using race and culture as primary determinants in their sense of political belonging and orientation, and who instead work to dissolve or lessen the thoughts, bonds, and commitments attendant to Black unity. Some, like the postmodernists, try to supplant Black unity with an attenuated, individualist longing that acts as a kind of currency one uses to negotiate her and his self-interests. Others simply declare outright that the post-racial or colorblind moment has dawned, ostensibly turning racial and ethnic identity and consciousness into certain anachronisms. Still others look to an array of contradictions—class, gender, sexuality, and so on—bedeviling American society, and pose any number of them as moderating biases that essentially eclipse race and culture. Altogether, the qualms about Black experience (and the values and ideas evolving therein) being *the* generative source-place for explaining Black political phenomena, serve mainly to augment the Western world's persistent disdain and obfuscation of Black agency. In no way, however, can the evasions and denials, anxious as they are, erase or negate the plain reality of Black political phenomena (that is, Black people conceiving and acting with political intent and effect, historically and contemporaneously). But, to paraphrase Cornish and Russwurm's call to Black people to narrate their own stories, the problem ultimately revolves around how these phenomena are interpreted and understood.

To which, recounting our own stories is especially urgent in the arena of politics, mainly because it is the space wherein authoritative decisions (rules, laws, policies, and regulations) and non-decisions emanate, affecting Black and human life in innumerable ways. There are, of course, antecedents (the period of the 1920s in Harlem, for instance) of heightened assertion of Black self-definition. But it was the during the 1960s Black revolt and embrace of Blackness that the pursuit of Black self-definition garnered substantive and systemic change. Incensed about higher education's role in Europeanizing human consciousness, and wanting to immobilize and thus halt its unwanted infringement on Black thought, Black college students in the late 1960s rose up and pushed for curricular and administrative change, demanding, among other things, that curricula and faculty properly reflect Black historical and cultural experience, and with the appropriate administrative structures to house and support them. Studies of Black political experience, of course, preceded these challenges; however, it was in this crucible of resistance and struggle for Black Studies that the disciplinary initiative of Black Politics was born.

The birthing of Black Politics was undeniably difficult, one filled with hushed disapprovals as well as discordant tirades from antagonists bent on decrying Black political experience as not lending itself to credible study, excepting, of course, when it mimics White experience. Notwithstanding the birthing pains, headway was made during its embryonic years of 1968 to 1971 in generating new conceptualizations of Black experience, but it was not sustained. Nearly a half a century has passed since those heady, inaugural days of Black Politics as an intellectual and academic challenge, and still the birthing pains have yet to sufficiently subside so as to allow for organic growth, development, and maturity to occur. One might even argue that disciplinary (in the sense of field of study) Black Politics has all but come to a standstill, resulting in it being regarded as little more than an academic nuisance by some or as an insipid stepchild of American (White) Politics by others. Never mind that there are now sizeable numbers of Black political scientists busying themselves in studying Black political phenomena. However laudatory these numbers (and their scholarly output) may appear, the fact remains that this still offers little cause for us claim an easy victory. Perhaps a hearty, celebratory dance should only be occasioned when we are certain that Black Politics stands squarely on philosophical and conceptual sources rooted in Black historical and cultural experience.

But a careful accounting of Black Politics as an academic and disciplinary enterprise underscores what a precarious undertaking it has become. The shortcomings of disciplinary Black Politics are all the more distressing (and bordering on unchangeable) because Black political scientists by and large have abandoned their intellectual resolve and duty to evolve their own (meaning those rooted in Black experience) philosophical and conceptual perspectives. Such developments certainly raise questions about the nature and meaning of Black Politics as a disciplinary and intellectual endeavor. In our effort to expound on what is nominally called Black Politics, we will pay close attention to philosophical and conceptual concerns because they make up the basic tools with which the intellectual frames and ultimately analyzes and explains phenomena, including their political dimensions.

THE SEARCH FOR A RELEVANT BLACK POLITICS

Critical analyses of Black intellectualism are always appropriate, for it helps us to sort out its meaning, responsibility, and role. In a real sense, Black intellectuals have yet to come to terms with attending to the tasks history has imposed on them, which is, broadly speaking: to chart new and fruitful directions for the consecration of harmony and balance; to create lucid understandings of Black experience from the historical and cultural images and materials of Black people themselves; and, in the specific case of Black political scientists and analysts, to transcend the wholly Eurocentric orientation to examining and interpreting the sociopolitical universe.

Not that there were no self-conscious attempts by some to break away from the Eurocentric straightjacket, and thereby purge from our midst (or, at least, moderate their social import) the Black parodies of White consciousness and intellectualism. The forerunners of a disciplinary Black Politics yearned to kill the slave mentality, which, by training and force of habit, never tires of aping European conceptual schematics. As pioneering insurgents, these intellectuals were very much cognizant and appreciative of the historical moment of the late 1960s and early 1970s, which was, in the prudent teachings of Maulana Karenga (1993), a time of rediscovery and reclamation of heritage.

Riveted by the spirit of seizing the time, these pioneers staged a divorce of sorts from the protocols of White political science and its premier governing organization, the American Political Science Association (APSA). Unfortunately, as it played out over subsequent decades, the intended break up turned out to be just a short-lived estrangement, as Black political scientists largely made their way back to what in reality was always an incompatible, asymmetrical, disharmonious, and abusive relationship. We should note that whereas practically all Blacks in political science reneged on parting ways with the exploratory protocols of White political science, their rebel-compatriots in psychology did extend their scholarly revolt into a full-fledged branch of study in which African ideas and concepts frame their research and analyses (Nobles, 1986; Myers, 1988).

Notwithstanding the insurgency's collapse, the logic that induced and propelled it merits reflection because it helps the process of discerning and elaborating a more appropriate meaning of Black Politics. We should note that although the detriments of racism (qua institutional racism and its related tyrannies) in the academy and society helped induce insurgent actions, they could never supply the underlying and governing principle for sustaining a disciplinary Black Politics. What we mean here is that disciplinary Black Politics per se is not wholly reducible to the obliteration of these detriments. Racist practices in the academy could very well end tomorrow such that more Blacks obtain faculty appointments (perhaps even commensurate with the Black percentage of the national population) and still European intellectual dominance would continue. The old numbers game in which a little color is added here and there in the name of diversity in no way defined the full measure of the insurgency. Black people know from painful experience that there are Black beneficiaries of diversity-style programs who are quite adept at parroting European ideas and programs.

We should be a bit more precise on this point, however. Surely an urgent concern in Black political thought and behavior is the eradication of oppression—racial, class, gender, and so forth. Hence the emergence and enthronement of resistance as a core value in Black political experience. Resistance naturally acquired an honored status in Black experience because it is the one core value that is unequivocally correlated with oppression/domination. As the saying goes, wherever one finds oppression, one will also discover deep reservoirs of resistance. Yet, in saying this is not to elevate the oppressions to the point where they are given epistemic and ontological primacy for evolving and determining the full range of meanings of Black Politics. The situational context of Black people living under White racial domination, while providing ample fodder for Black Politics to examine and explain and challenge, tells us, for instance, virtually nothing about the substance of Black governing styles and traditions or about Black conceptions of what is good and beautiful. The canonical literatures of American (White) politics ritualistically magnify this deficiency via their wide-ranging and unending denials, distortions, and caricatures of Black people and traditions. Thus, as we consider the subject of Black Politics, it would behoove us to bear in mind the early counsel of Mack Jones (1971, 1977) and Ron Walters (1973), both of whom advised that we build a Black political intellectualism on top of Black historical and cultural foundations.

Jones (1971) stands out among the early pioneer-insurgents in launching Black Politics because he recognized the vital role of philosophy (read: orienting assumptions and values) in framing both our understandings and the nature of our analyses. Indeed, Jones viewed philosophy as the heart and soul from which political meanings derive—be they theories or ideologies, and their residual connotations (their elaborateness notwithstanding). Strain though we may, we can never reach a state of detachment from one philosophical tradition or another, or combination thereof. Hence, the crux of the problem, according to Jones, is that the Black political scientist is unduly enamored with the White worldview (European conceptions of reality) and, in so being, is unusually careful to steer clear of critically challenging its predominance in structuring social reality. In acquiescing thusly to White conceptions of reality, Jones continues, the Black intellectual invariably "define[s] progress, responsibilities, etc. in terms of white interests; militant sounding rhetorical flourishes notwithstanding" (pp. 24-25). Making a related argument, Walters (1973, p. 203) expresses doubt about the utility of quantitative approaches (the staple of White social science) to adequately deal with Black culture, whether it be for explanatory or prescriptive purposes. This leads him to argue for the diminution (not elimination) of the Black technician's (one who is wedded to her or his disciplinary assumptions and tools) role in Black liberatory discourses when she or he is not guided by a liberation orientation. Moreover, Walters believes "a balance between substance and technique, is preferable, and that the deficiencies in white social science are revealed when, in dealing with Black life, the analyst comes prepared only with methodology" (p. 202).

There can be no doubt about what this capitulation to White ideas (codified as philosophy and social science technique) portends for Black struggle, for it far exceeds being just an inconsequential blip on the long road to Black freedom. In the best case scenario, surrendering to White assumptions generates a pragmatism-only logic in which Black strivings for social change and freedom are circumscribed to fit into the sociopolitical world as defined by Whites. Personal experience drove this understanding home to me. I recall once bringing up (alright, I confess, I was advocating) the subject of culture (as in African concepts and values) and its relevance to Black intellectualism and struggle to a decorated Black social scientist at a university lecture sponsored by, get this, its Black Studies unit. Annoyed that I would raise the "taboo" subject of African culture in polite White company, the esteemed scholar invoked the snappy, put-down and, I surmised, pragmatic response declaring, in effect, that the Black struggle is about securing jobs for Black people. In the spirit of openness, I gave him the benefit of the doubt, and took his reply as a heartfelt call to enhance the standard of living for Black people, of which I would never contest.

But surely there was much more in his retort than what he verbally enunciated. It was as if he was being haunted by the European-contrived interference demons—fear, self-absorption, inferiority, memory loss, indifference, and ignorance—whose objective is to inject and spread the dreaded complicity and duplicity viruses into Black hearts and minds. The infected Black host of either one, or both, can always be counted on to sabotage and suppress, among other things, the self-affirming tenets and expressions of the Black movement such that the best one can hope for is the expansion of employment and educational opportunities, ala the highly touted "pragmatic," "realistic," and "responsible" socio-political posture that Jones (1971) says bedevils Black struggle. Accordingly, never are the Blacks to assert an emancipatory logic that exalts African experience, African identity, and consciousness. Never are the Blacks to question or challenge the European usurpation of conceptual and moral space. Never are the Blacks to champion epistemological and ontological realities which are not pre-cleared (white-washed, that is) by the self-congratulatory guardians of so-claimed European philosophical primacy. As one might expect, in being so restrained in this never-never world of acquiescing to European constructs of reality, Black imaginings of independence are severely, if not fully, compromised.

In this light, the more recent usage and popularization of notions like diversity, inclusion, and multiculturalism by elite Whites make perfect sense. In the name of White hegemony, the language and meaning of diversity and multiculturalism are contested territory to be duly commandeered and used to extend and fortify White rulership. Offering the perfect foil, the terms diversity and multiculturalism instantly signify moral uprightness and evenhandedness on the most recognizable (on the surface) level: the number of Blacks, Browns, women, and others joining an organization in which they were previously excluded or under-represented. Was this not the scope of advocacy of our decorated Black intellectual, who lambasted the use of African values and concepts in Black liberatory discourses? Certainly quantity-driven considerations must be pursued and enacted, for they are contributory to the process of bringing about equality and social justice; however, one might suppose that the social change process ultimately turns on the question of *quality*. Nearly two decades of Clarence Thomas (and, more generally, Black conservatism) on the High Court should be convincing enough to encourage us to place a higher premium on quality.

Too often, as is common in the diversity and multiculturalism policy debates, many Blacks end up ceding to the White appropriation of meaning. When this happens, to use a worn-out cliché, we generally get the proverbial "killing of two birds with one stone" whereby the interests of the White hegemonists and the Black pragmatists, strange bedfellows indeed, are realized. Not only does this tacitly endorse the maintenance of White domination, it also, as we have noted, provides the perfect foil in that White domination is no longer readily recognized as such a bad thing. Quite the opposite, under the aegis of diversity/multiculturalism, a so-claimed reformed White hegemony can assume the appearance of a benevolent social force whose modus operandi nonetheless is still hegemonic. In due course, cautions Jones (1977), this creates an unseemly state of affairs in which the Black intellectual as pragmatist becomes nothing more than a two-bit player in her and his own subordination.

In some respects, Jones' (1971) exhortation to Black intellectuals to construct a Black worldview and Walters' (1973) advocacy for a Black social science served as precursors for evolving a more explicit Afrocentric transcendence in Black Politics. In his critical, yet encouraging, call for Black analysts of political phenomena to perform the tasks of clarification and self-definition, Jones (1971) says:

> In my view, we as Black political scientists have not faced up to our responsibilities. We have not tried to understand the unarticulated (yet no less real) *Weltanschauung* [worldview] of white America and interpret it to the lay public; nor developed one of our own. Instead, we have been content to be "practical" in the context of the prevailing order. (p. 25)

Walters' (1973) vision of an ideology for Black social science is even more strikingly akin to an explicit Afrocentric statement:

> [I]t is possible to identify certain elements which contribute to an ideology for Black social science; they refer

to radicalism and conflict theory as well as an infusion of the substances of Blackness—Africanism, nationalism, history, cultural style, self-determination and consciousness of racism. . . . I believe this term ["Unity and Order of Blackness"] . . . to be comprehensive enough to include all aspects of a Black social-science ideology. (p. 198)

Walters (1993) demonstrates the utility of this approach in his pioneering case studies analysis of Africa oriented liberation movements in African diaspora settings. As he says:

[T]he Pan African analytical approach is an associated Black studies methodology in that it recognizes the dominant influence of the racial variable within the context of domestic relations, while the Pan African method recognizes the dominant influence of African identity, history and culture in the transactional relations of African-origin peoples in the Diaspora. (p. 46, his emphasis)

We now know, of course, that the early proposals put forth by Jones and Walters for a transcendent and vibrant Black Politics that "would put in sharp relief the self interests of blacks in America," such that "[t]he incompatibility of their interest—liberation— and that of American capitalism grounded in white supremacy would be obvious" (Jones, 1977, p. 16) never truly matured.

A more pointed call for an African intellectual transcendence did come to pass, however. Identifying culture (that is, philosophic values, concepts, and ideas) as the key variable to clarify and extend interpretations of sociohistorical, sociopolitical, and other human phenomena, a cadre of imaginative intellectuals self-identifying as Afrocentrists and cultural analysts (Maulana

Karenga's *Kawaida* philosophy and Molefi Asante's *Afrocentricity* emerged as the archetypes) invigorated the process of revolutionizing our understandings and knowledge in all areas of life activity. Arguably, their urgings for Black intellectualism to be centered or located (Asante, 2003, 1990) in the African historical and cultural experience provided instant relief (assuming one embarked on the process of evolving a centered consciousness) from the Eurocentric malaise encumbering Black intellectual strivings. Truly, an uncharted world of explanatory possibilities opened up for the Afrocentric intellectual, enabling her and him, Asante (2006) says, "to analyze human relationships, multicultural interactions, texts, phenomena and events, and African liberation from the standpoint of orientation to facts" (p. 153). The key point here is orientation (or consciousness), for first and foremost this is what shapes our analytical and liberatory visions.

Given the vivacity (and simplicity) of the Afrocentric idea, one is left begging the question: What explains the relative silence of Black political scientists on the question of (African) cultural orientation to sociopolitical phenomena? Before we tackle this question, we should reiterate the point that some intellectuals (the Afrocentrists) do ground their analyses in the culture concept; they, however, have done so largely within the Black Studies disciplinary domain. With few exceptions, most Blacks trained in political science have been either unable or unwilling to transcend the Eurocentric underpinnings of American (White) political science.

Carruthers (1999) candidly speaks to the pitfalls of this problematic in proposing "An Alternative to Political Science." Carruthers is among those who answered Cheikh Anta Diop's

(1974) charge to Black intellectuals to reconnect Africa with her classical Nile Valley heritage. In so doing, he focused on examining African philosophic concepts of governance and society. Carruthers' contribution to this endeavor is not narrow in the sense of desiring only to correct the falsification of human history, although this certainly is high on his agenda. Also chief among his concerns is the Eurocentric orientation of Black political scientists, creating what he describes as a dilemma (that is, loyalty to the race versus loyalty to the political science discipline). Doubting the utility of political science in formulating a liberatory Black intellectualism and behavior, Carruthers encourages Black intellectuals to envision an alternative, home grown reality/resource to draw on: "Black scholars who are interested in the politics of Europeans and what sometimes goes under the name of black politics should certainly have a radically different view of the Europeans who are targeting on the same areas of scholarly pursuit" (p. 81).

Furthermore, Carruthers' position does not advocate for the non-study of politics, or what he calls the clash of factions and interests. To do so, of course, would turn the Black intellectual into a non-player, a more or less naïve and imperceptive bystander in the urgent sociopolitical affairs of the day. As he says:

> Political science, which is nothing more than the study of the dominion of one group and its interests over other groups must be studied by Africans. The study of political science is one way of studying the worldwide system of domination that must be overcome. It is therefore useful to have black scholars study political science just as it is useful to study any pathology. However, such study in itself cannot provide

the guidance necessary for formulating answers, or even questions, concerning the ultimate world organization for which we should strive. Nor is it capable of recommending actions in which black people should engage. (p. 82)

Perhaps the problem as outlined by Carruthers is apt to affect Black analysts of sociopolitical phenomena more acutely not just because she and he make the realm of political affairs their primary focus, but also because she and he continue to remain faithful to the discipline's techniques. As such, the Black freedom movement cannot escape being subjected to challenges to both its direction and purpose. That these challenges also manifest as Black loyalties and affinities for European styles of governance and freedom—Machiavellianism and Madisonianism (Marxism, too)—undoubtedly impedes the cultural rediscovery and reconstruction processes so essential in the decolonization/liberation campaign. Let us now take a closer look at some of the details of this bleak situation.

HONOR THYSELF, AND IT WILL MAKE YOU FREE

Arguably, an intellectual inventiveness in Black Politics would be better position us to address a range of interrelated questions. First, what accounts for the problem of Black intellectual conformity? Second, what precludes Black political scientists and analysts from severing (or tempering) conceptual ties to the nobles of European thought—Plato, Machiavelli, Madison, Hobbes, Locke, Jefferson, Marx, and others? And, why hasn't the incisive and more appropriate analytical centrism been given greater place and space of authority and influence in our explanations of the sociopolitical world?

It might be somewhat presumptuous here to suggest that analysts of Black political phenomena have glimpsed the full import of honoring their own truths; certainly all have not, but some I suppose have at least sneaked a peep. The truths we have in mind are those which are embedded in the culture idea, the authenticating and affirming guidepost of Black realities. For the typical Black political analyst, the culture idea is basically a pesky irritant in need of ritualized adjustments so as to tame it, dilute its potency, and thus make it palatable (and serviceable) to the ruling White cultural/racial group. After all, Black cultural truths can never truly be eradicated, hence the pressing need to use, in today's postmodern rhetorical parlance, de-centering, de-essentializing, and deconstruction-like analytic categories to expedite the taming process. Moreover, concomitant with the European appropriation of diversity and multiculturalism (a disturbing development, to be sure) is the more invidious explosion of pop-culturalism as a mode of inquiry and explanation. This pop-culturalism (not to be confused with the unconscious and spontaneous synergetic intergroup developments that are naturally free-flowing) positively looks every bit the same as postmodernism in that it also self-consciously avoids linkages with Africa on epistemological grounds

Herein, again, is the crux of our problem: the failure of Black Politics intellectuals to either identify with or map out the contours of their own philosophic tradition. This definitional problem, all by itself, underscores the rather debatable use of the Black Politics nomenclature as a conceptual category. On what grounds does the Black Politics nomenclature stand? The prevailing view appears to be that all that is required for a study to obtain a Black Politics designation is for it to be focused on examining the political thought and behavior of Black people. In this way, the "Black" in Black Politics operates as a somewhat narrow signifier, signifying only that the subject matter (the Black political experience) be the determinative factor in the defining process. Relatedly, and what really exacerbates the definitional problem, is the view that Black politics (as thought and behavior) encompasses all Black people who are engaged in some manner of political expression, irrespective of what that expression portends for Black people and struggle. This view rests on the assumption that racial phenotype alone qualifies one to be a practitioner of Black politics.

Neither trend offers satisfactory insights on the meaning of Black Politics (the conceptual question) and Black politics (as thought and behavior). Of the first tendency—categorizing all analyses of Black political phenomena as Black Politics studies—there is little to suggest that there will be an appreciable divergence from the European investigatory and explanatory constructs in the way we examine and explain Black experience. In fact, up to now the prevailing, unchallenged practice has been what Ama Mazama (2006) appropriately calls "a 'Blackenization' of European disciplines—that is, the exploration of the Black experience within the confines of European disciplines" (p. 8). The second trend—classifying all Blacks engaged in some form of politics as practitioners of Black politics—in being open-ended to embrace all manner of Black politicos unwittingly leaves the Black movement vulnerable to some of the worse forms of opportunism and duplicity, which, unfortunately, are frequent despoilers of the movement.

Let us take the case of the new Black conservatives to illustrate the conceptual imprecision created by this definitional schematic.

Obviously, in the phenotypic or sociological sense Black conservatives are Black. But, is it so that their phenotypic identity-affiliation and the fact that they are politically engaged sufficient grounds on which to classify them as practitioners of Black politics? I believe one should answer this query warrants a no answer.

Our 'no' is supported by the attitudes that predominate among Blacks: When a broad cross-section of Blacks publicly excoriate U.S. Supreme Court Justice Clarence Thomas for being the whitest man in America as well as on the High Court, the Black appraisal rests on subordinating the weight accorded to skin color. In other words, skin color is but a secondary consideration. In this instance, the primary bases on which Black people's judgment stands are *value orientation* and *interest articulation*. Clarence Thomas and the cabal of Black conservatives—Thomas Sowell, Shelby Steele, Ward Connerly, John McWhorter, Armstrong Williams, and the like—openly and proudly self-identify with the values of the White worldview and, as such, are obliged to defend and extend the interests associated with it. Even so, Black conservatism leans heavily on its Black phenotypic identity-affiliation (its colorblind pretensions notwithstanding), certainly not to demonstrate fidelity with Black political values and interests but rather to impersonate as a "new and improved" pathway for Black people. One quickly discovers, however, that what is alleged to be a novel and pioneering course of action is in reality an "old and bankrupt" program cleverly repackaged in Blackface so as to come across as reasonable and respectable. The real problem, of course, is marked by philosophic orientation, not by phenotype. This is the essence of the Fanonian (1967) paradox when so-called Black politics (including its academic renditions) is rooted in European ideas and values.

Even though the descriptive-oriented focus is an untenable criterion for classificatory purposes, it nonetheless obtains in every political science department in American colleges and universities that offer courses (usually a solitary course) on the Black political experience, historically Black colleges and universities included. That this state of affairs persists speaks to the overpowering hold that conformity has on Black intellectualism. Whereas Black scholars in Black Studies departments theoretically can flee the intellectual plantation—note that Mazama (2006) reports the problem of conformity to be every bit a reality in Africana Studies—Black political scientists, by contrast, are particularly averse to making a Tubman-Douglass move for fear that this would offend their White masters and overseers and perhaps derail their careers.

Adding insult to injury, the typical Black political scientist still obtains her and his faculty appointment in the White academy via the joint appointment arrangement with Black Studies, with Black Studies having but perfunctory influence. Invariably, the appointee (save the Black subject matter focus) brings practically no meaningful interest to the philosophical dimensions of Black experience, particularly its pre-enslavement underpinnings. Hence, the underdevelopment of Black Politics persists. As such, said appointee's loyalties expectedly are geared to the disciplinary protocols of her and his home department, which wields the real power and accordingly dictates the terms of Black deference to White intellectual approaches. Plainly put, conformity is the price the White academy charges for recognition and career advancement. Meantime, Black Studies end up serving as recruitment tools to hire Black scholars having virtually no appetite to speak of for developing or evolving centered perspectives.

Whereas Black Studies arguably has more than a fighting chance to survive, evolve, and thrive, Black Politics really exists in name only, held together by the insufficient and unwieldy glue of Black political scientists examining the same phenomena— the Black sociopolitical experience. But if Black Politics has no binding glue beyond the subject matter focus, it would seem that all that remains for a Black Politics future is a continuation of what already exists: the rather unenviable status of marginality within the confines of American (White) Politics; however, by its very nature a marginalized Black Politics is a censored and emasculated intellectual project, and, as such, is not disposed to breaking substantially new ground in our understandings of the sociopolitical world, not to mention devising a liberatory intellectualism. At heart, a marginalized Black Politics is one operating on the epistemic and ontological terms as postulated in White Politics and experience, thereby placing its practitioners in the tragically discordant position of trying to make do with their philosophic presuppositions and explanatory categories.

NOTE

1 When I use an upper case "P" in the phrase *Black Politics*, I am specifically addressing intellectual, disciplinary, and conceptual concerns. When I use a lower case "p" in the phrase *Black politics*, I am speaking more broadly about Black political thought and behavior.

REFERENCES

Asante, Molefi Kete. (2006). "Afrocentricity: Notes on a Disciplinary Position." In Molefi Kete

Asante and Maulana Karenga (Eds.), *Handbook of Black Studies* (pp. 152-163). Thousand Oaks, CA: Sage.

. (2005). "Review of Michael Dawson's *Black Visions*." Retrieved July, 2006, from http://www.asante.net/reviews/blackvisions.html.

. (2003). *Afrocentricity: The Theory of Social Change*. Chicago, IL: African American Images.

. (1990). *Kemet, Afrocentricity and Knowledge*. Trenton, NJ: Africa World Press.

Bernal, Martin. (1987). *Black Athena: The Afroasiatic Roots of Classical Civilization*. New Brunswick, NJ: Rutgers University Press.

Carruthers, Jacob. (1999). "An Alternative to Political Science." In Jacob Carruthers, *Intellectual Warfare* (pp. 75-84). Chicago: Third World Press.

Cruse, Harold. (1984). *The Crisis of the Negro Intellectual: A Historical Analysis of the Failure of Black Leadership*. New York: Quill.

Dawson, Michael C. (2001). *Black Visions: The Roots of Contemporary African-American Political Ideologies*. Chicago: The University of Chicago Press.

Diop, Cheikh Anta. (1974). *The African Origin of Civilization: Myth or Reality*. New York: Lawrence Hill

Fanon, Frantz. (1967). *Black Skin, White Masks*. New York: Grove Press.

Harris, Norman. (2006). "Black to the Future: Black Studies and Network Nommo." In Molefi

Kete Asante and Maulana Karenga (Eds.), *Handbook of Black Studies* (pp. 16-29). Thousand Oaks, CA: Sage.

Jean, Clinton. (1991). *Behind the Eurocentric Veils: The Search for African Realities*. Amherst, MA: The University Massachusetts Press.

Jones, Mack H. (1971). "A Note from a Black Political Scientist." *The Black Politician*, Vol. 2, No. 4, pp. 24-25.

. (1977). "Responsibility of Black Political Scientists to the Black Community." In Shelby Lewis Smith (Ed.), *Black Political Scientists and Black Survival: Essays in Honor of a Black Scholar* (pp. 9-17). Detroit, MI: Balamp.

Karenga, Maulana. (1993). *Introduction to Black Studies*. Los Angeles: The University of Sankore Press.

Mazama, Ama. (2006). "Interdisciplinary, Transdisciplinary, or Unidisciplinary? Africana Studies and the Vexing Question of Definition." In Molefi Kete Asante and Maulana

Karenga (Eds.), *Handbook of Black Studies* (pp. 3-15). Thousand Oaks, CA: Sage.

Myers, Linda James. (1988). *Understanding an Afrocentric World View: Introduction to an Optimal Psychology*. Dubuque, IA: Kendall/Hunt.

Nobles, Wade W. (1986). *African Psychology: Toward its Reclamation, Reascension and Revitalization*. Oakland, CA: Black Family Institute.

Schiele, Jerome H. (2000). *Human Services and the Afrocentric Paradigm*. New York: The Haworth Press.

Taylor, Charles. (1985). "Neutrality in Political Science." In Charles Taylor, *Philosophy and the Human Sciences: Philosophical Papers* (pp. 58-90). Cambridge: Cambridge University Press.

Walters, Ronald W. (1993). *Pan Africanism in the African Diaspora: An Analysis of Modern Afrocentric Political Movements*. Detroit: Wayne State University Press.

. (1973). "Toward a Definition of Black Social Science." In Joyce A. Ladner (Ed.), *The Death of White Sociology* (pp. 190-212). New York: Random House.

Contributors

ADEBAYO C. AKOMOLAFE, PhD

Lecturer, Department of Psychology,
Covenant University
Nigeria

MOLEFI KETE ASANTE

President, Molefi Kete Asante Institute for Afrocentric Studies
Professor, Temple University
Philadelphia
Masante@temple.edu

GEORGE J. SEFA DEI,

Sociology and Equity Studies
OISE, University of Toronto
Toronto, Ontario
CANADA
george.dei@utoronto.ca

EKEANYANWU, NNAMDI T. PH.D.,

Director, International Office and Linkages
Covenant University, Ota, Nigeria
Email Addresses: nekeanyanwu@covenantuniversity.edu.ng
nnamdiekeanyanwu@yahoo.com

YVETTE ABRAHAMS

Commission for Gender Equality
South Africa

GORDON ONYANGO OMENYA

Department of History
Kenyatta University
P.o Box 43844
Nairobi, Kenya
Tel: +254723865833
Email: gomenya30@yahoo.com

AUGUSTINE NWOYE, PhD

Professor of Psychology and Fulbright Scholar
Discipline of Psychology
School of Applied Human Sciences
University of KwaZulu-Natal
Pietermaritzburg Campus
South Africa

PETER ONYEKWERE EBIGBO, PhD, NNOM

Professor of Psychological Medicine &
Consultant Clinical Psychologist
President Nigerian Association of Clinical Psychologists
Department of Psychological Medicine
University of Nigeria Teaching Hospital
Ituku Ozalla Enugu/College of Medicine
University of Nigeria, Enugu Campus

PAULO WANGOOLA

Founder and Nabyama[++]
Mpambo Afrikan Multiversity

IJEOMA CLEMENT-AKOMOLAFE

Lecturer, Covenant University
Nigeria

TSITSI DANGAREMBGA

Tsitsi Dangarembga is a Zimbabwean author and filmmaker.
She is the author of famous African novel, *Nervous Conditions*

AMA MAZAMA

Professor
Department of Africology
Temple University
Philadelphia

DARYL TAIWO HARRIS

Associate Professor, Political Science
Howard University
Washington, DC

Printed in the USA
CPSIA information can be obtained
at www.ICGtesting.com
LVHW021448101023
760608LV00014B/133

9 780982 532768